KU-178-744

WHAT ABOUT THE

BIG

STUFF?

ALSO BY THE AUTHOR

Don't Sweat the Small Stuff for Men
Don't Sweat the Small Stuff for Teens
Don't Sweat the Small Stuff in Love (with Kristine Carlson)
Don't Sweat the Small Stuff at Work
Don't Sweat the Small Stuff with Your Family
Don't Sweat the Small Stuff About Money
Don't Sweat the Small Stuff . . . and It's All Small Stuff
Slowing Down to the Speed of Life (with Joseph Bailey)
Handbook for the Heart (with Benjamin Shield)
Handbook for the Soul (with Benjamin Shield)
Shortcut Through Therapy
You Can Feel Good Again
You Can Be Happy, No Matter What

RICHARD CARLSON

WHAT ABOUT THE
BIG
STUFF?

Finding Strength and Moving Forward
when the Stakes are High

HODDER
MOBIUS

Hodder & Stoughton

Copyright © 2003 by Richard Carlson

First published in Great Britain in 2003 by Hodder and Stoughton
A division of Hodder Headline

The right of Richard Carlson to be identified as the Author of the
Work has been asserted by him in accordance with the Copyright, Designs
and Patents Act 1988.

A Mobius paperback

1 3 5 7 9 10 8 6 4 2

All rights reserved. No part of this publication may be
reproduced, stored in a retrieval system, or transmitted, in
any form or by any means without the prior written permission
of the publisher, nor be otherwise circulated in any form of binding or
cover other than that in which it is published and without a similar
condition being imposed on the subsequent purchaser.

A CIP catalogue record for this title is available
from the British Library

ISBN 0 340 82599 5

Printed and bound in Great Britain by
Clays Ltd, St Ives plc

Hodder and Stoughton
A division of Hodder Headline
338 Euston Road
London NW1 3BH

DEDICATION

This book is dedicated to everyone who has gone through big or painful stuff in their lives, and the selfless heroes who helped them get through it.

Acknowledgments

I owe a debt of gratitude to the following people:

My loving family: Kris, Jazzy, and Kenna for reminding me, every day, what's really important. I love you so much. My parents, Barbara and Don Carlson, and my sisters, Kathy and Anna, for the love they continue to share with me and for including me in their lives. It's so nice to laugh together after all these years.

A big thanks also to my dear friends Benjamin Shield and Joe Bailey for being willing to discuss the Big Stuff with me, as well as for their insights and unconditional friendship; to Mavis Karn for her incredible wisdom and willingness to listen—you have been very helpful to me personally. Also, a very special thanks to one of my lifelong friends and mentors, Marvin Levin. Thank you for your ideas, for always being there for me, and for your loyal friendship.

To the hundreds of people I've met, and who have been willing to share their stories with me about the Big Stuff in their lives.

To Leslie Wells, my brilliant editor, and to everyone else at Hyperion who has worked so hard on this book and who continue to believe in my message. To Patti Breitman, who has encouraged me to write this book for a very long time; to Linda Michaels for her loving persistence in getting my books into other countries; and to Nicole Walton for the tremendous help and support she has provided in my day-to-day life. I thank you all so much!

Finally, thank you to my dear friend Robert Faberman. After all these years, I think about you every day. You will never be forgotten.

Contents

Introduction

1. Learn from the Big Stuff 5

2. Ask Yourself the Question, "Will This Matter a Year from Now?" 11

3. Know That You Don't Know, and Then Step into the Unknown 17

4. Grieve Freely 25

5. Prepare and Let Go 33

6. The Dance of Divorce 41

7. Overcome Aging Anxiety 47

8. Become a Healing Force 55

9. Reflect on the Words, "You Must Be the Change You Want to See" 59

10. The Fiction of Failure 65

11. Illness and Injury: Are There Any Silver Linings? 73

12. Making It All Workable 79

13. Beware the Burden of a Busy Mind 87

14. Face the Truth with Loving-Kindness 99

Contents

15. **Surrender to Your Lack of Control** 107

16. **Do Not Enter!** 113

17. **Dedicate Yourself to Mindfulness** 121

18. **Know the Secret of Thought** 127

19. **Soften** 137

20. **Finding Life after Death** 141

21. **Admit to Your Common Ground** 147

22. **Let Go of Your Past** 151

23. **Survive Those Financial Setbacks** 157

24. **Catch and Release** 165

25. **Reflect on What You're Going to Want to Say— Before You Need to Say It** 171

26. **Straighten Your Patience** 179

27. **Be All You Can Be** 185

28. **Treat Others As If They Were Going to Die— Tonight** 193

29. **A New Look at Stress** 199

30. **Rely on Optimism** 207

31. **Cultivate Your Compassionate Heart** 217

32. **Listen to Your World** 225

33. **Turn Toward Your Religion** 235

34. **Retirement** 241

35. **Big Stuff and Moods** 251

36. **Meditation** 259

37. **Experience Calm Resolve** 267

38. **Forgiveness** 273

39. **Become Aware of the Mind-Body Connection** 281

40. **Happiness** 289

◆ x ◆

Introduction

You don't even have to say it. I admit it! I'm the person who said "Don't Sweat the Small Stuff . . . and it's all small stuff." Fortunately, a vast majority of it is small stuff. Most of the things that bother us on a day-to-day, moment-to-moment basis are of a relatively small nature. It still holds true that learning to deal with small stuff effectively plays a large role in creating a happier and less stressed life. I can make the argument that it might be the single most important ingredient.

However, there's no denying that "big stuff" exists. In fact, there's no escaping it either. Every single one of us will experience pain during our lifetimes. Some of the issues will be universal—illness, death, injury, and aging—while other issues will vary from person to person, such as drug abuse and alcoholism, financial pressures, divorce, or being a victim of crime, violence, or prejudice, and so forth. Big stuff will hit us at different times during our lives, with varying severity and in different forms—but it will be there. Some things are predictable, while others are totally unexpected.

On September 11, 2001, we saw how quickly life can change. Not only were thousands of innocent lives destroyed, but also our entire nation, and in some ways the entire world, was changed forever. Whether directed at a nation or at an individual, vicious acts of violence have this potential. The same is true regarding other big stuff such as an accident or a sudden diagnosis.

This book came about for a very special reason. Since 1997, when *Don't Sweat the Small Stuff* was released, I have received thousands of letters asking the same question: "What about the big stuff?" As I've grown older and hopefully wiser, I find myself asking this question too. This book is my attempt to answer it. Writing this book has been a tremendous learning opportunity for me, an important part of a lifelong journey. I've had the privilege of speaking to and learning from some remarkable people who deal with remarkably big things.

I approached this book as much from the perspective of a student as that of a teacher. I'm not an expert in this particular field. In fact, some of the issues in life are so "big" that I'm not convinced that anyone is really an expert or qualified to dish out advice. With that in mind, I want you to know that this is not a prescriptive book. Instead, my hope in writing this is that it touches a part of you where your own capacity for inner healing exists. I believe with all my heart that everyone, regardless of what he or she is going through, has the capacity to heal and to experience inner health. I've seen it time and time again. What I offer you is my best attempt to point you in this direction.

This is intended to be a book of comfort and inspiration. My goal is that you will feel inspired and hopeful, in order to do whatever is necessary to find peace and move on. For some, that might mean seeking help or friendship. For others, it could mean reading additional books, taking a course, learning to meditate, or turning toward your religion. My hope is that this book sparks your creativity and nudges you in a helpful direction.

I want to say a few words about a delicate subject. I encourage you, while reading this book, to stay open to your own lightheartedness and to the predicament of being human. Though the subject matter is serious and the stakes are high, I believe it's important to maintain a sense of humor and perspective. I say this not to minimize the severity of anything we must deal with as human beings, but as a way through it. When you look around at all the people going through big things, you'll quickly notice that those who fare the best are the ones who somehow manage to keep their perspective and sense of humor. At times, it's hard to see how they do it—but they do, and it's genuine. Part of it is that the best anti-dote to pain is joy. The more we appreciate life and experience joy, the better able we are to balance the pain and keep things in perspective.

It seems to me that there are several ways to approach the big stuff in our lives, whatever it happens to be. First, we can prepare ourselves by creating a reservoir of inner health. We can learn about the ways that our thinking, attitude, and behavior can sometimes inadvertently make things even worse, and by knowing that, we can avoid exacerbating our pain, at least to some degree. In the same light, we can learn to be hap-pier and more contented on a daily basis, thus providing much-needed balance to offset the pain in our lives.

We can learn to let go and become more accepting, therefore allow-ing our natural wisdom to take over. With practice, we can learn to access our mental health and experience inner peace, not only because it creates the immediate reward of having a happy and satisfied life, but also as preparation for the inevitable. To this end, I believe that learning to not sweat the small stuff actually prepares us for tackling the bigger stuff. As we get used to responding to life in healthy, effective ways instead of reacting to every little thing, it's as though we are training for bigger things. It becomes normal for us to be healthy. And that health comes in handy when the stakes are high.

We can also learn to be "proactively responsive." In other words, we can learn actual skills to apply in response to the painful events and aspects of our lives. We can, for example, learn to be more genuinely optimistic and to surrender and be open to our pain, rather than to fight it. There are skills such as meditation, yoga, and mindfulness that make surrender much more realistic. We can learn to pray, ask for help, and most importantly, to turn to God in good times and bad.

There's no question that we can learn to practice compassion and kindness in our daily lives. This practice not only benefits everyone else but also creates an inner immunity to pain. When you observe the helpers who respond to a natural disaster, an act of terrorism, or a personal crisis, you'll notice that they are the ones who fare the best by far. That is because they are focused not on themselves, but on what they can do to be of service. Their minds and hearts are filled with love. And love is the strongest healing force in our world.

As our wisdom deepens, so too does our capacity to deal with our own pain and to help others deal with theirs. I think it's important to note, however, that one doesn't have to be going through a life-or-death crisis to benefit from a deepening of wisdom. By focusing our attention and efforts on the deepest aspects of our being and on the most important aspects of life, we not only prepare ourselves for dealing with pain, but just as importantly, we learn to treasure the gift of life. In some ways that's the most important thing to remember—that life is a gift. Despite the pain, the troubles, and all the big stuff, life is still a magical experience. Keep in mind that any strides you make toward learning to deal with the big stuff will reinforce your resolve in not sweating the small stuff!

I hope this book enhances your experience of living; that it brings joy to your heart and hope to your pain. My own hopes and prayers are that you will find peace in spite of it all, even when the stakes are high.

—*Richard Carlson*

1. Learn from the Big Stuff

There is so much we can learn from the big stuff in our lives. Whether it's something happy, such as a wedding, a new baby, or a celebration of some kind—or it's something very unhappy or tragic, an accident, illness, or death—there are always important lessons that can enhance our lives, and, if we pay close enough attention, have the potential to transform our world, one person at a time.

I was sitting with a friend at lunch about ten days after the terrorist attacks on the World Trade Center and Pentagon. With tears in her eyes, she said, "Did you notice that not a single person on any of the hijacked planes who had the opportunity to make a phone call called their stockbroker?" Far from being facetious, she was making an obvious but very important point. When the stakes are high, only one thing matters: love. No one is concerned about their weight or the way they look. They aren't upset that life isn't perfect. They aren't fretting about high taxes, the liberals or conservatives, previous conflicts, disputes with neighbors, or a lack of parking. They don't care about the rates of return on their investment portfolio. They aren't focused on any of their grievances. Indeed, the only thing that matters, when it *really* matters, is love. The question is, "Why do we treat life as if it doesn't really matter right now?"

Christopher Morley was right on target when he said, "If one were given five minutes' warning before sudden death, five minutes to say what it had all meant to us, every telephone booth would be occupied by people trying to call up other people to stammer that they loved them."

Weddings remind us of the importance of love. It's always nice to see couples attending weddings, hand in hand. It's as if the ceremony in honor of another couple has the effect of connecting us to one another. It reminds us of our loving feelings and encourages us to reflect on the nature of love and relationships. Wouldn't it be nice to see those same couples walking hand in hand more often? Why don't they?

A friend once shared with me that when she had her baby, both her parents were present at the hospital. You might think, "What's so unusual about that?" It was unusual for her parents, however, because they hadn't spoken to each other in more than ten years. The birth of their grandchild brought them together. They spoke, almost like long-lost friends. The bitterness and awkwardness softened and was replaced with a reverence for the gift of life and of love. There was no effort involved. Neither one was trying. All that happened was that both of them realized that there is so much more to life than the petty things that keep us separate. Wouldn't it be nice if we could remember this on a day-to-day, moment-to-moment basis? What's to say we can't?

In an earlier book, I told a story about Jim and Yvonne, who were unhappily married for more than thirty years. One day they were given the news that Jim had cancer. What was really interesting was that, before knowing this, the two of them lived side by side in an almost constant state of irritation. Both were bothered and dissatisfied a great deal of the time. Jim said that their love for each other had been lost many years earlier.

You've heard similar stories before, but it's worth repeating here.

The moment they found out about the tumor, both of them experienced a sudden shift in their consciousness. Very simply, they had a change of heart. The anger, bitterness, and impatience were instantly replaced with a sense of love and perspective. They realized that, beneath the superficial and self-destructive habits they had developed, they really did love and need each other.

Had their love really been lost? If so, where did it go? Is it possible that the two of them had simply been focusing on the wrong things and that it took a big event to wake them up? It's my feeling that the love they felt after discovering the life-threatening illness was always there for the taking. Is there some way that we can see this possibility in our daily lives, before being delivered bad news? Why not?

Big stuff also teaches (or reminds) us of life's short duration and preciousness. Attend any funeral, and what do you hear? Undoubtedly, there will be plenty of thoughtful (and accurate) reflection about how quickly life passes us by.

Not too long ago, I attended a high school graduation party in honor of one of our friends' daughters. The thing I remember most was the loving way in which so many people who knew the new graduate for most of her life said essentially the same thing, which was: "I can't believe she's all grown up. It happened so fast." One minute we are playing in the sandbox; the next minute, we're finishing high school. Similar words were expressed at the last retirement party I attended, another "big" event. Friends and colleagues, as well as the honored guest, said words such as, "It seems like yesterday that Fred was working in the mail room. How did all those years go by?"

Why do we so often forget to enjoy the process of life while it's unfolding? Why are we so preoccupied with rushing through everything? Why are we in such an enormous hurry—but then saddened when it's over? We rush to grow up and get through things—and then wish we could do it over again. Is there a way to slow down and enjoy the process? Is it possible that, if we were to do so, we wouldn't have the same regrets?

The third gift, so often learned from various big stuff, is the importance of kindness and generosity. It's awesome to witness the loving generosity exhibited after a painful tragedy. The outpouring makes us proud to be human. People often give "until it hurts." After a tragedy, I've seen little children put their favorite toys in boxes and send them off to families in need. It's not at all uncommon to see emergency personnel as well as everyday people doing extraordinary things, risking their lives to save others, often complete strangers.

Not too long ago, a friend of ours had a baby. The most remarkable thing happened. The new mother was inundated, not only with beautiful gifts, but also with premade dinners from virtually everyone in the neighborhood. There must have been enough family meals for at least several weeks! Others chipped in to clean her house and do various other chores. The kindness was almost as beautiful as the baby (well, not quite)!

Last year, one of my wife Kris's good friends was married. It was a beautiful celebration. Something else was amazing as well. I was touched at how readily Kris was willing to get on a plane and spend most of a week helping her friend with the preparations. Even though it was one of the busiest times in her entire life, her response was, "I'm so happy to do it." And she meant it. She loved every minute. While she had been able to find almost no time for herself in previous months, she was somehow able to give several days of her time to someone she loved. I've spoken to so many women (and men) over the years who have done similar things for friends when it involved something "big."

Being kind and generous is so natural and brings us such joy. Is there some way we can bring that kindness and generosity to our daily lives? I believe we can, if it's a priority.

Whether we're personally involved or not, big stuff is all around us, all the time. I often think that big stuff is to "understanding," as school is to children. In both cases, the information is there, ready to take us to new heights. But it's also true that we must be willing to learn.

2. Ask Yourself the Question, "Will This Matter a Year from Now?"

In **_Don't Sweat the Small Stuff,_ I suggested that we ask the** question, "Will this matter a year from now?" The implication, of course, is that most things will *not* matter a year from now. And if they won't matter, what's the point of being upset today?

About two weeks ago I was meeting someone for lunch. At least I thought I was. The problem was, the person I was meeting never showed up. As I had gone out of my way to make time to meet with this person, I was getting a bit impatient and annoyed. Then, I remembered the question—and my reaction began to soften. It's not that reminding ourselves of the relative importance of things is a panacea that will prevent us from ever becoming upset. It's just that it helps to put things in better perspective.

There is another important side to this question, however: There *are* things that will matter a year from now—the big things.

When you look back a year from now, will it matter if you have taken good physical care of yourself? Will the time you will have spent (or didn't spend) with your loved ones matter a year from now? Will it matter a year from now if you save and invest some of your money? Will it matter if you spent at least a reasonable amount of time doing those things that are truly important in your life? If you meditate, pray, or stay dedicated to your spiritual practices, will it make a difference? Will it matter a year from now if you, or someone you love, dies, becomes very ill, or suffers a serious injury? The answer to all of these questions is, "Of course it will."

Asking yourself variations of this question, and reflecting on the answers, is a powerful way to gauge the relative significance and importance of some of the events and circumstances of your life. Generally speaking, if something passes the one-year test, it's a good indication that it's worthy of your time and attention. If not, perhaps it's not worth prioritizing, over and above that which is necessary and practical.

I was talking to Lily, a busy working mom. She told me that she had been in the habit of compulsively saying yes to any number of requests for her time. She was overcommitted at work, at the kids' schools, and with her community projects. She said that because she "had it pretty good," she felt guilty saying no. It wasn't any one thing that had taken over her priorities and dominated her time. Rather, it had been dozens of small commitments, combined, that had done her in.

After a death in the family had shaken her, Lily began to reexamine her life. One of the most significant changes she reports to have made was her new use of this important question. She began to ask herself, "Will this use of my time matter a year from now?" She realized that though it's relatively easy to rationalize how something would matter a year from now, the truth is that only a handful of things really will.

She began to filter out a few of the commitments that had been preventing her from spending her time in the way she knew she wanted to. She learned to say no more often. Sure enough, her life started to change for the better.

I've found that many people have used this question in a similar way, including myself. I know how easy it is to become overextended, even without the commitments that can't pass the one-year test. That's why it's critical to ask the question, "Will this matter a year from now?"

As a result of reflecting on this question, my life has changed in many ways. While I'm more hesitant to agree to certain requests, or to begin certain projects, I'm far more inclined to say yes to those things that really matter. For example, the reality of the changes that took place in my children over a one-year period hit me very hard. I realized the obvious: I don't get a second chance at spending time with my nine-year-old or my twelve-year-old. One year from now, they will be ten and thirteen. Each optional decision not to spend time with either one of them has a very real consequence.

One Saturday when neither of my kids had any plans, I had intended to spend the day cleaning out the attic. Despite the fact that it's not very much fun, I was determined to do it. I had even written it in my appointment book, and boy, did it need cleaning!

I was getting ready to start the project when my twelve-year-old daughter, Jazzy, said, "Hey, Dad, what are you doing today?" I let her know that I was going to be busy up in the attic. "Oh," she said, "I was sort of hoping we could do something together."

This is one tiny example of the importance of asking the question, "Will this matter a year from now?" Obviously, it's unrealistic to think you could indefinitely postpone all household chores or other types of requests. Clearly, we can't, and probably wouldn't even want to. However, in many instances, we do have a choice in the matter. This was one of them. In our household, it's somewhat rare that the kids don't have any plans with friends on a Saturday—or a soccer game—or anything else! I had the power to make a choice.

I closed the attic door, certain that the mess would still be there another day—which it was. We ended up taking a family walk instead, then watching a movie together. Needless to say, it was well worth the trade-off. A year later, I'm still really glad I made that decision.

The value of applying the one-year standard is that it encourages us to look at each circumstance independently as opposed to reflexively, or in a knee-jerk sort of way. In other words, instead of reacting by saying "I don't have time" or "I'm too busy" to your spouse, girlfriend, or child, you'll take an extra moment to evaluate the situation. You'll be more inclined to find the time (if it's truly important to you).

On the flip side, we're more careful to evaluate each situation before saying yes. When asked if you can do something, you should ask yourself two questions. First, "Is this something I have to do?" And second, "Is this something I want to do?" If you don't answer yes to at least one of these questions, you'll probably learn to say no more often. In the process, you'll begin to create more time for those things that really matter. After all, what's "bigger" than time itself?

I've found that I've become a happier and more genuine person as a result of keeping this question in the back of my mind, because now when I say yes, it's no longer likely to be out of obligation. Whether it's doing someone a favor or carpooling for a school field trip, if I say I want to do it, I usually really mean it. This means I have far less regret and almost no resentment toward others because, more often than not, I'm doing things by choice.

One of the problems many of us face is that we confuse our priorities with a sense of urgency or obligation. We have twenty items on our "to do" list and feel compelled to complete them. So we rationalize by saying to ourselves, "I'll spend more time with the kids when I get through this list," or "I'd love to volunteer at church, but I don't have enough time these days," or "I'll start exercising next week, after my schedule clears."

Meanwhile, items on the list might include cleaning the garage, doing some errands, visiting a distant acquaintance (out of obligation) who happens to be in town—or whatever. We might sit on certain committees or volunteer for other things that, upon more careful consideration, don't mean as much to us. The point isn't to say that these things might not be important, but rather to suggest that many of the ways we spend our time, if we're really honest, are optional. Our intent is to do it all—but our priorities are left behind because they lack a sense of urgency.

My best friend, Benjamin, and I don't exchange gifts during the holidays, and here's why. Initially it was his idea. He told me, "Knowing that you won't be spending your precious time walking through shopping malls, trying to find something for me, brings me more joy than anything you could ever buy me!" The best part about this is that he really means it! He knows that shopping isn't something I enjoy, especially when there are big crowds. Think about his gift to me for a moment. Each year, he literally gives to me the one, two, or even three hours of time it would take to drive to and from the appropriate shops and find him the perfect gift.

I heard a story that broke my heart but that also speaks well to the point of this strategy. A "busy" man who juggled too many things had been trying to find time to visit his ailing mother in the convalescent hospital. He kept saying, "I'll see her tomorrow." You know the rest of the story. She passed away before he made it back.

Most of our stories aren't this dramatic, of course. They are usually far more subtle and have to do with day-to-day decisions about how we choose to spend our time and energy. It's important to remember, however, that our lives are made up of the way we spend our minutes, hours, and days. Our time is precious, and we can learn to treat it as such. Asking the question, "Will this matter a year from now?" is a great place to start.

3. Know That You Don't Know, and Then Step into the Unknown

I was speaking to a man who had been, in his words, "cheated and taken advantage of" by his business partner. To make matters worse, the man happened to be one of his now-ex-best friends. He felt betrayed and hurt, angry and resentful. Since the time of the incident, he had spent over a year wracking his brain for a logical reason, searching for an answer that would relieve his pain. He was determined to "know" why things unfolded the way they did, to "figure it out." He had even entered therapy to come to grips with the whole ordeal.

Yet, it seemed that no matter how hard he tried, the end result was always the same: more frustration. The more he insisted on "knowing," the more confused he became. He became cynical and felt he would never trust again. He was experiencing a case of circular thinking.

By what he described as a stroke of luck, he was encouraged to attend a lecture focusing on, among other things, the realization that there are almost always reasons for things we simply don't understand—and it's okay that this is true. The point was that by making peace with the fact that we don't know, we can let go of the past—however painful—and move on.

When I was young, I wasn't a very good speller. My dad used to tell me, "Richard, it's not necessary that you know how to spell every word. It's only necessary that you know which words you don't know." He was right, of course. That's what dictionaries are for. As long as you know that you don't know a word, there is no problem. You simply look it up! A similar dynamic holds true in many of life's challenges: It's not always necessary to know something. It's most important to know that you don't know, and that it may not even be necessary to know a particular thing.

Just as knowing that you don't know how to spell a word opens the door to an answer (in this case, a dictionary), admitting that you don't know what to do—or why something happened—also opens doors yet to be discovered. It takes a little faith and patience, but the answers will emerge. By stepping toward the unknown, instead of fighting and resisting it, you pave the way for new answers to unfold.

When people are dishonest, unethical, untrustworthy, or deceitful, such as what was alleged in the above story, factors are at work that we cannot see. The world and its inhabitants are filled with conflicting agendas, inner drives, and needs that can lead to disappointing, even evil, results.

Initially, the man who felt betrayed by his former friend thought to himself, "So what." He asked himself the obvious question: "What are we supposed to do—forgive evil acts simply because we don't understand the motives? What kind of superficial psychobabble is that?"

As time went by, however, he began to understand the deeper meaning of what the lecturer was trying to get across. Human beings are incredibly complex creatures. We have all experienced pain and disappointment and are filled with competing and conflicting desires. Often, our motives are unconscious. This means we sometimes do things without the slightest awareness of why we do them. Some of us have had horrible role models and have been taught some very negative and destructive habits. Our vision of the world is tainted with negativity, self-interest, and insecurity. To one degree or another, we're all subject to internal damage that taints our judgment, compassion, and even our ethics.

A person's need to prove himself "right," for example, can be so intense that he will criticize in front of others those he loves most. He will try to put them in their place. He does this, not necessarily because he doesn't love that person, but because his overidentification with needing to be right is so much a part of what he thinks he is and what he identifies with. It can be an unconscious drive or habit that, quite literally, runs him. When someone says or does something that threatens his "rightness," he springs into action to defend his unconscious pride. He will say or do practically anything to, once again, prove himself right.

It's unfortunate but almost inevitable that we will meet, become friends with, engage in business with, and possibly even marry someone who has been similarly damaged. The details will differ, but the damage will be there. The damage may have been caused by either upbringing, learned behavior, genetics, or whatever. Who really knows?

A mentor of mine likened it to a person who is, in a metaphorical sense, in an emotional wheelchair. Just as a person who is confined to a wheelchair isn't able to walk, a person who is emotionally crippled may be incapable of acting differently from the way they do—irrespective of how distasteful that may seem to you or me.

The man who cheated his friend may be so overidentified with his own self-interest, or with appearing successful, that he is virtually incapable of treating people fairly and conducting his business in a consistently ethical manner. The fact that his "victim" was a good friend could not overshadow his shallow insecurities.

The difference, of course, is that it's easy to have compassion for someone with a physical handicap. We can see it. It's visible. It makes sense to us. On the other hand, a person with an "emotional handicap" has an invisible problem, which is harder to understand. We can't see anything except the effects of it.

So what good does knowing this do us? Putting this understanding into practice is, of course, difficult. It has absolutely nothing to do with excusing a person's behavior. For example, the man whose friend had cheated him was considering pursuing legal and/or criminal charges. Instead, the insight is intended to allow us to make peace with the fact that, no matter how much we wish it were otherwise, there are many things we simply don't know—or understand. And we never will.

The first step toward inner peace, then, is admitting the fact that we simply don't know certain answers.

The second step toward inner peace—the way to reinforce and secure it—is to embrace the unknown rather than resist it. The more we make peace with the fact that we don't know, and the more we step into it and toward it, the sooner we will be at peace ourselves.

For most of us, change is scary—whether we're getting married or divorced, having a child, moving away, changing jobs, or leaving a relationship. It's all pretty frightening because it's different. We don't know exactly what's going to happen or how to predict the outcome or the future. The unknown takes us out of our comfort zone.

Sara's husband died in a car accident. About a year later, her friends and family insisted that it was time for her to step out, to meet new people, even to date. She had met someone she was initially interested in. Though she wanted to go out with him, she was too scared. Like Sara, sometimes we are in pain, bored, lonely, or frightened. But something inside of us would rather stay with the familiar, even though it's painful, than step into unknown territory.

I was listening to a story about lions being rescued from a dangerous environment, a burning forest for example, and transported in a cage to a new place. The new living environment was "perfect" in every sense of the word, to a lion. It was full of his natural prey, and water was plentiful. There was natural beauty and safety in every direction. It simply couldn't be improved upon from the perspective of a lion.

But when the cage was opened, the lion refused to leave. Even with the door wide open, he would retreat to the back corner. Any attempt to encourage him to walk out toward total freedom was met with an angry and threatening growl. To a lion, what could be worse than being confined to a cage? There is only one thing: his fear of the unknown. He would, literally, rather die in the cage than step into the unknown world.

This is a near-perfect metaphor. Most of us are like that lion, except that our cages are mostly self-created. One of the most dramatic and sad examples is a battered woman returning to her abusive husband or boyfriend. She knows that to stay is pure hell, but leaving is often perceived as so frightening that familiarity is chosen over the unknown.

There are hundreds of less severe yet important applications where fear of the unknown dominates our attitude and decision making. An acquaintance was experiencing deep pain in his marriage. His love had long been lost in the mutual bitterness and resentment that had developed between him and his wife. They had developed a functional way of being together that, on the most superficial level, appeared to work fairly well. The bills were mostly paid, the house looked pretty good, and the kids were growing up.

But inside, his spirit was dying. There was no connection or intimacy—none whatsoever. Conversations were often polite, but habitual. Listening to each other had long disappeared. Neither knew of the other's dreams.

As painful as it was, it was at least familiar. To address the issues would be, to use his words, "to stir the pot." It would be dangerous and risky. He didn't know how she would respond. Maybe she would be devastated. Perhaps she would want a divorce. Maybe she would take the kids. It could ruin him financially. It was all so frightening, not worth the risk of change.

In painful situations, the key to increased freedom is to first acknowledge the cage. How can we get out or become free if we don't even know (or acknowledge) that we are trapped? Although the cage is often wrongfully described as being safe, it is in reality filled with anguish. Yes, it is familiar; but no, it is not safe.

Sometimes, the pain must be almost unbearable before the desire to become free is activated. This is why an addict must often hit bottom before he or she seeks help. When the pain is awful but somehow bearable, the familiar cage is misrepresented as being safe; it's seen as the way life should and/or needs to be. It's only when the pain crosses the line and becomes unbearable that action is taken.

Risk can be difficult to evaluate objectively. It can be risky to jump off a roof. You could get hurt, break your leg, possibly even die. Yet, if the house is in flames, the failure to jump means an almost certain death. My acquaintance considered it extremely risky to bring the pain of his marriage out into the open. There was the actual risk of things getting worse. He imagined divorce, counseling, fighting, hurt feelings, financial hardship, lawyers, kids being taken away—all sorts of other things. How can one evaluate these risks? How real are they? It's hard to tell. Perhaps it's pure guesswork, or speculation.

But to remain in the "cage" is to guarantee continued suffering. The risk is 100 percent. To stay in his cage, to remain silent, to keep up his image of the status quo, is to guarantee pain. And the pain will only get worse.

Perhaps the "safest" answer after all may be to go ahead and take the risk. Often when the first step is taken outside of the cage, one wonders what all the fuss was about. Not always, but frequently, the freedom, relief, or at least hope that one feels is instantaneous. The first day of sobriety, the first safe night away from the abuser, the first date after losing the one you love, is experienced as pure joy.

All that is required to become free is the willingness to acknowledge the unknown as being less risky than the familiar—and to take the step. When this occurs, the unknown will be perceived in a different light. It will be seen (and experienced) as that which keeps life alive and fresh. The willingness to step out of your comfort zone becomes your way of becoming free.

The hardest part is the first step. Once that first step has been taken, however, your world begins to change. Things that seemed so frightening begin to seem more like an adventure. You suddenly realize that being the first to reach out—or to apologize—was worth the risk. Taking that leap of faith in a new career or business venture is now seen as an opportunity that really could be realized after all, despite your earlier doubts. You begin to see new options that were invisible. You start to try new things and open your eyes to new possibilities. You travel to new places, and your life becomes richer and more meaningful.

The world is a mysterious place. It's tempting to think that whenever something is unknown, it's necessary and wise to avoid it. And while there are times when this may be true, it's also the case that stepping into the unknown may be the very best alternative. Being open to this possibility brings wisdom and peace to your life. I hope that the next time you "don't know," you'll see that, just maybe, it's okay after all.

4. Grieve Freely

For the most part, we live in a very repressed society when it comes to grieving. There are certain religions that encourage it more than others. Other than those isolated pockets, however, it's allowed but encouraged only in small, controlled doses. Sadly, I met a man whose brother had died in a skiing accident. The two brothers had worked in the same building. The surviving brother said that in the first day or two after the accident, he received a great deal of support in the way of cards, flowers, and condolences.

When he returned to work after a three-day weekend, however, virtually all the compassion stopped abruptly. His coworkers seemed uncomfortable with what had happened and clearly didn't want to talk about it any further. There was an almost irrational rush to fill the dead brother's office with a new person. There was massive denial—almost a conspiracy—to pretend that everything was just fine.

The silent message in the office seemed to be: "It's time to move on. Let's get back to business." No one actually came out and said it, which made the message even more confusing and painful.

In describing this silent group behavior, I would take it one step further. I would say the unintended, fear-driven message to this grieving man was: "Bury your pain. Don't think about it anymore. Run from it, and it too will disappear."

There are many examples in life in which an individual or a group has decent intentions, but subsequent actions create a negative, unintended consequence. Think of all the codependent alcohol providers, popping a beer or pouring a glass of wine for their alcoholic partner. They do so not with any malicious intent. In the vast majority of cases, they are oblivious to what they are doing and the part they are playing. To them, they are simply offering their loved one something he or she wants, something of comfort. They are helping their partner to relax.

Dealing with grief is way up there on this list of events that can create unintended consequences. Being uncomfortable with death and loss makes it almost impossible to be a supportive friend, regardless of how much you would like to be one. Inevitably, your words or actions (or inaction) can cause more harm than good. Your discomfort will come out in unsuspected ways. You might say, for example, "Everything will be all right," but at the worst possible moment. Or you might try to rationalize the loss with logic instead of heart. For example, you might say, "It was his time to go." While your intent may be loving, your words may be received like salt in a wound.

By becoming more accepting, open, knowledgeable, familiar, and truthful with grief, however, two things will happen. You will become more comfortable with the subject and with the process. In turn, you will be better able to "be there" for others during their grief, and you will be better able to "be there" for yourself when it's your turn. Always keep in mind that grieving isn't a matter of "if," but of "when." Everyone will experience grief. And, like the coworkers in the above example, everyone will be around others who are experiencing grief. It makes such good sense to prepare yourself, to the greatest extent possible, for this inevitability.

There are many great books on death, grieving, healing from

grief, and related topics. I encourage you to read them before they are necessary, or, of course, if it's necessary, to read them right now. Among my all-time favorites are *Who Dies?* by Stephen and Ondrea Levine, *On Death and Dying* by Elisabeth Kübler-Ross, *When Bad Things Happen to Good People* by Rabbi Harold Kushner, and *Awakening from Grief* by John E. Welshons. I consider all of them "required reading," not only for learning how to deal with death and grief, but also for learning how to live life to its fullest. Though they deal with intense topics, these are not depressing books. I see them as uplifting, inspirational, and hopeful.

In addition to reading about grief, there are hospice centers with loving and supportive personnel and volunteers scattered throughout the country. I encourage—in fact, I urge—you to look into what resources may be available in your community in the way of classes, support groups, or lectures. Check out the library or the Internet. Ask friends if they know of any special resources. When you ask, you'll find that more people have been through grief than you can possibly imagine. And most people who have are very willing to help.

By taking time right *now* to open your heart to grief, you will be more prepared to help others and to help yourself. In the process, you'll open yourself up to a world of richness, depth, and inner fulfillment that is impossible to experience without doing this preparation.

What I have learned, in my own life, is that the most healing and helpful grieving exists when, instead of running away, keeping a stiff upper lip, denying or pretending in some way, I move in the opposite direction. We turn toward our grief. We face it head-on, straight from the heart. Instead of turning away, we investigate with genuine interest the nature of our grief. What does it look like? What does it feel like? Is is the same or does it change? By investigating our grief, slowly and consistently, instead of fighting it, or running from it, we befriend it instead. We develop a workable relationship with grief.

My youngest daughter was involved in a scary experience. A

dear friend of hers was lighting a piece of incense when her sweat-shirt suddenly caught on fire. Instinctively my daughter immediately smothered the fire with her hands, pounding it into submission, thus not allowing the fire to spread. It was out in a matter of seconds and, by the grace of God, neither she nor her friend was hurt. My daughter's friend was very brave and thanked Kenna for her courageous action.

Unlike a fire, trying to extinguish grief is the worst thing you can do. It makes sadness and grief less accessible and more difficult to work with. Instead of being right there on the surface where it's workable, it festers and grows into an even bigger and more painful obstacle. That's why I say, Grieve freely.

The need to grieve will not go away because you run from it or turn in the other direction. You can't pretend it's not there just because it's time to "get on with your business." Burying something only puts it deeper in the ground. Burying your pain only deepens it and makes dealing with it even more difficult. Running from pain makes pain the enemy. It encourages us to look at pain with anger and repulsion. This, in turn, makes us push it away even harder. It's a vicious cycle.

Grieving is a natural process that extends far beyond the topic of death. We live in a world of constant change where nothing stays the same. Every experience has an end, as has every thought. Every accomplishment will end, as will every relationship. It's natural to try to hang on and even cling to things, especially those things, experiences, and people we love.

Some of us can hang on for a long time. We can "be strong" and push away the pain. Someone dies. It's sad, but we get through it. We're tough. There's a loss, then another and another. We keep a stiff upper lip and somehow keep going.

But at some point, which is different for each of us, it all becomes too much. There is a sort of dying into the reality of life that takes place at some point in our lives. In my opinion, this is the first step toward healing.

For true healing to take place, we must acknowledge the pain that exists, and that has existed in our lives. I'm not necessarily talking about a commiseration session with a friend or counselor, but rather an ongoing reflective investigation of that which needs to be grieved.

There are as many levels and degrees of grieving as there are people who need to grieve. The seriousness of one type of grief doesn't negate the need for another. Here's what I mean.

For a short period of time, I was having a difficult time accepting the fact that my daughter had become a young woman. Many parents go through this as their kids grow up. I knew it was normal, but it still hurt. I missed our special times together when she was young— running through the park, renting boats at the reservoir, playing games, and so forth. I was her hero. But then it happened. She had come to that time in her life when she would rather be on the phone with her friends than playing Candyland with me.

Meanwhile I heard about a mom and dad in our community who had lost their child to a freak accident in a swimming pool. Their pain must have been unbearable; I can't even imagine it.

I think it's important to honor the grieving process rather than to minimize it simply because there are others going through even more painful experiences. In other words, while one couple must grieve the loss of their child with unimaginable pain, it doesn't negate or remove the less serious loss that I had been experiencing or that you may be experiencing. I had enormous compassion for what those parents were going through—my heart ached for them. But to pretend that I too wasn't in pain would have been a serious mistake and a disservice to myself. Just as there is always going to be someone better looking, younger, stronger, faster, richer, or whatever else, than you are, there is also always going to be someone who is experiencing greater pain than you.

If you are in the midst of great pain, it's critical that you grieve freely now. On the other hand, if you're not, don't let the fact that you're not currently suffering discourage you from becoming familiar with the process. If you're lucky, you can "start small," if there is such a thing! You can build on your inner willingness to relate to your pain a little differently, with loving-kindness and openness instead of harshness and bitterness.

In some ways, it seems ironic that turning toward that which we have always run away from is the answer. Yet what I am learning and what I have been experiencing is that the more I am willing to "investigate" my pain, to look directly at it instead of hiding from it, the softer and more workable it becomes.

As pain, anger, and sadness come up, try to treat them with compassion and mercy instead of loathing and hatred. The feelings are there, waiting to be acknowledged. Pushing them away, hating them, and wishing they would go away doesn't work anyway. More of the same will only create more pain.

Grieving freely and relating to your pain in a different, more compassionate way can be a little like speaking a new language. It's difficult at first. But also like learning a new language, the learning curve and early rewards can be high. What you quickly realize is that it takes great energy and determination to hold back our fear and pain when our natural tendency is to grieve. When we open our hearts and acknowledge and look at the pain with kindness and compassion toward ourselves and our pain, we have a chance to relate to it a bit differently. We are softer and kinder to our pain and to ourselves. We learn to treat ourselves and relate to our grief with mercy instead of with a controlling iron fist.

A valuable by-product of learning to grieve freely is that we learn to live more fully. This is certainly another reason to start the process now, even if there is nothing monumental going on at this time in your life. When we feel safe in our grieving, we learn to relate to all our daily pain and frustration in new and healthier ways. When anger comes up, for example, we can recognize it without necessarily acting on it. Or we can acknowledge our feeling of envy or jealousy and move on. It doesn't have to control our lives. For me, the investigation of my pain has helped me deal, not only with the most serious aspects of life, but also with the most mundane. I'm better able and more equipped to deal with traffic jams, unexpected hassles, and difficult and frustrating people.

I once spoke to a man who was experiencing incredible grief. He had been holding it inside and trying so hard to keep it all together. Finally, he sought the help he needed through a support group. Within hours, his aching heart began to ease. He had sent love and kindness to that which hurt so badly. He had no idea that he had been treating himself with such mercilessness. It was that newfound willingness to send love that began the process of healing. Over time, he reinforced that love and remained as open and accepting to his pain as he could.

If you are in pain, please find someone to help you; someone who can be with you while you grieve. Maybe you can find a support group for people experiencing similar pain. Or perhaps you have a good friend or even a counselor who can help. Know that you are not alone in your grief and that it's not only okay, but ideal, that you grieve freely. God bless you.

5. Prepare and Let Go

Many of us worry about some big things that are yet to come or might never come. We worry about finances, natural disasters, emergencies, terrorism and acts of war, health, aging, illness, death, and catastrophes, among other things. Some things we have a capacity to prepare for, at least to a small degree. Other things, of course, are totally beyond our control. I'm not suggesting here that preparing yourself means being paranoid, but rather that preparing yourself mentally and materially helps eliminate some of the obstacles that get in the way of letting go.

When we prepare ourselves for certain calamities, we give ourselves a better chance of feeling secure, maintaining a sense of peace, making it through safely, and hopefully letting go of our worry.

When we talk about preparation, there are essentially four types of people. There are those who prepare but, despite their preparations, can't let go of their worry. Then there are those who don't bother to prepare but who worry nevertheless. There are also some people who don't prepare for much of anything, but they don't seem to worry about much either. I would make the argument here that a total lack of preparation (whether one worries about it or not) is somewhat selfish because it means that, in an actual emergency, this person would require assistance that might have been unnecessary, had he or she taken the time to prepare. My dad always taught me that each of us is, ultimately, part of the solution or part of the problem! In my mind, when you're not prepared, you are indeed a part of the problem.

Finally, there is a category of people I'd like to encourage you to become one of. Specifically, it's the type of person who commits to making wise and reasonable emergency preparations, and who is informed about what to do, yet at the same time, who backs up these efforts and this attitude with a confident dismissal of worry.

To "prepare and let go" is your best possible defense, for several good reasons. Let's begin with the obvious. Being prepared or not can often make the difference between life and death for you, your family, even friends and neighbors. Having an emergency plan that you have practiced many times can save your life during a fire, earthquake, or other natural disaster, or even during a human-caused emergency such as a robbery. It's important to know exactly what you would do, and how you would get out, protect your children (if you have any), and stay safe, depending on where you are during the crisis. It's important that you know how to turn off the gas or propane in your home, and that you're aware of any other safety precautions you should take during or after a crisis.

Having a working transistor radio with fresh batteries can help keep you informed about what's going on, should other communication devices requiring electricity be shut down or inoperable. It's also critical to have an adequate supply of fresh water, food that will keep for a long time, a can opener, warm blankets, a few fire extinguishers, a change of clothes, and any essential medication prescribed by your doctor that could be difficult to replace on short notice.

Having other things can also be potentially very important—things such as dry matches, candles, extra flashlights, and an emergency medical kit. Some people want to have a little bit of cash set aside as well, and a cell phone, again with a charged battery. All these things, and any others that you can think of, should be kept in a safe place that will probably be accessible during a crisis. The exact configuration—the specifics and the amounts of your supplies—will depend upon your individual circumstances and just how prepared you want to be. I've met some people who have enough supplies for a day or two, and others who are prepared for several months, should that become necessary.

Beyond the obvious importance of self-preservation, there is another reason to be prepared. During an emergency such as after an earthquake or hurricane, supplies in the immediate area can be limited. Stores, warehouses, and distributors can be damaged or completely shut down. This shutdown can create panic, because, obviously, anyone who hasn't taken the time to prepare will need to take immediate action. Depending on the size and nature of the crisis, as well as where it is taking place, there could be thousands or even tens of thousands of people scrambling for the essential things they will need to get through the next period of time. The more people who panic or who even need things—and the fewer the places there are to get them—the worse the problem will be.

Other than a heroic act of saving another person's life, perhaps the single most important, unselfish thing we can do in a scary situation is to be fully prepared. Thus we can stay out of the way and not be part of the problem. The fewer people who need to scramble to obtain essentials, the more order there will be among us. Furthermore, if you have food and water and other essentials set aside, and your neighbors don't, you'll be in a position to be helpful. They will be less panicked as well. The simple act of being prepared can make you a hero, and it could literally save someone's life.

Knowing the importance of good preparation, why not prepare now, before you actually need to? It's very easy and will take a few hours at most. Lately, I've noticed that classes are being offered on the best ways to prepare for different types of emergencies. Why not consider taking one of these classes and talk to others as well, about what they have done to prepare?

Prepare while it's not an emergency, when you have the time and you're not feeling scared, and while there are plentiful supplies available. If you have kids, be certain to share with them what you are doing and educate them on the plan. I just heard a beautiful story about a family of five who escaped a horrible, destructive fire. They were completely unharmed, and the parents attributed their survival almost totally to the specific fire plan they had practiced less than a week before.

Can you imagine what would happen, at a community level, if everyone was adequately prepared for an emergency? It would ensure that the greatest number of resources, and the least chaotic environment, would be available for emergency workers, police and fire personnel, and others to help those in need. In certain situations, you too might be available to help or rescue others, assuming you weren't one of the people scrambling for supplies. Every one of us makes a difference, and I can't think of an argument against being prepared.

Beyond the "prepare" side of the equation, however, it's also important to "let go" of your fear. Now that you've prepared and have a plan, you can rest assured that you have done everything that you can do. This being the case, it's time to let go.

Worrying about things we have no control over is counterproductive. It makes you tense—which, in turn, ruins your judgment. When you are worried, you live in a state of fear. This makes it difficult, if not impossible, to be loving, helpful, and kind on a day-to-day, moment-to-moment basis. And being kind is what the world needs most at this time. We need living examples among us who are confident, loving, kind, courageous, and generous. As individuals, being excessively worried about our personal and national safety doesn't support these ideals. When we're too worried, we tend to be less generous. We're so concerned about our own needs and fears that we forget about others. There are exceptions, such as immediately following a national crisis, when people can be extremely generous, but generally speaking, we are usually more stingy with our time and money when we are focused on ourselves and our own worries.

When you're not overly worried, you trust that everything is going to be okay. It's therefore easier for you to reach out to others and to be an example of someone who isn't frightened. You intuitively understand that giving and receiving are two sides of the same coin. The more you give, the more you receive. You trust your heart instead of only relying on your head. Other people see the way you live your life and begin to trust that it's okay to be generous and kind themselves. Your lack of fear spreads a positive message.

On the flip side, one of the problems with excessive worry is that it's also contagious. When you're worried, you tend to discuss your fears and commiserate with others about those fears. We then focus too much on what's wrong with the world, instead of remembering how much good there is as well. This spreads worry and negativity, which compounds the problem and makes us feel even more insecure. Too much worry makes people suspicious and cynical. When our children see us worried, then they too become frightened. It creates a vicious cycle, and the best way to help is to step outside the confines of that cycle.

Beyond all the negative practical aspects of fear is the simple truth that worry interferes with the quality of your life. Rather than being awestruck by the beauty of life, you focus too much on its potential dangers. You have fewer experiences because of fear of what might happen. Worry interferes with spontaneous joy. It keeps us tense and on guard. It makes us far more reactive, which in turn negatively affects all of our relationships, personal and otherwise. Our patience is affected, as is our temper. When we worry too much, it's harder to see the innocence in people and to remember that, although there are obvious exceptions, a vast majority of people are decent and loving.

An absence of worry doesn't mean an absence of preparedness, nor does it mean you don't care. We all want our government and our military to be in a constant state of readiness. Likewise, we want our police, firefighters, and other emergency workers to be ready to help within a moment's notice. We want our doctors to be on call should they be needed. We too want to be ready should something happen.

It's wise to prepare for retirement, for contingencies, and for emergencies. When we are prepared, we are ready. That's all we can do. When we live our lives, not from a place of fear, but from a place of calm, prepared wisdom, we are clearheaded and ready to respond to anything if needed. Knowing this is very comforting. You can live with inner peace when you know that you have put the odds in your favor. And your own inner peace actually contributes in a significant way to the peace of the world at large.

Worry is a mental process that exists independent of what we are worrying about. In other words, the worry can exist regardless of how prepared or unprepared we are individually, as a community, or as a nation. This is critical to know, because if you believe that the only cause of worry is that which you worry about—and you believe that your worry isn't tied to your thinking—then there will be no way to put those fears to rest. Let's face it: Our thoughts can create more worry, even if we are ten times more prepared than actually necessary.

This doesn't mean there aren't legitimate things to worry about. It's just that it's important to know that worry itself is something we do to ourselves, within our own thinking. It's not bad. It's just important to know where it's coming from in order to create the possibility to let it go. Worry is one of those things that tends to magnify and feed on itself unless and until we can recognize the role that our thinking is playing in the process.

Many people equate being worried with caring, as if the two are interconnected. To some extent, I disagree with this notion. While it's certainly true that there are appropriate times to worry about those we love, it's also important to know that worry is not synonymous with love. In fact, when you describe or think about love or caring, what words do you use? To me, words like *gentle, kind, trust, relaxed, selfless, giving, supportive, listening, willing,* and *hugs* come to mind. What about you?

On the other hand, when you think of worry, the opposite adjectives come to mind: words like *tense, untrusting, cynical, suspicious,* and *on-edge,* to name a few. I bring this to your attention as further justification for attempting to eliminate, or at least greatly reduce, your sense of fear. It's always easier to get rid of something when you see it as harmful instead of as an asset.

Whatever you do, don't pretend that you have no fear. It's not necessary, and it's not the best way to get rid of fear anyway. The most effective "fear-buster" that I'm aware of is to acknowledge the fear fully, but rather than running from it—or reacting to it—the technique is to turn *toward* the fear, face on. You can even talk to it like this: "I see you, fear, and it's okay that you're here. I am, however, prepared to give you less significance. From now on, when you surface, I'm going to dismiss you more quickly."

My own experience has been that the fear will probably continue to come up from time to time. When it does, ask yourself if you are as prepared as you can be for the types of concerns that could manifest themselves. If you're not, decide what action you are going to take, and when you are going to do it. Then be sure to prepare.

If you have already prepared, however, stay as lighthearted and detached as possible as you gently but confidently dismiss an excess fear you might have. You might think of your fear as you would a tape recorder, playing tapes that are no longer necessary. That's what I did. After too many years of worrying too much, I realized it was time to switch off the tape, or at the very least, lower the volume. The metaphor has been helpful.

My advice here is simple. Do everything within reason to prepare for the multitude of things that "could happen." Do so calmly and wisely, and make sure you are using sound judgment and wisdom, and not reacting from paranoia.

Once you're adequately prepared, remind yourself, frequently at first, that you have done everything you can from a practical standpoint. The more confident you become about your own preparedness, the easier it will be to let go. The remainder of your preparedness occurs in your attitude and thoughts. It has to do with seeing the value of letting go of your fear so that you can fully enjoy your life. By preparing and letting go, you will not only be helping yourself, but you'll also be making a valuable contribution to the security of your community and to everyone's sense of well-being.

6. The Dance of Divorce

While listening to the radio today, I heard someone suggest that the best way to deal with divorce was to never have one! I suppose there is some truth to that; however, it's a bit unrealistic. In America, close to 50 percent of all marriages end in divorce, and most people have had at least some direct experience with it—parents who are divorced, friends or family members or colleagues.

When I titled this strategy "The Dance of Divorce," I did so with no intent to minimize the seriousness of the end of a marriage. I consider divorce to be one of the most difficult events a person can endure. I've known many, many people who have been through the ordeal, and although some felt it was the best, if not the only possible, solution, not one of them thought it was very much fun.

I use the word *dance* because dealing with divorce is a flowing, alive process. It's a matter of finding a delicate balance among conflicting emotions and interests. People going through, or having been through, divorce have reported to me feelings of love, hate, jealousy, bitterness, hopelessness, fear, anger, and the need for revenge, all at once! No wonder it's a confusing time.

At the same time, the "dance" often involves children. So many questions need to be addressed and answered. Most important: "What's in the best interest of the kids?" But there are others. How will we share the time, responsibility, and financial needs of the children? Where will they live? How do we deal with broken hearts, blended and extended families, and new relationships? The list goes on and on.

Then there is the issue of "stuff." How do we divide the money, assets, and the things? Who gets what? That's not fair, and so forth. You're constantly in the position of walking the tightrope between being fair and reasonable on the one hand, and making sure you protect your interests on the other. If all of this combined isn't considered a form of a "dance," then I'm not sure what would be!

If ever there was a time when it's important to keep your heart open, it's during and after a divorce. Yet, this is one of the times when a person is most tempted to slam it shut. Stubbornness arises in the heart and mind, and one easily retreats into negativity. How can we prevent this from happening?

I once spoke to a group predominantly composed of divorced people. Many of them had gone to great lengths to heal from the painful breakup of their marriage. They had read books, seen counselors, gone to seminars, support groups, and so forth.

I asked the audience three questions. First, "Have the healing processes you have engaged in since your divorce been helpful?" Overwhelmingly, the audience said that their efforts had, indeed, assisted them in healing. It seemed that there were many different methods and sources that were generally, and in some cases very, effective. The second and third questions required a slightly more thoughtful response. I asked, "How many of you believe that when you are at 'your best,' and in a loving space, that you are (and were) able to effectively implement the good advice you received, regardless of its source?"

One by one, every person in the room raised his or her hand. My final question addressed the other side of the coin. "How many of you feel that when you are 'at your worst,' in other words, when you are insecure and reactive, that you are or were able to follow any advice, regardless of how sound it might be?" Predictably, no one raised his or her hand.

My conclusion, and what I shared with the group, was identical to the conclusion I have come to about many different aspects of life. It is that, ultimately, the single most important ingredient in helping someone heal from divorce is that person's ability to develop his or her sense of well-being. You'll get no disagreement from me that other factors are very important—our friends, support systems, legal counsel, cooperation of our ex-spouse, good books, even a therapist, to name just a few. But when you think about it, nothing is ultimately very helpful if someone doesn't have a healthy state of mind. And conversely, when we have one, we can get through just about anything.

Human beings have essentially two modes or mind-sets that we operate or live in, with, of course, some shades of gray in between. We have what you might call a healthy mode, and another, which you can think of as reactive.

When we are in our healthiest state of mind, we "dance" with life. We're in the flow of things. We're patient, wise, thoughtful, and kind. We make good, sound decisions. We treat others with respect and compassion—and we treat ourselves that way too. We make adjustments when necessary, and are flexible in our thinking.

Reflect, for a moment, on your own life. Can you recall times when you have remained—even for a moment—in a healthy, calm state of mind, despite difficult circumstances?

Our reactive state of mind is quite different. In fact, if you're anything like me, there are probably times when you wonder how the same person can respond (or react) so differently to a remarkably similar set of facts. One moment we can handle something really well, even when it's "big." But the next moment we fly off the handle!

In a reactive state of mind, we are less patient. Instead of being effortless, our thinking is difficult. We churn and struggle. We are quick-tempered and judgmental. We are frustrated and hard on ourselves and others. Our problem-solving skills are limited, as are our perspective and vision.

It's helpful to notice and acknowledge the difference between these two ways of being (or states of mind) because it gives you a "home base" and a starting point; it gives you something to work with. It's very comforting to know the power of your own state of mind because, unlike so many other factors involved with divorce, it comes from within you. You have some capacity to control it.

Sometimes it's hard to believe, but ultimately we are the source of our own love. In the beautiful audiotape course *To Love and Be Loved* by Stephen and Ondrea Levine (published by Sounds True), the Levines spoke of a woman who said, "My mother can't allow me to love her." They pointed out something that took me some time to digest. In a very compassionate tone they pointed out that, "Actually, she can't stop you from loving her."

Our healthiest state of mind is that strong. It's a state of mind filled with love. When we are in it, we feel secure and at peace—to some extent regardless of what's going on around us. This is our most natural state of mind.

Everyone gets reactive, and at times it seems we're always that way. And there's nothing wrong with this, nor am I aware of any way to completely eliminate it. But if you've ever felt the peace of your mental well-being, then you know it's in you and can be found again. Simply knowing that it's there is half the battle. By acknowledging the existence of a healthy state of mind, you can learn to trust it, and access it, more often. And this is key regarding divorce: When you're in a healthy state of mind, you'll know who to turn to, who your friends are, and what to do. That's not a pep talk, it's the truth.

Ironically, the way to access your inner health and strength is not by "trying," but by letting go. The idea is to clear our minds and let go of our analytical thinking when it's getting the best of us. When we do, and as we quiet down, a natural, orderly flow of thoughts will begin to emerge, including insights on what to do next. It's this quieter place where our deepest wisdom exists.

You'll notice that when you are in your healthiest state of mind, life will seem pretty manageable and effortless. The decisions and actions you need to make will flow, as if you are dancing. You will see right to the heart of the matter and you will act accordingly. On the other hand, when you slip into a more reactive state, you'll feel overwhelmed and stressed. The key is, you'll *feel* the difference.

My dear friend and coauthor of *Slowing Down to the Speed of Life*, Joe Bailey, equates our thinking to a walkie-talkie. He says we are either on "talk" or "listen." The metaphor suggests that we are either in a healthy state or a reactive one. And just like a walkie-talkie, in order to shift from talk to listen, it's necessary to know which mode you're in. But once you do, all that's necessary is to let go of the button, and the shift occurs automatically.

So it is when we're thinking. When we're reactive, churning, and trying too hard to figure everything out, the key is to recognize that we're doing so. Then, like silt settling in a pond, we do nothing except ease off and wait. Relax and trust that your wisdom will kick into gear. It requires no effort, but it does require faith, humility, and patience. It requires faith because you must trust that your wisdom and healthy mind-set do in fact exist. It requires humility because it's often hard to admit that effort is not the answer. Finally, it requires patience because even though the process is simple, it's not as easy as it sounds.

After Sally's divorce, she was bitter and cold. She described her ex-husband as difficult and uncooperative. He tried to make her life miserable. Her mind tried to make sense of what had gone wrong, but it couldn't. Most of the time, her thoughts were focused on hatred and revenge.

She resisted the idea that a state of well-being was possible when forced to deal with such a jerk and while her life was so difficult. What she learned, however, was that it was possible.

The first step was recognizing when her mind would launch into familiar territory. She even came up with a name for it—Apollo Sally. Time after time, she would catch herself after liftoff. Thoughts such as "That jerk, I hate him" would spread like wildfire.

Slowly, she learned to put out the fire before it became too big— and in time it was totally contained. She said that she had learned an important lesson: Any success she did have (or would have in the future) was despite her anger and fear, and not because of it.

She did not give up her "right" to be angry, and, in fact, she was quite angry at times. She still had to go through the process and deal with the divorce—but it was less a struggle and more a dance. She still had moments of regret, stress, anxiety, and frustration. But there was a lot less, and it didn't last nearly as long. Things were not perfect—far from it. Her ex-husband was still difficult—but she admitted, not quite as difficult. She had learned new responses to old problems.

Divorce, like many of the larger issues in life, is complicated, painful, and, at times, messy. One thing is certain, however. If you can dance with it, making the necessary adjustments along the way, you can and will get through it. Give yourself plenty of time and space, and remain compassionate toward yourself. There is a part of you that is stronger than any of your problems—even this one.

7. Overcome Aging Anxiety

I was sitting at an outdoor café in downtown San Francisco.
Four elderly men were at the table next to me. I don't remember ever
seeing four people who seemed to be having so much fun. They were
laughing so hard that I thought one of them might fall off his chair!

During a break in the laughter, one of the men stood up and
excused himself. A moment later, a woman sitting at the table next to
the remaining three men turned toward them, smiled cheerfully, and
asked, "How old are you guys anyway?" It appeared as though she
was simply being friendly and curious. I shared the joy she was feeling from simply being in their presence.

In one of the most dramatic, sudden shifts in attitude I had ever
seen, one of the men became visibly distressed. In an angry, defensive sort of way he responded, "We're in our eighties, why?"

It was easy to see what had happened. Whereas a minute before
he was simply living life and enjoying his friends, he had now started
to think about his age. The unintended consequence of the woman's
(very innocent) question was that it took this man out of the
moment and into his head. He started to think about it. Instantly, he
became self-conscious. Everything else became a lesser priority, as
age was now the target of his thoughts.

How can it be that the same person, being the same age he was a moment earlier, can instantly transform from being lighthearted, content, and full of joy—to being serious, depressed, and full of self-pity? It couldn't be inherent in age itself because, if it were, the concern would be there all the time. Plus, many people are fully content with their age—no matter what it happens to be. Some people claim they are much, much happier being older than when they were younger. And, of course, many cultures around the world not only value but actually honor the most senior people in society.

It's so strange. Many of us spend our early years racing to grow up, and our later years wishing we were younger! The only consistency is dissatisfaction with whatever age we happen to be.

I don't think there is any way to purchase a cure for "antiaging anxiety." If there were, we'd already have it! Billions of dollars are already spent trying to look and feel younger and to either postpone or deny the inevitable. Money is spent on everything from food, nutrition, exercise programs and equipment, and supplements, to special clothing and plastic surgery. There are classes, support groups—you name it, it's there. And the promise is always similar: If you take this product, or buy it, you'll feel younger or you'll look younger—or even "you'll stay younger." The problem is, even if it works—temporarily—the core issue, anxiety, is still there.

Before I continue, let me go on record as saying that I'm a huge fan of many things that will make you look or feel better—or that can help you feel better about yourself, relative to your chronological age. I believe in and am appreciative of modern science and feel we should take advantage of the strides in medicine, physiology, and nutrition whenever possible. In fact my own doctor, Dr. Timothy Smith, whom I consider a genius, wrote a definitive book on reversing the aging process called *Renewal: The Anti-Aging Revolution*. If you haven't read it, I strongly encourage you to do so! I believe we should take care of and honor our bodies, as they are a gift from God and the temporary home of our soul.

That being said, I think it's important—once we've done all we can to keep ourselves healthy and vibrant—to become at least somewhat detached from our age and our body. I remember my dad sharing this wisdom with me many years ago when he jokingly said, "If you wanted to guarantee yourself an anxiety attack and a great deal of ongoing pain, then be totally attached to staying young. Fight it all the way. It's a game you can't win, so if you want to be depressed, this is a great way to go about it."

He has an extremely healthy perspective about aging and takes as good care of himself as anyone I know. Yet, at the same time, he's completely at peace about the fact of aging. When we talk about it, he jokes with me by saying, "I'm really good at accepting things that I have absolutely no capacity to change." I can attest to the accuracy of that statement, and to some extent, I feel I've done a pretty good job in those areas of my life as well.

A few months ago, a friend of mine asked me to fill in for an injured player on his "Over Forty" basketball team. Enthusiastically, I agreed to play once a week. It had been years since I had touched a basketball, but hey, how tough could it be?

It turned out to be an extremely humbling experience. Out of the many teams in the league, and certainly with regard to my new team, I was the worst player on the court! But more than that was the physical beating I took. My forty-year-old body couldn't do what it used to, and when I came home that night, Kris couldn't decide if she should tease me—or hug me! So she did both.

I had to laugh at myself as one of my favorite lines came to mind: "If you don't have a sense of humor, it just isn't funny." At some point, you have to be able to step back and get a little perspective. You can't take it too seriously. Michael Jordan isn't worried about my comeback! Bodies are going to do what nature intended for them to do—age. Again, there are wise things we can do. Everything from stretching and exercise to diet, supplements, and attitude can help, but ideally we need to develop a healthy balance between holding on and letting go. We don't want a fearful mind-set to interfere with the quality of our life.

There is only one way that I'm aware of to completely rid yourself of aging anxiety. It's not something you buy at a store. Rather, the solution is spiritual in nature and is tied to perspective.

The solution involves seeing yourself, not as a human being having a spiritual experience, but the other way around. It's important to see yourself, as Wayne Dyer puts it, as "a spiritual being having a human experience." Having this "inside-out" perspective creates a sense of inner ease and takes the pressure off of us to feel as if one age is better than another.

The truth is, one age is *not* better than any other. That's not true because I say it's true or because I want it to be true. It's true because age is neutral. It is exactly as it is. You and I are exactly the age we are right now, and we are the perfect age. Our thoughts, of course, can convince us that it's a lot more serious than that, but that's all they are—our thoughts. Our thoughts, for example, tell us it's better to be forty than fifty. Then, each year, our thoughts come up with a new preferred age.

In the spiritual world, however, there is no age; there's just now. Our body is right here in this moment, and life is nothing more than one moment after another, after another. We can make a big deal out of being any particular age, and our minds can play horrible tricks on us about the whole subject, but time will simply continue to be "now."

Living and aging in the now is one of the most perplexing puzzles we face. On the one hand, it's so darn simple. What could possibly be more straightforward than being right where you are—right now? On the other hand, it's not so easy. Our minds are so used to reminiscing and fantasizing about the past or how nice it would be to be young again. Or we think about—and get frightened about—the future. We're getting older. What's it going to be like? Will we have regrets? We can come up with hundreds of thoughts that can cause us great anxiety.

One of the most fabulous books I've ever read is *A Parenthesis in Eternity* by Joel Goldsmith. As the title suggests, our human life is lived within the parentheses. As long as we are thinking about our body's problems, predicaments, and especially about our age, we will be concerned about them. It will seem like there is a lot at stake. It can even seem like an emergency because there is so little time within those parentheses. So if that's all you identify with, it can be pretty terrifying. The goal becomes one of two things—either to slow down the journey toward the end of the parentheses, or to make them farther apart.

On a spiritual level, however, time is unlimited. We are not these bodies—we are *in* these bodies. What a difference it makes to see it this way. We step into and inhabit a body—we live our life as a human being—then we depart this body. But the "me" isn't the body.

Meditation is the best way that I'm aware of to get in touch with the part of us that lives outside the parentheses, the part of us that doesn't need a body. As we quiet down from within, we touch a part of us that never ages. Once touched, the panic is gone and is replaced with a peaceful sense of acceptance. We are able to identify with that part of us that observes our body aging without overidentifying with it. We become the witness rather than the witnessed. We can still protect our body, nourish and take care of it, honor it and appreciate it. But we don't fret as much about its impermanence.

In meditation, we connect with the moment (which is this moment) that exists between any sort of recollection or reference to our past—and any concerns, hopes, or anxieties about the future. We get in touch with right now. In that moment, which anyone can learn to connect with, we see that our chronological age is irrelevant. We're simply right here, as we were when we were nineteen, and as we will be when we are eighty-nine.

Once we've connected to this comforting place through meditation or some type of quiet reflection, or perhaps even through a simple insight, it's easier to apply it to your life. You start to notice when you are giving significance to thoughts that pull you away from this moment. You make the connection between your thoughts of aging—and your feelings of aging. You realize that it's impossible to feel old without thinking "old thoughts," which is exactly what happened to the man in my earlier example, who was offended, then frightened, by the woman's question regarding his age.

Years ago, an insightful teacher of mine was giving a lecture in which he demonstrated how this dynamic works in day-to-day life. In a comical way, he pretended to look into a mirror and began flipping his hair. "Hmm," he said, "it looks like I'm getting more gray hairs." A few seconds later he continued. "Boy, I feel old. And what a coincidence. I feel old only seconds after thinking I was old."

The audience laughed because all of us could see that he was absolutely right. Whenever we have a thought about our age, take it seriously, and give it significance, we feel the effects of that thought. Without thoughts, there is nothing to be concerned about. We're just living our lives the best we can.

The bad news is, the thoughts *aren't* going to go away simply because we color our hair differently, get plastic surgery, or lose a few pounds. Neither will they go away because you want them to go away, or because you attempt to "will" them away with a positive attitude. Having an affair with a younger partner won't help either, nor will getting into better shape. No matter what you do, or how hard you try, your aging thoughts will return again and again.

The good news is that any thoughts you have about your age are still just thoughts. As long as you relate to them as thoughts—instead of as reality—you will be able to enjoy whatever age you happen to be. When the thoughts arise, you'll see them for what they are—and you'll drop them, or at least give them less significance.

Think about the logic for a moment. There are plenty of twenty-nine-year-old men and women who are absolutely paranoid and convinced that they are over-the-hill or getting old. You have to ask yourself the million-dollar question, "Is the problem really that person's age, or is it their thoughts about their age?" And if you agree that it's clearly not about age, but of one's thoughts, then the question becomes, "When does this change?" Does age suddenly become the "real" factor when one turns thirty, forty, fifty, or sixty?

These are very important questions to reflect upon because, once you're convinced that the solution has nothing to do with your actual age, you're a moment away from eliminating all concerns you have about aging. You'll apply the same standard to yourself as you would to a twenty-nine-year-old person, and for the rest of your life, you'll be free.

8. Become a Healing Force

At times, we all need others to lean on. We want others to be there for us, to listen and to understand. Feeling connected to others who not only care for us, but who are also equipped to embrace us and make us feel safe, is one of the ways we get through life in one piece.

It's also important, however, to become a healing force. What this means is that you become the person that others can rely upon as well. You're there for people during times of need, or when they simply need someone to talk to. You become the "giving" part of the giving-and-receiving circle.

Being a healing force does not mean becoming a martyr. It doesn't mean you always have to be the one who is strong and wise. Nor does it suggest that people turn to you because you sugarcoat reality or pretend that it is different from what it actually is. In fact, sometimes one of the worst things you can do for someone in need is to try and "make things okay" when they are not. Imagine, for example, the wife who has just lost her husband—or the boy whose dad died the day before yesterday. The last thing in the world they would want you to tell them is that "everything is fine." Everything is not fine. The same might be said when a person loses his job or his financial security. During times like this, unfettered optimism is not only unhelpful, it's obnoxious.

Instead, those who are a healing force are simply available for others and really "there" when needed. They are available to listen. They know that not always, but often, the most important role they play is that of listener—not advice giver. They have a well-developed sense of presence. This means that they aren't preoccupied with themselves or with a predetermined agenda. They don't plan out what they are going to say, how they are going to say it, or how they are going to be of help. Rather, they are spontaneous in their efforts, adjusting to the situation.

Someone who is in the healing mode is more interested in consoling than in being consoled; more concerned with listening than in being listened to. She or he cares more about understanding than about being understood.

There are many ways to become a healing force in the life of others. Once you have the intention and see the importance of being a healing force, perhaps the most powerful way to do it is to quiet down your own mind. As you do, you become more available for people. You are less scattered, and you become a much better listener. You become one of those people who are often described this way—"When I'm with her, I feel as though I'm the most important person in her life." People sense that you have that quality of being able to drop everything, even though you can't or don't always do so.

Another way to think of quieting down your mind is to temporarily turn down the volume of your personal thinking. When we deactivate our thinking, including our judgments and evaluations, we open the door to our potential to help others.

Keep in mind that our thinking will always create the reality we are perceiving and experiencing. For example, when we feel hurried, we have hurried thoughts: "I don't have time right now—I'm so busy." This is important to know because, just as people sense our impatience, they can also feel our patience. Just as they feel our judgments and opinions, they also sense our love. When you understand the influence your own thoughts have on the way you are feeling, you will be setting the stage to be available to others. When you're experiencing peace, those whom you are with will feel it too. Your own quiet mind will become a tool to help.

Have you ever been with a physician who has a good bedside manner? Or a good counselor or a good friend who genuinely would rather be with you than anywhere else in the world during that moment? If so, you've been with someone who had learned, at least during that moment, to not allow her thoughts to rob her of her own mental health. Think about it for a moment. Imagine sitting with that doctor, and instead of being present with you, she was preoccupied with the swimming pool she was having built in her backyard. Can you imagine the difference in her effectiveness as a healer? It's the difference between night and day. The same person with the same credentials, background, and experience is either a loving, healing force in your life—or simply another person who doesn't care. The only difference is the attention she gives or doesn't give to those thoughts in her head. This factor cannot be overstated.

It's the identical dynamic for each of us. When our minds are clear and available, we become a healing force for others. Whether it's our five-year-old child telling us about the mean kid at school, or our good friend telling us about her husband who is having an affair, we are either a source of healing and love—or we won't be. The determining factor will be to what extent do we allow our own thoughts to interfere with our ability to listen and be available?

When you are a healing force, you become highly intuitive and can sense when you are needed. Never forcefully, but sometimes gently, you reach out to others, even before you're asked. You might, for example, make a phone call or write a letter to see if there is anything you can do. Or you schedule time for someone, even if it's not convenient. Your efforts are rarely received as overbearing because when you are a healing force in someone's life, you are perfectly willing to back off. Your intent is to be of help, and you realize that sometimes the best way to be of help is to keep a distance or give someone some space.

The final component of being a healing force for others cannot be ignored. The truth is, it's also one of the best ways to help yourself through any situation. It's almost impossible to be worried, anxious, or angry when your primary focus is being of service. When Mother Teresa was asked, "How can I help myself?", she responded by saying, "Go out and help someone else." I don't believe she's ever been proven wrong.

9. Reflect on the Words, "You Must Be the Change You Want to See"

We all want change, of course. Most of us would love to see a more peaceful world, a world filled with love and kindness, generosity, compassion and forgiveness. We witness "big" acts of cruelty and hatred, and say to ourselves, "Those people must change." We see businesses being unethical or greedy. We see individuals being selfish or unkind. We witness impatience, self-interest, or a lack of tolerance and feel saddened. We accurately and correctly point out to others, and remind ourselves frequently, of how awful things have become.

It's interesting, however, that while we desperately want and demand others to change, we strongly resist doing so ourselves. Instead, we justify our own anger and frustration by saying "They started it" or "They must be the first to change." Without even knowing it, we use entirely different standards to judge others than we use to judge ourselves.

The real truth, however, is that we must, as Gandhi said, "Be the change we want to see." If we want a more peaceful world, we must become more peaceful ourselves. If we want an ethical world, we too must commit to being truly ethical. We must be loving, kind, and generous. We must be the ones, you and I, to stop the cycle—even and especially when it's hard to do so. By being peaceful ourselves, and making peaceful decisions, we demonstrate to others that peace is, in fact, possible. We pave the way.

While it's so very easy to point the finger at others on any number of issues, it's far more difficult to look in the mirror and admit, "I too am part of this problem." But having the courage to do so is the first important step toward transforming our world. Being willing to look at our own imperfections and our own contributions to the problems we face enables us to see ways of being of greater service. We become part of the solution.

Being willing to examine ourselves helps us realize how much we are all in this together. I'm not at all suggesting that we be hard on ourselves by looking at or focusing on our flaws. It's not about finding fault with yourself but rather about recognizing that we are all, as Zorba the Greek once said, "The whole catastrophe." By taking an honest yet very compassionate look at ourselves, we see that we all have both good and bad in us. We all have strengths and weaknesses. Once we admit this, but not before, we can begin to see others in a more innocent light. It becomes possible to have perspective and to forgive.

The day in 2001 when America and thousands of innocent people were attacked was as painful a day as any other in history. Unthinkable violence and cruelty, needless pain, and so much suffering occurred. We found out firsthand how difficult it is to respond to hatred with anything other than hatred. Those of us who have advocated that other nations respond to violence with the attitude, "You must be the first to reach out," or, "You must be willing to put it behind you to give peace a chance," found it virtually impossible to be that way ourselves.

Over and over again, I heard very thoughtful and usually level-headed people saying, "I know we're not perfect and we make many mistakes—but I want revenge." It was as if they threw in the "I know we're not perfect" part to make themselves look as though (or to convince themselves) they really are willing to look at themselves. But the reflective part is dismissed when hatred and frustration take over. Unfortunately, what is required in order to find peace in ourselves and peace in our world is much, much deeper than that. It's like the difference between thinking it would be fun to be an Olympic athlete and actually being one.

I do not pretend to have good answers, and I am well aware of the difficult questions regarding how to deal with violence. I do know, however, that more hatred—whether when dealing with nations or with individuals—will not solve the problem. We must find a way, individually and collectively, to become more loving. And in order to do so, we must be willing to look at our own tendency to hate and to accept anger as a viable solution.

This wisdom applies not just to horrible tragedies but also to everyday "big stuff" as well. How many of us have either been involved in—or had friends who were involved in—a nasty divorce or child custody battle. Personally, I've seen plenty of men and women demanding that their ex-partner change for the better. Yet anger, resentment, and bitterness dominated their very essence. How anyone could think there was any possibility that such anger would encourage another person to be kind in return is, if you think about it, pretty ridiculous. Yet we've all done it.

How could it be that remaining angry ourselves—no matter how justified it may be—could create peace in our world? Each of us is important. The feelings we live in—and the actions we take—are contagious. When we strike out at others, others will want to strike back. Feeling resentful tends to bring that feeling out in others. I've yet to see someone respond to my anger with a gentle response such as, "You've convinced me to change my attitude, my way of thinking." To the contrary, my distrust, cynicism, anger, and frustration have been met, 100 percent of the time, with a similar response.

Buddha said, "Hatred does not cease through hatred at any time. Hatred ceases through love. This is an unalterable law." When has it ever been the case that violence and hatred did not perpetuate and increase the cycle of violence and hatred? There have been instances when pure strength and domination ended a military conflict, of course, but I can't think of a single exception where the anger, hatred, and suspicion have disappeared.

This is why this is such an important issue. The root causes of violent acts are hatred and anger. We must eliminate this hatred and anger, one person at a time, if we are ever to live in a totally peaceful world. Obviously, we have control over only one person in our lives—ourselves. To the extent that we can become filled with kindness, compassion, and forgiveness, we can become an instrument of peace, a model of the ways things can be.

It can be so difficult to forgive. Yet, anger poisons the soul. It has even been said that "anger is often more harmful than the injury that caused it." On a personal level, I know this is true. I have been mad at people, feeling betrayed and unable to forgive. Over time, however, I realized that the pain I experienced was far greater than the acts I was angry about. The acts were over and done with, a memory of the past. The anger, on the other hand, lived on, day after day, until it was eventually forgiven.

When genuine forgiveness *has* taken place, however, the heaviness of heart is gone forever and replaced by a deep inner peace. Robert Muller said, "To forgive is the highest, most beautiful form of love. In return, you will receive untold peace and happiness."

Indeed, Muller was right. While I may not choose to be in contact with certain people ever again, I am always in relationship with them in my mind. That is why it's so critical to forgive fully. What I have learned is that forgiveness often has provided me with more joy than would have occurred had the "betrayal" or injury not occurred to begin with. It's that powerful.

10. The Fiction of Failure

I believe that at some level, most of us are intuitively aware that there is no such thing as failure. At the very least, we acknowledge that what we have learned to label as "failure" is actually an absolutely necessary part of the process of life. Nevertheless, when a result or effort doesn't turn out the way we'd like it to, we tend to dismiss this wisdom as being too "theoretical" or even superficial. Over and over again, I've heard people say, "I can see that *those* other disappointments were necessary, but *this one* is different. I'll never live this one down."

The fear of failure comes out in many subtle ways. I often wonder how many ventures never get off the ground because of this fear. How many classes aren't taken? How often do we avoid introducing ourselves to a potential new friend, reaching out to someone, trying something new, asking for help, going beyond our comfort level, or simply thinking outside the box? Being frightened of failure can be the difference between getting started and not getting started, but it can also be the difference between winning and losing. It's an important topic that affects both the quality of our lives as well as our effectiveness and level of success.

It's a real gift to be able to know that failure is nothing more than a fiction cleverly disguised as disappointment. Once you realize that's all it is, an entirely different world begins to emerge. You'll become less frightened and more inclined to try new things more often. You'll be willing to take appropriate risks with less fear, become more adventuresome, and have a more interesting life. Most importantly, you'll respond to adversity with more confidence and wisdom.

The reason I refer to failure as fiction is because, once the alleged failure has taken place, it can remain alive only in your thoughts and imagination. This isn't to deny the event happened, nor does it minimize its importance. This doesn't suggest in any way that it wasn't extremely disappointing or that it didn't have lasting impact. It's simply pointing out this truth: Events that occurred in the past are over and done with, and the only way you can be a "failure" is if you think you are a failure.

Here's a vivid example. Suppose a surgeon performed five thousand successful operations during her career. However, the day before she retired, she made a minor mistake during her very last surgery. Had her colleague not stepped in, her patient could have been injured. Luckily, everything worked out fine.

The surgeon, however, didn't think so. To her, she had suddenly become a "failure." She was thinking, "Not only could I have hurt my patient, but I can only imagine the lawsuit that would have resulted." Over and over again, she played out all the worst-case scenarios.

After her retirement, she became more and more depressed. She couldn't stop thinking about what had happened. Though she wasn't always thinking about it, from time to time the event would cross her mind. When it did, she would take her thoughts to heart and become despondent. Her husband, friends, and colleagues all tried their best to reassure her that she had been a successful surgeon and that her competency was unquestioned. Yet, ten years later she was still depressed.

I'm hoping you're already thinking, "Obviously she wasn't a fail-ure. That part was all in her mind."

Even though it's more obvious when someone else is involved, it's much more difficult to see it when it involves us. Our thoughts are very convincing. When we think of ourselves, or of one of our efforts as being a failure, there's a tendency to think that those thoughts are real.

But if you step back for a moment, you'll probably agree that it's nonsense. The degree of "failure" is totally dependent upon the thoughts and perceptions of the thinker. After all, one surgeon to whom the same thing happened might think to herself, "Wow, only one major mistake in twenty years—pretty impressive." Yet a sur-geon like the first one would think the absolute worst. If it's not up to the individual's thoughts, then what determines the degree of "failure"?

The hardest part of describing this is that I don't want it to seem as if I'm excusing the mistake. I'm not. The mistake occurred. The surgeon did the very best she could, and if she were to perform any additional surgeries, she would surely learn from that mistake. The question is, "How does one move on?"

I met a law student who failed the bar exam. He told me that the last three years had been a total waste of time and that he was a "mis-erable failure." My question is, "Who decided this?" There are thou-sands of other future lawyers who fail the exam but respond by saying, "Oh well, I'll take it over and do better next time." I'd guess that 100 percent of them are disappointed, but only a handful of them would become depressed.

Years ago I trained for and ran the San Francisco marathon. About three weeks before the race, I met a man who had injured his ankle. He referred to himself and his training as a "total failure." He said he had spent two years training "for nothing." You could tell that he took his thoughts about his injury very seriously. You could actually witness his thoughts bringing him down.

In all of these cases, the solution is the same. Without minimizing the disappointment, the person involved has only two choices. He or she can either trust in and take seriously the thoughts that arise about the so-called failure, or he or she can recognize them as thoughts. If they were able to do so, they could respectfully and gently dismiss the thoughts merely as "thoughts," not reality, and get on with life.

When you question the validity of failure as a legitimate concept, you begin to experience the magic of nonattachment, one of the greatest gifts life has to offer. Before I go on, let me assure you that nonattachment has nothing to do with not caring or with being apathetic. Instead, it's about doing your best, putting the odds in your favor, working hard toward your goals—but simultaneously letting go of the results. You become more involved in the process, but less attached to the fruits of your labor. You still want things to go your way, but you're not dependent on it for your survival and peace of mind. You lose all sense of desperation, replacing it with gentle confidence.

I sometimes describe this as "holding on tightly, but letting go lightly." To do so creates enormous emotional freedom. It suggests giving something your very best, 100 percent of your effort, putting your heart and soul into whatever you're doing—but at the same moment being willing to let go of the outcome, or the end result. It means knowing, beyond any shadow of a doubt, that when something doesn't match your expectations, hopes, dreams, or vision, all it means is that the universe has something else in store for you. Much more than wishful thinking, this is the way life really works—and it's the best way that I'm aware of to be happy and effective.

I'll admit that, had I heard someone say this twenty years ago, I might have rolled my eyes and said, "Oh, sure." But I've had too many disappointments, and have witnessed too many other people's disappointments, to have any lingering doubt. In other words, what appears on the surface to be a disappointment or a failure, is just that—the surface. What lies beneath is the mystery.

Think about the ocean for a moment. As beautiful as it is, all you can see from the shore is the surface. But under the water is an amazing universe full of awesome surprises. The fact that we can't see it doesn't mean it's not there.

Having faith in this mystery, or the unknown, is the doorway to freedom. We can learn to trust that just because we can't see an acceptable reason or an explanation for something in this moment, doesn't mean it's not there. We begin to know that despite the disappointment we feel, and even the pain, there is within each experience a gift, something to learn, or even an opportunity. We will get through whatever it is we're going through.

Attachment is like having a ball and chain around your ankle. It creates fears and encourages us to "overthink" our lives with too many preferences. We think, "What if the deal doesn't work out?" or "What if she doesn't like me?" We start to believe that the only way to be happy is if everything works out and goes as planned. If that's not pressure, I don't know what is! The more you trust in those thoughts, the more pressure you'll feel.

Nonattachment, on the other hand, gives you enormous confidence and takes the pressure off. It's like the proverbial weight off your shoulders. The fear of failure is a huge distraction that interferes with your concentration and enjoyment. Without this fear, the sky's the limit!

In retrospect, it's usually fairly easy to see that every mistake we made, as well as each disappointment or "failure," as we might have called it at the time, was necessary in order for us to be where and who we are today. I spoke to a researcher who had failed his English class in high school. At the time, it seemed like a catastrophe. He felt that his dream of becoming a teacher was shattered. Because of this "failure," however, he changed his direction and became interested in science. Since becoming a researcher, he has contributed to the saving of many lives, and he absolutely loves his profession. Was his so-called failure really one? I certainly don't think so.

You could say the same thing about practically everything. I met an extraordinary man who got into some serious trouble while in college. After being embarrassed, he learned from his experiences and vowed to become a giving and loving person. Years later, he became what I would call a "human angel." There was no question in his mind that his "failure" had been the single most important jump start to his evolution as a human being. Thousands of people benefited from that jump start. He wouldn't have wished his mistakes on his worst enemy, but was his college experience really a failure after all?

Personally, I failed to get into one of the colleges that I was considering, and at the time, I was quite disappointed. Yet if that had not happened, I wouldn't have met Kris and wouldn't have my family. Plus, I loved the school I attended. I suspect many things would have been different had I been admitted to the other school. Was not getting in a "failure"?

I met a woman who dropped out of high school and became addicted to drugs. Her parents (and most everyone else too) called her a failure. For years, she struggled and experienced a great deal of pain. Eventually, however, she became drug-free and has since become totally committed to helping young people stay away from drugs. She told me that had she not experienced such great despair, she would have never been in a position to be of such service to others.

The secret is to bring the wisdom that you will almost certainly feel in the future, into the now. The idea is to know that what appears to be problematic, or even hopeless, isn't.

Again, I'm not talking about saying "Oh well, so be it" when things go wrong, as if you don't care. Instead, I'm encouraging you to become more detached and philosophical about perceived failures. I'm suggesting that when something happens that you don't like, instead of labeling it as a "failure," you banish any doubt that you'll bounce back and that eventually everything will be okay. As your thoughts bombard you with negative reinforcement, learn to dismiss them as you would flies at a picnic. Some of the most powerful methods for inner peace are the simplest.

It's interesting to experiment with the notion of banishing your doubt. You can remind yourself that there is always an answer, even when we can't immediately see it. When doubts arise in the mind, we can learn to recognize and acknowledge them, and then gently let them go. Each time it happens, go back to trusting the unknown. Trust that you'll know what to do next, when the time is right.

Over time, you'll develop greater confidence in your own inner intelligence. Instead of trying to force answers or solutions, you'll learn to quiet down in order to know what to do next. Being inwardly quiet doesn't stop your mind from thinking; rather, it activates a deeper intelligence, which some people call wisdom.

Learning to appreciate inner stillness fosters your ability to be patient, which in turn reinforces your confidence that an answer is just around the corner. So many times the best and wisest answers come not from our intellect, but from this quieter place. When we are still, we tap into what is sometimes described as "universal intelligence." No one really knows where this comes from, but wise people throughout history are certain that it exists. It's very comforting to know of this deeper intelligence. It allows you to trust that if you're quiet enough—and patient enough—the appropriate solution is just around the corner.

One of my favorite descriptions of life is that it's just "one mistake after another with a little time in between." Despite its humor, this is a pretty accurate way of seeing things. If you think about it, it's true. We make mistakes, we (hopefully) learn from them; we make adjustments and move on. At some point, there will be another mistake, and so forth. In the meantime, everyone else is going through the same process. Your parents are making mistakes, as are your friends, neighbors, children, coworkers, and everyone else.

Notice that the above description says "one mistake after another" instead of "one failure after another." It's not necessary to see our mistakes or the things that go wrong as failures. Mistakes are so much a part of life that they cannot be avoided. In fact they are what allow us to make adjustments in our lives and to learn. Without them, life would probably cease to be very interesting.

I think the greatest lesson is this: Failure is an illusion that is generated and reinforced by our own thinking. Two of my favorite quotations about thinking are these: "We are what we think" and "What you think, so shall you be." Let's not think of ourselves as failures—because we're not!

11. Illness and Injury: Are There Any Silver Linings?

In *Anatomy of an Illness*, Norman Cousins writes, "What I do for myself comes out of my philosophy, not out of my science." As a layman, unfamilar with medical science, that's the best that I can offer as well. The thoughts and ideas here stem from my own intuition into the nature of healing on a spiritual level, and have nothing to do with medicine.

My first major personal experience with illness was when I was thirteen. I had an emergency appendectomy that was done in just the nick of time. My parents were out of town, and I had been home sick, thinking it was the flu. Luckily for me, when my mother came home, it took her about five seconds to determine that this was much more serious. Into the car we went, zooming off to the emergency room.

Even though it's been almost thirty years since that experience, there were a few doctors, nurses, and medical staff personnel that stood out like shining stars on a clear, dark night. To these special people, this was obviously more than a job. They really cared. From my perspective as a teenager, they were true healers, and their compassion and love shone in their very being—you could see it in their eyes.

The people I'm talking about were highly present, meaning they were "right there" with me. More than what they said, their presence was very comforting and reassuring. Knowing what I know now, I'm certain they were terribly rushed for time and overworked. However, they didn't come across that way. Instead they would take an extra minute to sit by my bedside and an extra few seconds to look me in the eye. When I've been with others who are sick or hurt, I've always tried to remember what I learned before, during, and after my own operation—that a compassionate heart and someone who cares can be as important to a patient as any medical intervention. As I've gotten older, I've tried to seek out doctors for myself, and for those whom I love, who have this extraordinary quality of compassion.

The past few years have been interesting for me on a physical level. Overall, I've been very lucky. I developed a back problem, however, that I can only describe as mysterious and excruciating. It was similar, only worse, to the back pain that ended my college tennis career years earlier.

At first, the most frustrating part of the back injury was that I couldn't do the things I was used to being able to do. I had been forced to temporarily halt my physical rituals, such as vigorous exercise, as well as my yoga practice. Later on, that frustration turned to fear as I started to believe it would last for the rest of my life. I have been extraordinarily fortunate in that my injuries are on the mend.

While I don't pretend to clump my now ex–back problem or any of my subsequent other injuries into the same category as something much more serious, I did learn a great deal about myself in the process. Interestingly, when I've shared my experience with others who were far more sick or injured than I, they often confirmed a shared thread of humanity. Rather than compare notes on who was sicker or more injured, it was healing to simply share from the heart, instead of from the mind.

Through being sick and injured and, to a much greater extent, watching and being with others who have also been ill, I've learned a great deal about what I'll call the "silver lining" of illness or injury. Incidentally, the Silver Lining Foundation in Aspen, Colorado (no affiliation to myself), was cofounded by former tennis star Andrea Yeager. It is an amazing, heartfelt organization that allows kids to temporarily "escape" from their life-threatening illnesses, such as cancer, for some awesome adventures in nature. I'm not generally into commercials, especially within my own books, but I encourage you to check out their Web site and perhaps even consider making a financial donation. It's: www.silverlining foundation.org

When I refer to "the silver lining" of illness or injury, I'm not, in any way, making light of the subject. I'm not saying, "Look at the bright side." It's much subtler than that. What I've learned and what I'd like to share with you are a few of the nuggets of wisdom that almost always seem to be reinforced through illness or injury.

One of the first and most striking observations we can make as a result of being sick or injured is that we are not our bodies. We are the soul, which resides within our body, but not the body itself. One of my favorite spiritual teachers, Ram Dass, would peer into someone's eyes and say, "Are you in there? I'm in here. What's it like in there for you?" It's an entertaining way to emphasize the fact that we are spiritual creatures here on earth—sharing a human experience in these containers we call bodies. For whatever reasons, part of the experience of having a body is that it has problems and, eventually, wears out. Specifically, bodies get sick and hurt.

Even people who have undergone enormous physical pain and discomfort have reported that it has been extremely helpful to not overidentify with one's body. In other words, while it's important to be kind and respectful of our bodies, and to take good care of them, it's also helpful to be slightly detached from them, to "know" that "they" are not "us."

Although my own physical pain has been minimal in comparison to that of many others, I have to agree that detachment has been the key to keeping my sense of perspective. Knowing that I am *in* my body, but that I'm *not* the body, has been very comforting. This knowledge has allowed me to soften to my pain, and even to keep a sense of humor about it. One night I returned home after a basketball game with the guys. I was hobbling around and was in quite a bit of discomfort.

Half-kidding, Kris said, "Richard, I sure don't remember sports being this difficult for you twenty years ago when we first met." Indeed, she was right. I was (and am) the same person, but despite my best efforts to stay in shape, I'm not the same body. As I pulled myself over to the couch, I couldn't help but smile at the "predicament" of being in a body. Instead of tightening around my pain and sending anger and hatred in its direction, I relaxed and let go. I'll always be grateful to have a body, and I'll do whatever I can to take good care of it. I won't, however, make the mistake of believing that this body is who I really am. As Joy Thomas says in *Life Is a Game; Play It*, "The body needs no healing, but the mind that thinks it is a body is sick indeed."

Along similar lines is the subject of humility. For some of us, there's a certain arrogance that comes with the luxury of perfect health. Without even knowing it, we assume that aches, pains, illness, and even aging are things that happen to other people—not us! Obviously, deep down, we know that illness and aging are inevitable, but in the absence of present evidence to the contrary, we tend to remain in denial. So in a way, illness and injury wake us up to our shared humanity. They can act as catalysts to compassion, reminding us that despite the surface differences, deep down, we're all in the same boat, or at least a similar one. To some degree, this helps us become less self-absorbed, kinder, and more generous.

There are few things in life more inherently geared to reminding us of our own mortality than illness or injury. They reinforce to us how fragile our bodies are and how quickly life passes us by. When we or someone we love is injured or seriously ill, we are reminded to think of each day as a gift—which it is. Rather than taking life for granted, we take a close look around and marvel at the wonders of our ordinary day-to-day life. Many of our so-called problems that looked so huge and overwhelming take on a lesser significance.

My grandma Emily once said to me, "It's actually a good thing that God created aches and pains. They encourage us to be grateful when we're feeling good." I thought this was a pretty wise way of looking at physical discomfort, particularly because she suffered from a painful case of arthritis.

Recently I bruised both of my kneecaps. As they started to heal, I reflected on my grandmother's wisdom. It was amazing how grateful I became for the gift of being able to walk. An interesting question is, "Why wasn't I consciously grateful for this gift prior to my injury?" I encourage you to ask yourself similar questions. Are there ways that you too are taking certain gifts for granted?

Finally, even if you are very sick, don't discount your chances for a full physical recovery. As you know, this wasn't meant to be a strategy on physical wellness. And even though the ultimate healing occurs in the heart and not the body, it's nevertheless important to acknowledge the miraculous power of the mind-body connection. It's my feeling that there is always the possibility of a turnaround. This is true even when the doctors and other experts disagree.

I began this strategy by quoting Norman Cousins. Since *Anatomy of an Illness* is one of my all-time favorite books demonstrating the power of the human spirit, then perhaps it's also a good place to conclude. Toward the end of the book, Cousins says, "My body has already carried me far beyond the point where the medical experts in 1954 thought it would go. According to my calculations, my heart has furnished me with 876,946,280 more heartbeats than were thought possible by the insurance doctors."

12. Making It All Workable

What if there was a way, almost irrespective of what you were going through, that could make emotional pain more workable? I'm not talking about taking the pain away or denying its existence, but rather seeing and experiencing it with a different perspective. While this is a lofty suggestion, I believe that there is a way to accomplish this.

Imagine a tiny snowball being rolled down a mammoth ski run. When it starts, it's no larger than your fist. If the mountain is steep, however, and a few other ideal conditions exist, then that snowball could grow quickly as it travels down the hill.

After only a few dozen feet, the snowball grows exponentially and rapidly gains speed. It goes faster and faster, becoming bigger and bigger until, hypothetically, it is totally uncontrollable and destructive.

This is the precise nature of our thinking. Even the most painful thoughts start out small. But they fester and grow with attention. Like a snowball, when they are small, thoughts of all kinds are workable and manageable. If you were to kneel down a few feet below the snowball after it was launched, you could scoop up the snowball and crush it or even throw it back up the hill. If you were a quarter mile down the mountain, however, that same snowball might very well crush you! The key, of course, is to catch the snowball as early as possible, before it has a chance to gain much momentum.

I knew a woman who, before marriage, had a number of platonic male friends. She was absolutely open with her fiancé and made it perfectly clear that she intended to keep her treasured friendships after marriage. She was specific and honest in the way she presented her intent. To her, keeping her friendships meant occasional meetings for lunch, dinner, or coffee. She welcomed her fiancé to join in her friendships and did nothing in secret because she wasn't trying to hide anything. A very open, friendship-oriented person, she even went so far as to tell him that one of the things she loved about him, and one of the reasons she wanted to marry him, was that he was okay with her female *and* male friends. He agreed and repeatedly assured her that it would never be a problem. He said he was "very supportive" of her desire to maintain all of her friendships.

However, almost immediately after they were married, her friendships became an issue. The husband would fly into jealous rages and would sulk for days when she made plans to see a friend (even when she invited him to join them). He wondered why she didn't want to spend all of her time with him. "Why?" he asked. "Am I not enough?" He felt betrayed, bitter, and suspicious.

The two of them eventually made it into counseling, and one of the things they learned was to meditate. Their counselor wanted to show them how small stray thoughts and feelings could, quite innocently, get out of control, almost like a brushfire that starts with a single spark. A spark, of course, caught early enough, can be put out with your fingertips, whereas a brushfire can be a disaster.

The counselor explained that a person like her husband could have lingering insecure doubts in his mind about faithfulness, fidelity, and the meaning of marriage. They might be so small and rare that he wouldn't even notice them. In other words, they would be brewing and affecting him, but he wouldn't have a clue.

Because he didn't notice them, however, and recognize them as thoughts, they could grow, multiply, and become more common. It's as though the thoughts would sneak up on him, shooting him in the back. All of a sudden, without even knowing why, he would be overcome with emotion and react, often flying into a rage—or falling into despair.

It's easy to see how this could happen. If we're not paying attention and don't know what to look for, our thoughts can take over our emotions as quickly and surely as that snowball rolling down the hill! By the time we notice what's happening, it's too late. It's no longer workable. It's too big and too much to handle.

But what if you were to notice the first signs of those thoughts? What if we recognized what was happening when the snowball (thought) was still a snowflake falling from the sky? What if we were to catch that snowflake with an open and gentle hand and treat it with loving-kindness? Believe it or not, I'm not trying to be poetic here! I'm simply pointing out the power of noticing thoughts and feelings at their earliest stages. Doing so allows us to treat them with kindness and wisdom. We can look at them honestly and with perspective. We can learn from them and make intelligent, appropriate choices and decisions.

If you think about it, this not only makes spiritual sense, but it's also one of the most practical tools imaginable. Its applications are vast and effective. What if you noticed fearful thoughts about taking on a work-related project when they were still tiny? What if you could see the subtleties of the fear? What if you could reflect on them wisely, see them for what they are, and relate to them differently? It would be so much easier to be courageous. You could either seek some advice about how to overcome the fear, or maybe even let it go—instead of allowing that fear to become huge. It could be the difference between taking on the project, even if you were a little scared, and making up an excuse as to why you "can't do it." It can be the difference between procrastinating and getting started. I've found that it's very easy for fearful thoughts to become thoughts of paranoia. Likewise, it's easy for anger to turn to resentment. The easiest and best way that I'm aware of to be able to work with any of this is to catch it early. That way, it usually won't seem so ominous.

The jealous husband was not only able to save his marriage, but he was able to get over his jealous tendencies as well. Through meditation (to which I will devote an entire strategy in this book), he learned how to quiet his mind. Although it had been there all along, for the first time in his life he was able to see the mental activity that he had never been able to notice before. He described his mind as a massive traffic jam. Through meditation, he was able to substantially reduce the traffic so that he could see individual automobiles. Prior to that time, his mind was so chaotic that it felt as if these cars were simply one huge line of steel.

There's a deeper level to this as well. Through quieting our minds, we also learn the distinction between thinking only in terms of "content," versus beginning to relate to it in terms of a process. In other words, most of the time we have a thought such as, "That's not fair." If we relate to it *only* as content, it can quickly become overwhelming, even frightening. We analyze the thought and have judgments about it. We add to it with more attention. Other thoughts feed and justify it. We respond to the content with anger, fear, and even hatred. We might judge ourselves harshly and say to ourselves, "Why am I thinking these horrible things?" Or we might justify it by saying to ourselves, "That really isn't fair."

We think about "what it means," give it our focus and even more attention. It stays with us as it grows and takes on more meaning. Certain thoughts can even haunt us, as was the case with the jealous husband. It wasn't his fault. It was simply a case of his thoughts festering without his awareness. Then, all of a sudden, it seems so real and pressing. Because we're relating to it as we are, we tend to give it lots of significance. It's there, so we think it's important.

The identical thought, however, in a quieter mind can be seen and related to quite differently. It's recognized early on as being just a thought, simply as part of a process. It's much less personalized. Instead of "that's not fair" becoming an emergency, "that's not fair" is recognized as just more thoughts swimming in the mind. Because they are not as threatening now, they can be dealt with more effectively. For the first time, you have a choice in how to respond. It doesn't have to be a crisis. You have some emotional space. You can decide whether it's necessary and in your best interest to take any given thoughts further, to the next step. Or you can drop it. This isn't about letting something slide by when it's really important. It's about being freed from the prison of the mind. It's about not having to be upset simply because a thought has entered your head.

One of the most fascinating aspects to a quieter mind is that it allows thoughts that were previously unconscious to become conscious. Because of the quiet, and because thoughts are being met with acceptance, the unconscious is somehow less frightened about showing itself. New thoughts and ideas that you have never experienced before will begin to surface.

An acquaintance of mine shared a dramatic example of this with me. He said that when he learned to quiet his mind, he quickly realized that his entire life had been about seeking approval. His career choice and most other major decisions had little to do with what was in his heart. They had everything to do with pleasing others. Whereas previously he had been completely blinded to his tendencies, they now became totally obvious to the point where he could actually laugh at the way he had been living. Over the next year, he made several major life changes, all for the better.

Quieting down my mind has allowed me to become much more

honest and compassionate with myself. I've been able to see the ways in which I can be, at times, impatient and unkind. I've been able to relate to some of my old habits in new ways, often breaking them altogether. While many different people and approaches have helped me during my lifetime, nothing has been more effective to me personally than learning to quiet my mind. It has enabled me to see my own patterns, including the destructive ones—as well as solutions to most of my problems. I have a long way to go, but I trust in the power of quiet.

I once met a recovering heroin addict. He had been through numerous drug treatment programs, all of which had been very helpful. However, only when he learned to quiet his mind could he completely give up drugs. He claimed that he had been sober for five years. He realized that his impulses, real as they were, started with a single thought. He learned to relate to those thoughts as "thoughts," instead of as desires. He would recognize them, treat them with compassion, tell himself it was going to be okay, and let them go. He said that he learned to relate to his "drug thoughts" as if he were gently putting a paper boat in a swift river and allowing it to drift away.

There are so many things, big and small, in life that have the potential to upset us. The advantage of learning to quiet down the mind is that even when something is big, important, and painful, we are able to see where some of that pain is coming from, and not always, but often, we can make positive changes.

For example, I met a woman who told me that she "hated" her mother, who was about to die. She had dozens of reasons and felt entirely justified in her hatred.

Very gently, I suggested she sit quietly and allow her mind to be still. She did nothing more than sit there for a few minutes, breathing and being quiet. Even though her eyes were closed, I could see the tears streaming down her face.

After a few minutes, she opened her eyes and, while crying, told me that she realized that the hatred wasn't worth it. She felt forgiveness toward her mother and told me she was on her way to see her and "make things right." And although this seems like a magical transformation, it's pretty simple to see how it could happen.

It seemed to me that she had dozens upon dozens of thoughts that were justifying one another. She was taking them all very seriously. It's not that she wasn't justified in her anger or that she didn't have any "good reasons." She simply realized that the tremendous burden of the thoughts she was holding on to didn't outweigh the benefits of her desire to improve her relationship with her mom—before it was too late. All she did was take the time to look at the nature of her thinking a little differently. She realized that simply because she was thinking the thoughts didn't mean she couldn't relate to them differently, or even drop them altogether. It was as if she saw the innocence in herself at the same time that she saw the innocence in her mother.

I hope you'll experiment with this idea of recognizing your thoughts early on, before they have a chance to control your responses or even bum you out. Mostly it's a matter of paying closer attention to what's going on inside at any given moment—and rather than allowing those thoughts to randomly grow and develop, you decide if and when you want that to happen. I have found this strategy immensely helpful and empowering, and I hope you will too.

13. Beware the Burden of a Busy Mind

One day, each of my two kids had a couple of friends over at our house. It was close to dinnertime and everyone was getting hungry and impatient. I rushed to get something started on the stove.

I turned the burner on full blast and threw some pasta into the pot. I was cooking it as fast as possible and quickly putting in the other ingredients as well, which included a variety of vegetables.

The result was a disaster. Some of the dish was overcooked, while other parts weren't done at all. None of it tasted any good. To make matters worse, I made a huge mess in the kitchen, food was all over the place, and I ended up having to start over. In my haste to save time and move quickly, I had created additional work for myself, and the kids ended up having to wait even longer to eat.

In carpentry, there's a saying: "Measure twice, cut once." The idea is that if you take a tiny bit more time, and be careful and attentive, you'll usually avoid wasting time, energy, and money. Instead of making unnecessary mistakes, you'll get it right the first time.

Looking back, it's easy for me to see that had I stayed calm and taken an extra five minutes to prepare the kids' meal, they would have loved the way it turned out—and in the long run, I would have saved myself time, energy, and even the money spent on wasted food.

Becoming aware of the burden of a busy mind is something that can make an enormous difference in your life. Personally, this strategy has made me calmer, happier, less reactive, and more effective. It's easy to learn this, and when you do, you may find yourself saying, "I can't believe I used to live that way." You'll be astounded that you could function as well as you did with a mind so full of thoughts, ideas, and calculations, all going on at the same time, many conflicting with one another.

Becoming aware of the potential damage and the toll that a busy mind creates is in some ways similar to becoming aware that cooking too fast works to your disadvantage. In both cases, there's a sense of urgency and speed, and in both cases even though they are easily justified, it becomes clear that they interfere in their respective ways with the quality, enjoyment, and effectiveness of the end result. We appear to be doing a lot, but in reality, our efforts are getting in our own way. There is a lack of order, a duplication of effort, and we're making things more confusing than they have to be.

Think about your home, for a moment. Most of us would probably agree that there's an ideal amount of stuff—furniture, knick-nacks, decorations, art, towels, clothes, pots and pans—when everything fits nicely. At some point, however, when you cross a certain line, the result is clutter. There's a point of diminishing return. While some clutter might not be so bad, and we certainly all have our own tolerance levels, it's still fair to say that at some point it begins to interfere with the sense of order, beauty, and organization in our homes. It becomes too crowded and more difficult to find things. You end up misplacing your keys, wallet, and other important stuff because everything is such a mess. It becomes harder and harder to find places to put things, and it's much more difficult to keep the house clean. It's simply too full.

This is a great metaphor for the way we treat our minds as well.

There is a huge tendency, in many of us, to have way too much going on inside our minds, at the same time. It's too crowded in there. After all, consider what we have happening within our individual heads at any given moment.

There are all the plans about our future. What are we going to do with our life? What's going to happen later today, next week, next month, and next year? How will we get all of our work done, get the kids to soccer practice, and pick up the dry cleaning, all before five? "Whoops, I forgot to call Bill," we think to ourselves; and, "I've got so much going on at work." Meanwhile, we're planning our son's birthday party and trying to remember where we put our receipts as tax time approaches! At the same time we're thinking, "How will I survive when I retire and get older? How will it all come together?"

In our minds, this can get very complicated and involved. Our thinking is relentless. Hundreds of thoughts and decisions about various things are all vying for our attention. There is conflict among our thoughts. "I want to buy the stereo, but I'm trying to save money." Then there are all those thoughts regarding what others think about us.

There's also memory—all the things that have happened to us in the past. There are the recent memories such as the argument we had an hour ago, as well as the long-term memories such as what happened to us when we were kids. Then there are our hour-to-hour schedules, our daily to-do list. Even if we have sophisticated electronic planners, we've got most of it in our heads as well. We're constantly altering this list as well as evaluating how we're doing. We add things, check off others, and make adjustments. Then there's good old-fashioned worry. What could happen to us—what could go wrong? How can we prepare for the worst? Throw in a few resentments, goals, and fantasies, and pretty soon it's just too much.

The tricky part about detecting a busy mind on an ongoing basis and having the desire to get rid of it (or at least limit it) is that, first of all, it seems totally "normal." You've probably always had a busy mind but never considered it to be problematic. Plus, almost everyone else suffers from the same problem. Our minds are like sophisticated computers on information overload. Eventually our wires get crossed, which creates some sort of crash or malfunction! Most of us become so accustomed to it, however, that we don't give it a second thought.

Secondly, having a busy mind is not only socially acceptable but in many ways, it's also admired. We look up to people who "have a lot on their plates" and "many balls in the air." We might even be proud of the fact that we, ourselves, have so much on our minds at any given moment, and that somehow we can keep it all together. There's no doubt about it. It's tough to get rid of something that we admire.

Finally, a busy mind seems so necessary. How could we possibly function in our "busy" world with our "busy" lives if our thinking minds weren't going full steam ahead, every waking moment?

An overactive mind can be very deceptive. When something is bothering you it might, on the surface, seem obvious that the source of the problem—the culprit, so to speak—is whatever your attention is on at that moment. Suppose, for example, you have a fight with your spouse. She says something that bothers you, and you fly into a rage. Instantly, you react. You get caught up in the drama and even more agitated. Mentally you're arguing and rehearsing your responses. You're convinced she's to blame. You're right—and she's wrong.

The question is, "Would you have been so easily bothered and reactive had your mind been clear and calm?" It's hard to know for sure, but it's certainly worth considering. As it was, your mind was probably spinning in a dozen different directions. You were tense and on edge before she made the comment that upset you. You felt pressure, and your head was full of concerns totally unrelated to your relationship with your spouse. Looking back, it's easy to see that practically anything could have set you off.

Think about the pressure of living like this—your mind always full, constantly calculating. You've got it all, right there, on the surface. It's one thought after another, after another—all day long. Like a mental game of Ping-Pong, your thoughts are flying back and forth. You are anything but centered.

There are numerous benefits to having less on your mind at any given moment. The first has to do with the way you'll feel. As the sheer volume of data, information, planning, worries, figuring out, and wondering is reduced, even slightly, you will feel as though you've just stepped out of a dark cave and into the sunlight. You'll feel a sense of spaciousness, lightness, and freedom. To me, it's the mental equivalent of having a cluttered desk—with papers and folders stacked to the ceiling—suddenly cleaned up and organized. You'll feel a sudden sense of clarity, as if you can see light at the end of the tunnel; the forest through the trees.

You'll also become less tense and reactive. Because your mind will be quieter, you won't feel the impulse to "jump" at everything that goes wrong or is unexpected, or overanalyze every thought regarding the slightest hitch in your plans or expectations. You'll be able to pick and choose which thoughts to give significance to, which ones to honor with your attention, and which ones to attach less significance to, or to simply drop or dismiss.

One of my favorite metaphors on the subject of a busy mind is to think of an elevator that has reached its capacity of sixteen persons or 2,500 pounds. As long as the rule is honored and the number of people doesn't exceed the capacity, the elevator operates safely at a high level of efficiency. Although it's crowded in the elevator, it's not packed, and the passengers remain relatively comfortable. The riders continue to cooperate with one another, moving out of one another's way when necessary.

If you were to cram an additional twenty people into the elevator, however, all hell would break loose. The passengers would become irritated and edgy, and the elevator would no longer be safe. Riders would get in one another's way, and the sheer volume of passengers would endanger the very process of traveling up and down the elevator. There would be claustrophobia, anger, confusion, and chaos.

Our mind is similar to that elevator. There is an optimal level of mental activity whereby we remain relatively relaxed and operate at high efficiency. Life doesn't get to us too much, even when things go wrong or when the stakes are high. I know that when my own mind is free and clear, I can keep my perspective pretty well. I can receive what could otherwise be seen as "irritating news" and take it in stride. When my expectations aren't met, I'm usually able to deal with it. What's more, when "bigger," more significant things come up, I'm usually able to think clearly and responsively in the moment.

When our "thought capacity" is on overload, however, the results can be, and often are, disastrous. Little things start to bother us. There is too much to keep track of, and we become frustrated and confused. Just the other day, for example, I was standing next to a stranger who appeared to have too much on her mind. I could see it in her eyes and hear it when she spoke. She seemed distracted and tense as she paced nervously back and forth, glancing constantly at her watch. Her thoughts and words were all over the place. The two of us were watching a soccer game, and the referee made a questionable decision. I have no idea whether or not his ruling was fair and correct—it didn't matter. This woman, however, couldn't get beyond it. She screamed at the referee and started pacing back and forth even faster than before, mumbling about the "stupid referee" and the unfairness of life.

On the surface, such small stuff might not seem that important, but cumulatively over time, it makes an enormous difference, especially when the stakes are high. Imagine the clarity and wisdom that are needed when we are dealing with really big stuff. A friend, for example, is hurting and needs help. If you have "a thousand things on your mind," how helpful are you going to be?

Suppose your bills are getting out of control and you're overextended financially. What you need most, of course, is crystal clear thinking. That way, you can make the needed adjustments and come up with an intelligent plan. What if, instead, your mind is filled with worries and overall busyness? You could easily panic and even exacerbate the problem with poor decision making.

I think of a busy mind as the early stage of nervousness, irritation, and stress. It's the breeding ground for overreactions and poor decisions. When looked at in this way, it's seen as being undesirable, which makes it easier to be motivated to turn down the volume and velocity of our thinking, to rid yourself of the grips of a busy mind.

The key to calming down and quieting a busy mind is to trust that, if you do, everything will be okay. If you empty your mind, you won't be turning it off. It will still be working. In fact, it will be smarter and work better and more efficiently, just like the back burner of a stove (remember my pasta)! A wise, intelligent, and orderly thought process will take over, and the appropriate thoughts will emerge when needed. As Joe Bailey and I discussed in our book, *Slowing Down to the Speed of Life*, it's comforting to remind yourself that when it comes to your thinking, "less is often more." It's also helpful to know that mental health is our birthright.

I was jogging along the sidewalk one day, tripped on the curb, and skinned my knee. What a mess it was. There was blood all over the place. Luckily it didn't feel quite as bad as it looked.

When I returned home, I cleaned the wound and put a bandage on it. I then pretty much forgot about it and went on with my day.

Later that night, some eight or nine hours later, I took off the bandage to clean the wound. Much to my surprise, the large cut had already begun to heal. A scab was forming, almost before my eyes.

The question I asked myself and that I pose to you right now is this: How do our bodies know how to do this? If you step back and think about it, it's remarkable. We don't try to fix or heal it—it just happens all by itself. Somehow, our bodies know what to do. The same dramatic healing process applies, in many cases, when we break a bone or sprain an ankle, as well as to countless other things that happen to us. It's an everyday miracle in action.

My experience has been that mental health and resiliency are remarkably similar. They are the mental or spiritual equivalent of having a healthy immune system. We don't have to learn how to "have it" because it's already there. Obviously there are many times when it evades all of us, such as when we get caught up in our thinking and lose our perspective—but it never goes anywhere. Think about it. Where would it go? Instead of going anywhere, it simply becomes hidden, much like the sun behind the clouds.

You've probably had the experience of having an idea or solution come to you, as if from out of the blue. Out of nowhere, you have an insight; the perfect thought pops into your head at exactly the right time.

What I'm suggesting is that instead of these insights occurring randomly—once in a while, by surprise—we can learn to make them more of a way of life. Each of us has the capacity to learn to relate to life from a calmer, wiser perspective. Instead of being scattered and feeling rushed, we can operate from wisdom and feel peace. Trusting in our own innate intelligence instigates this process.

The implications of trusting in this process are invaluable. It suggests that we don't have to try so hard, every moment of every day. We can let go of the need to keep everything at the forefront of our minds at all times. Instead, we can learn to trust that if we relax, the appropriate thoughts and ideas will come to us at the right time. This doesn't mean we don't pay careful attention to our schedules, keep a day planner, or think things through. It has nothing to do with losing our "edge." In fact, any edge we have is greatly enhanced. All we're really doing is learning to let go of and release many of the thoughts that are weighing us down; the extra ones that we don't need at any given moment. It's like letting go of a tight fist or taking off a heavy backpack.

The way to begin is to pay calm attention to the level and volume of activity going on in your mind at any given moment. Simply pay attention. Don't judge what you observe, or be hard on yourself. As you spend time observing your own thinking, you will find yourself becoming more "present." You'll feel the peace that comes from training your attention to be where you want to be at any given time. If you're reading, for example, you'll be focused on the content. If you're playing tennis, you'll be fully engaged in the game. If you're having a discussion, the person you're with will feel that you are right there with her.

Notice how much of your mental content is surprisingly unnecessary. For example, while you're sitting down talking to a friend, see if you can notice how other thoughts want to distract you. I was talking to someone just yesterday, when my own thoughts started to bombard me! There wasn't any actual emergency to deal with. They were just random thoughts reminding me of all the things I had to do that day. Every one of them was totally unnecessary at that particular moment. In fact, all they were doing was interfering with the one thing I *was* actually doing—having an important conversation with someone with whom I had an appointment. My thoughts, however, were trying to convince me that this appointment wasn't worthy of my attention, but all my other appointments were.

That's the nature of our thinking. It will sacrifice your concentration and joy in whatever you are actually doing in favor of everything else you are going to do later, or have already done, or even those things you are simply worried about. If you think about it objectively, it's bizarre and extremely ineffective. In this instance, it helped me to know what was happening. Rather than continue my conversation, totally distracted, I was able to let go of the unnecessary thoughts and refocus my attention. Personally, I'd rather have a five-minute nondistracted conversation than a full hour of mental busyness and distraction.

I titled this strategy "Beware the Burden of a Busy Mind" because being aware of the burden is half the battle. Beyond that, all that's necessary is to gently drop the thoughts that aren't needed at any given time. That's it: Just notice them, and let them go.

Know that your thoughts will still be there, and that they will reemerge if and when they are needed. For example, in the conversation I just mentioned, I had confidence that if I dropped my "busyness," meaning my unnecessary thoughts, and could simply focus on my current conversation, then when it was finished my memory would provide me with what I needed to do next. And that's exactly what happened.

A moment-to-moment busy mind is a huge burden. If you can limit this burden even slightly, you'll be amazed at this new source of creativity, as fresh ideas and insights become more common. As you trust in a quieter, less distracted mind, you'll also be amazed at how much calmer you can feel and how much more perspective you can develop. Then, when big stuff happens, you'll be ready. You'll be able to see exactly what is happening with heightened perspective, without the burden of dozens of smaller issues dominating your attention.

Over time, this awareness can become second nature, even normal for you. As you empty your mind in this manner on an ongoing basis, you'll create much-needed mental space that is the source of peace, insight, relaxation, wisdom, and happiness. As you create space between your thoughts, you'll find it easier to notice when there's too much on your mind.

I'm convinced that an overactive, busy mind is a true burden that interferes with our natural wisdom, common sense, and happiness. I hope that as you become familiar with the peace and joy that come from having less on your mind, you too will agree.

14. Face the Truth with Loving-Kindness

This strategy has been one of the most important concepts I have ever introduced into my life. I'll admit, up front, that it wasn't easy to get started. Initially, for me, it brought up many doubts and fears, some of which I didn't even know I had. But after some practice and patience, it has provided me with great strength, confidence, and courage, as well as a practical way to directly confront anything that comes my way.

One of the easiest and perhaps most understandable coping mechanisms we use, as humans, is suppression, or looking away from problems. Another way of saying this is, we pretend that something isn't so, or that we don't notice it to be so. I refer to this as "understandable" because it's related to our inherent "fight or flight" response. Typically, when we perceive something to be frightening or threatening, we do one of two things. We either strike back in retaliation, or we run for cover.

For example, we might be furious at someone in our family and may have been so for many years. Rather than face the truth and look it in the eye, we go about our business. We either avoid that family member or we put on an act when we are around them. In the name of wanting to maintain a level of family peace, we pretend that things are other than they actually are. We might very well be polite, but inside, we are fuming. There is a disconnect between what we are presenting and what we are actually experiencing. This type of relationship can be functional but never fully healed or as genuinely loving as it could be.

Sometimes we engage in passive-aggressive behavior. This means that we say, or do, mean-spirited things that on the surface may not seem to have anything to do with any anger or frustration on our part. We'll put someone down with sarcasm, for example, or we'll show up late, creating stress for that person, but always appearing very sincere. We might even say, "Oh, sorry about that." This way, we don't have to appear as though there is any negative intent or ill feelings on our part. We get to be aggressive but don't have to admit it. That's why it's called "passive." It's not blatant, and sometimes it's not even intentional. In any event, regardless of our actual inner truth, we can act as though nothing is wrong.

The problem with this type of self-deception and lack of truthfulness is that it's disingenuous and ultimately self-destructive. In addition to any negative impact you may have on another person, you also end up deceiving yourself and, most importantly, perpetuating the cycle. The reason is this: No matter how much we may wish it were otherwise, the truth is still the truth. It's still there, and it is what it is. Whether it's anger at a family member, self-doubt about your own abilities, or fear of the unknown (or a known risk), your feelings are right there, waiting to be dealt with. And until they are recognized, they aren't going to go away.

Your thoughts might involve regret from the past, sadness from a failed relationship, disappointment from a loss, or any number of other things. The truth is, however, that the thoughts, memories, and feelings you have about these things are still a part of your life, whether they are present in your mind, or even when left unattended in the background. They can be with you, hiding at a slight distance, yet just powerful enough to cause havoc, frustration, and confusion in your life. Until they are recognized, acknowledged, and dealt with in a straightforward and healthy way, they will continue to make their presence known in a variety of subversive ways.

For example, your unacknowledged fears will run your life and keep you from doing things. You won't sign up for certain activities, take risks, or meet new people. Your anger and resentment will poison your relationships and your ability to love and forgive. You'll be reactive or resentful but won't know why. Your tiny bit of greed or self-interest will encourage you to act in slightly unethical ways. You'll never know why people don't fully trust you. All of this, and more, is because we don't want, or can't face, the truth. None of this suggests that we are bad people, or that there is something wrong with us. It's simply a result of an unwillingness to look at those parts of ourselves, those thoughts that we fear or find unacceptable.

So what do you do with a nagging fear that never seems to go away? What can you do about your deep resentment about that person who took advantage of you? How can one ever overcome the sadness that came about from a hurtful or even traumatic experience?

As we have already seen, the practice of mindfulness involves being aware, in a nonjudgmental way, of what is really going on in the moment. So, for example, you breathe in and become aware that you are, in fact, breathing. As you breathe out, you pay attention to the fact that you are breathing out. You're fully aware of what's going on in the moment.

As you live your life in a mindful way and go about your daily business, many different thoughts and states of mind will surface. Some you will like, others you will not. You don't have to do anything different. Just be aware, mindful of what's happening. Rather than embracing only those states of mind that are pleasant, be open and willing to accept them all.

Notice when fear presents itself. It might be the fear of getting old, sick, or even the fear of death. Or it could be some old fear of failure visiting you once again; or maybe it's the fear that you're going to be alone, or that something bad is going to happen. Ironically, it's during these moments that you have a tremendous opportunity to grow and, ultimately, to reduce the source of your suffering. The trick is this. Instead of turning away from the fear, distracting yourself in some way, or denying its existence, turn directly toward it instead. Breathe in and say to yourself, "I'm breathing in." Breathe out and say to yourself, "There is that old fear again." I encourage you to actually talk to it, and when you do, be kind. Don't be concerned or even surprised that it's there. Instead, communicate with your own fear with loving-kindness. It will not hurt you, and it need not be your enemy. Instead of saying, "Go away and leave me alone," or pretending that it's not really there, be patient, as if it were an old friend. Investigate the fear, as if from a distance. Notice how it appears. Be detached, yet interested and attentive.

I sometimes think of my negative and fearful thoughts as being tucked away in a backpack that I wear on my back everywhere I go. Every once in a while, one of them comes out to visit me. What I've discovered is that there is no way, at least that I have found, to get rid of the contents of that backpack. However, I have learned to relate to that which is inside very differently. Whereas before I would try to keep the fear, anger, frustration, and regret stuffed in the bag, I now allow it to come out whenever it feels the need. In fact, in many instances, I (metaphorically, of course) unzip the pack and invite the thoughts out for a visit. What's really interesting to note is that the willingness to "let them out" is the very dynamic that keeps them from wanting to come out.

Some people describe the experience of "watching" their thoughts in this manner as being similar to watching a movie. They are simply the observer, watching the fears, jealousy, greed, hate, anxiety, frustration, stress, and whatever else happens to be on the "mind screen." They don't judge what they observe, or try to change it, but simply observe what is present. It's the simple act of observation that melts the negativity away and gives one's inner health the chance to surface.

It is resistance itself that keeps fear and other negative emotions alive and wanting to hang around. Our aversion to that which is uncomfortable keeps it coming back. It's like a rubber band. If we pull on it hard and then try to get away, it snaps back faster and harder.

When there is no resistance, however, there is no struggle. There is no fuel for the fire. When negative thoughts are recognized and the truth of the moment is acknowledged, without panic and without resistance, the edge is taken away. True, the first few times you do this may seem strange. After all, you are inviting for a visit the very things you have run away from, or avoided, for your entire lifetime. It's like inviting a neighbor you've been feuding with into your home for coffee. Your relationship with your own thoughts is similar to that relationship with your neighbor. Until you make the gesture, until you invite them in, the feud will probably continue.

However, as you practice and become more confident in this new way of relating to your thoughts of fear, anger, and pain, you'll notice that the pain will soften. It will never go away completely and it may not be pleasant, but it most certainly won't be so awful anymore.

I was having a difficult time working with someone on a project. We were experiencing more conflict than I was used to. There was an absence of flow and connection. Something seemed wrong. I began paying closer attention to what was going on within me. I noticed some old tapes playing in my head, thoughts of being taken advantage of, for example. I was also making a lot of negative judgments about this person.

Rather than trying to do anything about it, pretend it was otherwise, or demand that the other person behave differently, I simply acknowledged what was happening. "Boy, there's a judgmental thought—and another. And there's a fearful one too. Why are you visiting me today?" I asked. In a manner of minutes, it became obvious that my thoughts were bombarding me with "old stuff." But rather than trying to figure it out, or change what was happening, I simply let it be.

The healing experience that followed has proven to be somewhat common. The simple act of recognizing the thoughts, allowing them to be there without pushing them away and without trying to deny, change, or do anything with them, had the effect of lessening their impact. It was as if the thoughts lost their power to keep me upset, as well as their influence over my perspective and business judgment. As I became less reactive, I was able to make better decisions and to make the necessary changes in our relationship. Once I was no longer emotionally upset, I was able to make adjustments and to deal with the situation more rationally.

I remember the first time I confronted a bully without fear. I was only ten years old and had been very frightened by this person. Like so many other bullies, he fed on my fear. The more upset I became, the more he enjoyed bothering me. One day, at the suggestion of my mother, I looked him in the eye (in front of several other people) and very calmly and nonsarcastically asked him the following questions: "Do you really enjoy picking on people who are much smaller than you? Do you also pick on and beat up tiny little kids—or just ten-year-olds like me?"

I was totally helpless, yet from that moment on, the bully never again bothered me. In fact, he was hesitant to even come near me. By confronting him directly, face-to-face, with a calm, unfearful resolve, I was able to dismantle his need to pick on me. No force was necessary. No threats, muscles, or retaliation were required. What was required was a willingness to look directly at my fear.

I've discovered that our thoughts, fears, and frustrations respond in a remarkably similar way. When they are met head-on, face-to-face, with kindness, they will dissolve and become manageable all by themselves.

To me, this is the ultimate practice for the big stuff in our lives. We are all going to experience pain and grief. We will be separated from those we love. We will experience change and uncertainty. We will all experience loss, disappointment, and failure. The question becomes, "What will we do when it happens?" To me, the answer is difficult, but simple. When we lose something or someone we love, we will look directly at the pain. That way, instead of the pain coming at us, consuming us, and bombarding us from all directions, sneaking up on us at unexpected times, we will know right where it is because we'll be looking right at it.

Make no mistake about it. This strategy isn't about saying, "Oh there's pain," in a cavalier sort of way, as if that's going to take the pain away. It's about recognizing, acknowledging, and investigating the pain that enters our lives. It's about dealing with pain with kindness and compassion, instead of fear or aversion.

A woman I met was having an extremely difficult time dealing with the empty-nest syndrome. She had raised four daughters, and now they had all moved away. Her well-intentioned friends urged her to distract herself from her loneliness. She tried to keep busy and motivated. But the harder she tried, the deeper the despair and emptiness she felt. Time was moving on, but time alone was not healing her wounds.

At some point later on, she was encouraged to stop running from her pain and to stop trying to make it go away. Instead, she was taught to look directly at that which she feared most—loneliness—but to do so with compassion and loving-kindness. It was as if she said to her own thoughts, "Hi there, loneliness. I see you're still here with me." Rather than push it away, she welcomed the pain.

In a matter of days, the pain she had been experiencing for so long began to soften at the edges. Her biggest fears had been confronted, not with harshness or force, but with a gentle curiosity. Now that she had acknowledged and attended to her fear, her thoughts began to change and to become more positive. It was as if she had given herself permission to move on.

Facing the truth with loving-kindness is a powerful method for facing the things we fear the most. When we touch our fear, anger, or despair with compassion instead of aversion, our inner healing capacity has a chance to unfold. I hope you'll have the courage to look directly at that which causes you pain and to treat it with the kind of love that it really needs.

15. Surrender to Your Lack of Control

To me, one of the irony of ironies is that in order to feel "safe" in the world, one of the most important ingredients is that we must, in effect, give up. But it's not giving up in a defeatist sense. Rather, we give up the struggle that stems from imagining we have more control than we actually have.

To one degree or another, most of us have attempted to keep ourselves safe. Either consciously or unconsciously, we have imagined that it's somehow possible to adequately prepare ourselves in order to keep danger away. So we fight, build walls, resist, accumulate, stash valuables, live in cynicism, behave defensively, and otherwise set ourselves up and prepare for various forms of danger—real and perceived.

I knew of a man who, by all measurable standards, was very successful. He had everything a person could want. He had enjoyed great success, good fortune, and social prestige. He had a beautiful family and was physically attractive. He was healthy and very rich.

The trouble was, he was paranoid. He felt that he would be safe if he could only be "prepared." When asked what he was preparing for, he looked upon the questioner as if he were naïve.

Like most of us, he lived with the illusion that if one worked at it hard enough, it was possible to resist the laws of nature. He believed that control was possible, and he was relentless in his efforts. So he built and lived in a secure environment. He had the best lawyers money could provide. He had access to the best medical treatment. He sent his kids to the top schools and the best therapists. He hired a physical trainer so that he and his wife could remain fit and healthy. He had an ironclad, perfectly prepared prenuptial agreement and a very complex estate plan. His files and drawers were organized.

His days were spent watching over his fortune and trying to figure out even better ways to keep everything together. When there was a problem, he attacked it—head-on. He was always on his toes, on the lookout.

In a way, his wealth and good fortune worked against him. His money and power made it more tempting to believe he could protect himself against—well, everything.

Ultimately, of course, he could not. Life being what it is, things changed. His children grew up and rebelled. He had far less control than he imagined. His wife left him for a younger, more attractive man. The prenuptial agreement was helpful but not foolproof. His body aged, he became sick, and ultimately he died. After his death, his heirs fought over his money.

The reason I use a rich and powerful man as an example is because he, more than most, would appear to have beaten the odds. But like the famous actress who clings to her fame—or the physically attractive woman who ties her self-worth to her beauty—there is, in the end, unavoidable and certain pain.

But all of this is merely the external, easy-to-identify part of the illusion of control. The problem is actually much deeper and plays out in far more subtle ways in most of our lives. Because of our circumstances, most of us probably don't believe we can control everything with our money, power, or good looks! But there is still plenty we strive to control. And it's the attempt and, more specifically, the grasping at this control that is at the root of our anxiety and pain.

It seems to me that, more than anything, what most of us really want is a "certain" future. And there's a way in which we want this to be guaranteed. I don't necessarily mean financially certain, but rather, we want our world and our lives to be predictable. We want to feel secure about the future, to know what's going to happen—and to be able to control it. We want to be able to "hang our hats" on some degree of certainty.

This is, of course, very understandable. The problem, however, is that we live in a world of constant change, a world in which there is no actual security or absolute predictability. So the harder we resist, the harder we fall. The more investment we make in creating and demanding predictability, the more disappointed we are when our expectations and hopes are not met.

There are examples at every turn. We want someone to behave in a certain way, but they don't. We pin our hopes on a stock going up—but it doesn't. We want our children to take a certain path—but they choose differently. We need snow for skiing, but there is a drought. We expect to retire at a certain age, but the company we work for goes under. We want our friends' marriage to last, but they end up divorced. I could go on for pages.

As I mentioned above, it's ironic. The predicament of facing an uncertain future and an insecure world is best dealt with by surrendering to our lack of control. Indeed, the thing we least want to do is, ultimately, our only way out—our only true defense. Think about it. The burden of predictability is awesome and endless. If our primary goal is to be safe and certain, then change becomes our enemy. If getting what we want—the things, responses, outcomes, and all the rest—is essential to our peace of mind, we will never experience true or lasting peace.

When our response to change is aggressive or resistant, it's like being in a riptide in the ocean. The harder we swim, the farther we sink and the more helpless we become. The way out of a riptide is *not* to fight and resist. In fact, to do so greatly increases the odds of drowning. Instead, the way to free yourself is to let go and allow the tide to take you where it may. Once the tide has had its way with you, it becomes, in most cases, relatively harmless. It's then easy to make an adjustment, swim parallel to the shore, and get out of the water.

Keep in mind, you're not surrendering to the riptide because you want to drown. It's just the opposite. You surrender to the current because you want to survive. Your lack of resistance becomes your greatest strength.

Life is just like a riptide. It's going to do what it does, with or without our consent or approval. There will be plenty of twists and turns. At times it will be smooth—other times it will be rough. Always it will be largely unpredictable.

What I'm talking about here has absolutely nothing to do with downplaying the importance of making rational and practical preparations for the future. Obviously, it's wise to take good care of yourself and those you love. I'm a huge advocate of preventive health. I recommend yoga for many reasons, not the least of which being that you'll be less stiff as you age! I'm an advocate of lifelong education, not only because it's fun to learn, but also because a good education is often an essential tool for success.

I also carry life insurance to protect my family if I were to die unexpectedly. I believe in home security. I even have disaster supplies in the event of a natural or human-caused emergency. And I encourage you to do the same. I believe you should do everything, within reason, to put the odds in your favor.

This philosophy has nothing to do with rolling over and being a victim. It's not about allowing others to walk all over you, or about being passive. Instead it's about acknowledging the power of surrender. It's comforting to know that the future is not on your shoulders. And it's okay—in fact, desirable—that it's not. The solution is not to believe that you can somehow solve every problem that comes your way. Nor is the solution to believe that there is a way—if you were only to try hard enough—to stay on top of it all, or that you can anticipate and prepare for every twist and turn of the journey.

Whether it's making love, enjoying a play or some music, having a meal with a good friend, taking a walk by the sea, or doing any number of other enjoyable events, chances are you're right there, in the moment. The very fact that you're in the moment is what makes the experience so special. This is why memories can be wonderful, but generally they're not quite as great as the real thing.

The idea is to be "in" the moment instead of comparing it to other moments. Generally, when we are frightened, disappointed, or angry, we try to escape it in one of two ways. We either retreat into a memory because we consider it reliable and predictable. Or we imagine the future and either attempt to resolve the situation or create fear around it. Our mind spins and churns and searches for an answer. We don't want to be defenseless.

But as we acknowledge and embrace the importance of surrender, we feel safe to enter the moment—even when it's painful. Because we have acknowledged that there is nowhere to hide, we stop running. And for the first time we realize that the greatest safety isn't found in trying to protect ourselves from the moment. Rather it's found by being completely open to "what is."

Just yesterday I was talking to a woman who had just found out that her daughter had been caught using drugs at school. Her genuine sense of calm made me want to ask her to write a chapter for this book! She was at peace because she knew there was nowhere to hide. With unimaginable love in her eyes, she talked about how difficult it was to bring her child to rehab.

She reflected upon her own youth and some of the troubles she had experienced. In no way was she minimizing the seriousness of what happened. In fact, she was a model of "tough love" in action. She had a firm resolve about what needed to be done, and she was doing what was necessary. Yet at the same time, she had a deep sense of perspective. Although she knew her family life had changed, she was up to the task. She hadn't expected it, nor would she wish it upon anyone else. But she wasn't running from it, either—physically or emotionally. Rather than putting up a front, or pretending things were different from what they were, she was surrendering to the truth of the moment. Her surrender was enabling her wisdom to shine.

16. Do Not Enter!

Have you ever noticed how important signs are in our lives, and how seriously we take them? So often the meanings of those signs provide hidden life lessons well beyond their actual intention. Think for a moment about a few common road signs. How about Rough Road Ahead? The metaphor, of course, or suggestion could be to be aware of tough times approaching. Or, Caution. Again, you could take this one to mean, be careful. Sometimes, it's wise to approach life with our eyes wide open.

What about Reduce Speed Ahead? Who couldn't benefit from this advice in their life? What a great reminder for all of us, not just when we're driving, but in the rest of life as well.

Dr. Rhonda Hull wrote a great book, *Drive Yourself Happy*, filled with such metaphors. She suggests that when we see a sign, we can use it as a reminder of something else. It's almost as though the sign taps us on the shoulder, as if to say, "Keep this in mind."

One of the most meaningful signs of any kind, to me, is one of the most specific: Do Not Enter! How many times a day do you see these words? The meaning itself is self-explanatory. It's a command or warning that says, "Don't come in here." The sign might be announcing some sort of danger—or it could be protecting personal property. Or there could be some other reason.

To me, however, there is a powerful, life-enhancing message in the words Do Not Enter. And if you remember to use them during certain times, it can make the difference between internal suffering—anger, frustration, jealousy, depression, regret, worry—and a sense of peace. This is particularly true when we're dealing with difficult times.

In this instance, I'm suggesting that we apply the words Do Not Enter to many of the thoughts that we allow to enter our minds. Rather than granting unlimited free access to any thought that happens to want to be thought about, the words Do Not Enter offer a form of mental protection or barrier against potentially toxic thoughts. They are, very simply, a reminder that if we allow certain thoughts to take hold, they will almost certainly bring forth pain, confusion, or further aggravation. And although there are certainly times when it's necessary to think about something, it's more often the case—if you're really honest about it—that it's not necessary.

I once made this suggestion to an audience. A man stood up and objected. He said, "I see where you're going with this analogy, but it's a little too 'cute' for me." He felt that the issues he was dealing with were too important to be applying techniques such as this.

About a month later, I received one of the most humble, grateful messages I've ever received. It was from this same man. Apparently he had been able to overcome his own objections, see the relevance, and apply the words to his life. He claimed that applying the Do Not Enter concept had prevented his anger from turning to rage—and his disappointment to despair.

Often, the most effective techniques are not complicated at all. But though they may be described as being simple, they are not necessarily easy. Consider the wisdom of counting to ten before reacting. The simplest and shortest pause can make the difference between a knee-jerk reaction and an appropriate response. Or how about the wisdom of breathing before you speak? Taking a moment, even a fraction of a second, before blurting out a response, allows you to digest and fully understand what someone is saying to you. It allows the other person to feel heard, listened to, and understood. I was once told by a man that for every 5 percent he improved his listening skills, his marriage improved by a whopping 50 percent. I've been told countless other times that poor listening was a person's single biggest gripe in a relationship, and that the slightest improvement is extremely helpful.

I point out these examples to demonstrate that just because something is simple doesn't mean it's not powerful or effective. This is definitely the case with the Do Not Enter philosophy. Here's why.

Our thinking will always come back to us as a feeling. Suppose, for example, like the person I just described, you were thinking this technique is too simplistic. If so, you would, by definition, be feeling skeptical, suspicious, or cynical. On the other hand, if you see its relevance, you might be feeling hopeful or curious. A similar dynamic exists regardless of what specific content is on your mind. Imagine, for a moment, that you wanted to get really angry right now. How would you go about it? What would you have to do?

Obviously, in order to get angry, you'd have to think about something that makes you mad. Without those thoughts, or some other angry thoughts, you'd be out of luck—so to speak. Not that you'd ever want to, but what if you wanted to feel jealous? The only way would be to imagine or think about someone else having something you want—or taking it (or him or her) away from you.

One of my favorite examples of the connection between thoughts and feelings is that of someone reading a magazine. Suppose you were reading a story about a little girl and her pony. Although she was only ten years old, she had been winning national contests for several years. You might think, "Wow, that's really neat." If so, you'd probably be feeling uplifted, or even inspired.

On the other hand, you might think to yourself, "What a spoiled brat. She must have rich parents." If you thought this instead, you would be feeling cynical. What's interesting is that the words on the page were exactly the same. They didn't cause your emotion—your thoughts did.

Knowing this is extremely helpful and empowering. I'm not suggesting for a moment that there aren't physiological factors at play— I suspect that there probably are. Nor am I suggesting that one's background, genes, or circumstances aren't important, or that they don't play a role. However, that being said, a person can be predisposed to practically anything and still overcome it. The point here is that without negative thoughts taken to heart or taken too seriously, there is simply no fuel for the fire. Ultimately, your thoughts are the responsible party that determines how you are feeling.

A man shared with me a dramatic example of how his thinking brought an historical event to life. He had been very happily married for almost twenty years. He and his wife had three beautiful children. Other than a few ordinary complaints, he described his marriage as "very loving."

But then he found out!

About a year after they were married, his wife had had a brief affair. The affair lasted about a month and took place well before they had any children. She had never seen the man since that time.

He went completely nuts and started acting like a wounded animal (to use his own words). He wanted her out of the house and demanded a divorce. He said his rage went on for weeks. Luckily, he was willing to see a counselor.

Regardless of your personal view on infidelity, this is a dramatic example of the nature of thought. Twenty years of peaceful living erased by "the thought" of one's spouse having an affair.

"But it actually happened," you might say, and you're right—it did. In no way am I condoning or minimizing an affair, but instead,

I'm simply demonstrating the power and influence our thinking has on the way we feel. An event such as this was certainly real—it happened, but it had no impact on the husband until his thoughts brought it to life.

What makes this story even more interesting is the way he described his recovery. He had seen a counselor, who taught him to relate to his thoughts less harshly. He was encouraged to observe his thoughts instead of becoming lost in them. The effect was that he was able to step back from his thinking and decide, from moment to moment, which thoughts to allow in and which ones to apply the Do Not Enter policy to.

After a while, he became free of any misery, jealousy, or insecurity surrounding the affair. Often a thought would still come to mind about it, but he had learned to soften his response. He told me that he would "look" at the thought and say, with a smile, "I'd rather you went away." In other words, Do Not Enter. He had learned to make light of his own thoughts.

He began to experience a deeper level of relating to his thinking. He realized that his thoughts were just that—thoughts. And his thoughts, like everyone else's, will come and go. When you see your thoughts in this light, it becomes easy to become less reactive to them. It's the difference between being "in" a movie versus "watching" the movie. If you were in a bank being held up by bank robbers at gunpoint, it would be terrifying. If, however, you were watching a movie about a bank robbery, it might still be riveting, but you'd certainly be okay. In fact, unless it was a really bad movie, it would probably even be entertaining! That's exactly what begins to happen to your state of mind as you distance yourself from your own thinking. You will have many of the same thoughts but without being subjected to the same reactions.

It's important to know that this understanding isn't about pretending that something didn't happen or that you approve of something that you disapprove of. Rather, it's a perspective about your own power to determine how much significance you are going to give each thought—and whether or not it's in your best interest even to think about it at all.

Here's a personal example. I was in a conflict with someone and was in the habit of thinking about it too much. Every time I'd think about the problem—or the person I was having the problem with—I'd get uptight and angry.

At some point I realized that every time my thinking would turn in this direction, I had a very clear choice. I could think about the situation at that time, or I could hold up the Do Not Enter sign and back off. When I would choose to think about it, I'd bring it back to life. I would feel bothered and resentful, which would encourage more of the same.

On the other hand, the more often I dismissed it, the less relevant it became. What I learned was that my thinking about it had nothing to do with actually solving the issue. That was either going to happen or not, in time and on its own.

To be completely honest, the same thoughts continue to emerge, even to this day. The difference is that they no longer haunt me. I recognize their existence and, most of the time, simply dismiss them. Rather than being a source of distress, the very same thoughts are seen as harmless.

When you reflect deeply on the power of thinking, you can't help but realize that hatred, resentment, and nonforgiveness all stem from thought. I once questioned this fact and was asked, "If thinking isn't holding hatred in place—what is?" I've never been able to come up with an adequate answer.

Whenever we are dealing with an important issue in our lives— whenever the stakes are high—we are at great risk to "overthink," or to lack perspective about our thinking. Our thoughts will tend to dominate our attention, and each one will be crying out, "Think me." There will be so many thoughts, and so many of them will be painful that it's critical we develop the capacity for making checks and balances. In other words, we need to have a way to reduce the volume and intensity of any thoughts that are going to lower our spirits. That way, we will be more equipped to deal peacefully with whatever cards we are dealt.

The more we are able to recognize that our own thoughts can't hurt us without our consent, the more we will be able to keep them in perspective. And as this happens, we will be able to look some of them in the eye and, when appropriate, say the words, "Do not enter."

17. Dedicate Yourself to Mindfulness

One of the most dramatic examples of pure beauty that I have ever experienced occurred a few years ago in Connecticut. My plane landed very late, well after dark. My one-hour ride to my lodging accommodations in the countryside was very uneventful. After all, I couldn't see much. My vision was limited due to the darkness.

The next morning, however, was a very different experience. I woke up, quite unexpectedly, to the leaves of autumn. From the second I walked out the door, the landscape felt almost surreal. In every direction, including above me as well as at my feet, were unbelievably beautiful leaves, both in the trees and on the ground. Unlike anything I had ever seen before, the bright colors had the effect of heightening my senses to a new level of appreciation and awareness. It made everything around me seem so alive. I was so much more aware of my surroundings.

The practice of mindfulness is very similar on an emotional level in the way it affects our daily lives. It brings to the surface aspects of ourselves that are usually hidden in some way, or that we are frightened or ashamed of, embarrassed about, or simply unable to admit or deal with. But it does so, not in a way that is scary, difficult, or painful. Rather, the truth of the moment is able to unfold in an unthreatening, accepting manner. We're able to "see" and to accept what is.

Mindfulness also has the effect of making us far more aware of what's really going on around us. The best way I can explain it would be to say that it's like suddenly waking up from a deep sleep. Or it's as if someone has just turned the lights on after years of total darkness! Nothing around you has changed. It's just that you're seeing it for the first time. Even things that you did see before, you begin to see more clearly and more accurately. Imagine looking around and noticing things that were previously hidden from your awareness and finally being aware of your environment like never before. It's the experience of becoming alive, fully aware of the moment, as it really is.

The ramifications of being more "awake" are awesome. You find yourself more interested in ordinary things. Nature is more beautiful and mysterious. You're able to see others more clearly as well. You can see their innocence as well as their beauty. You become less judgmental because you become more accepting of the way people are. This in turn makes your relationships better and more loving because, as we all know, other people love it when we are accepting of them, when we are able to love less conditionally.

Although I still consider myself a real novice, one of the most dramatic changes that has occurred for me is that I now feel a new dimension of calm in my life. Whereas before I was, if not frightened by some of the thoughts or states of mind that would "pop up" into my awareness, seemingly out of nowhere, I was at the very least concerned by them. My overall experience was that some thoughts and feelings were okay, but that others were unacceptable. The problem I had, which is the same problem most of us have, is that whether we believe certain thoughts and feelings are unacceptable or not, they are still going to be there from time to time.

That's a scary way to live because our sense of well-being becomes totally dependent upon which thoughts happen to be in our minds at any given moment. Since we're usually only reacting to our thoughts after the fact, instead of being aware of them as they are unfolding, our relationship to them is quite destructive. We are at their mercy. If things are going well and our thoughts are happy, we do fine. But as soon as our circumstances shift or become more diffi-cult—and our thoughts become anxious or angry—we feel the nega-tive effects. We become scared or we react. Sometimes we pretend we don't feel the way we do—or we bury our feelings through work or alcohol or drugs. We're frightened by the thoughts that are in our minds. We forget that we're the one producing the thoughts in the first place.

Mindfulness is an enormously effective way to make peace with every aspect of yourself. Rather than being freaked out or stressed by your own worries, for example, you can learn to acknowledge your worried thoughts and feelings without being overly concerned about them. You begin to look at them instead of reacting to them.

The essence of mindfulness involves becoming aware of what's going on around you and, most importantly, within you, at all times. You start with your breath. As you breathe in, you're aware that you're breathing in. As you're breathing out, you're aware that you're breathing out. Simple enough? Not really. Try it for about a minute, and you'll soon discover that it's a lot more difficult than it sounds.

Our thoughts randomly jump from planning to solving, or wor-rying to figuring to fantasizing—and back again. It's as if each thought is yelling out to us, "Think me." "No, think me." "Hey, come over here, this thought is important." And all the while, we're not fully aware of all of this mental activity. Again, we react to the mental activity—but we're not aware that we're producing it. Our attention isn't at all used to being aware of one phenomenon for very long, even something as simple as our own breath. Instead our attention is scattered and our mind is all over the place.

When we are able to train our attention, even slightly, to be aware of our breathing—while we're breathing—we begin to feel a sense of peace and calm. Instead of racing every which way, zooming from thought to thought, worry to worry, plan to plan, we remain to a large degree centered, in the present moment. The thoughts we need will still come to mind, but in a far more orderly manner. As a result, our mind calms down and becomes quieter. It then becomes easier to focus on those thoughts that are serving us, and those that we need, rather than being at the total mercy of an agitated mind.

As you live each day, there is no need to do anything different. Instead, simply pay attention to your breath, which is with you twenty-four hours a day. Simply be aware of your breathing while you go about your business.

As this becomes easier with practice, begin to observe or pay attention to the thoughts and reactions you have to what's going on around you. Suppose, for example, you're driving and someone cuts in front of you. Instantly, your thoughts turn from whatever they were thinking—to anger. Perhaps you think, "What a jerk. No one knows how to drive in this city."

All you have to do is notice the thought and recognize it. You don't have to *not* think it. You don't have to push it away or pretend that you didn't have it. Nor do you have to be concerned about it. Simply allow it to be there. Be aware of what you're thinking.

You can even say to it, "Hi there, angry thought." Sounds a bit corny, I know, but you'll be amazed at what will begin to happen. As you begin to recognize your thinking in this way, you'll start to relate to it differently; it will be less of a big deal. You'll notice that all thoughts simply come and go. They're here for a moment, maybe a bit longer, then they fade away. No big deal. No need to be frightened or angry—or even frustrated. In fact, ideally you'll want to be kind to your thoughts that you recognize, even the scary or painful thoughts. Say to them, "It's nice to see you again."

Your awareness of your own thoughts, along with a total lack of resistance to them, will take the sting out of the experience. Instead of "How dare that driver behave that way? He should lose his license," you'll notice the angry thought forming. You can then dismiss it or not, but either way you'll have the choice.

The magic of mindfulness—which is that same dynamic or recognition that works with "small stuff" like dealing with a bad driver— is also extremely helpful when the stakes are high. It's very comforting, for example, to notice and acknowledge fully your sadness or grief. Rather than run and hide from it, or deny it, you can turn right toward your pain. Look it in the eye, not with aggression or fear, but with compassion and kindness. Gently, and with love, face your pain with mindfulness.

Noticing and facing our pain in a mindful manner helps us create a sense of spaciousness in our hearts. It gives us a place to rest, an inner place to turn to. It's ironic, but when we stop running from our pain, turning away in fear and horror, we are able to face it more freely. The pain, in turn, softens, and we are able to see that this too shall pass.

18. Know the Secret of Thought

Sometimes the greatest "secrets" are those that are right in front of us. This is certainly true with regard to the secret of thought. I refer to it as a secret because it's almost always overlooked. Yet there it is, with us every second of every day.

In each of my books, I've tried to emphasize the power of our own thinking. I've tried to point out how our own thoughts make us "sweat the small stuff." Our thoughts are also the most important factor in determining our level of happiness, the quality of our relationships, and how we feel about ourselves. Letting go of our thoughts is what helps us get over things, whereas focusing on them is what keeps them alive. Never has an understanding of the power of thought been more important than it is right now—when we're dealing with big stuff.

We are all thinkers. There are no exceptions. Our thinking is what ultimately determines whether our experience of life is positive or negative. We have all heard of people whose lives seem extremely difficult. They have been through hard times, had painful experiences, and lived with great hardship. Yet, through it all, they have a sense that life is okay. They experience inner peace and a sense of optimism regardless of what's going on around them, irrespective of their external circumstances.

There are many others who have been blessed with beautiful lives. They enjoy some degree of privilege, good health, nice parents, a loving family, perhaps even children. They may be attractive, strong, wealthy, and intelligent. They live in a beautiful environment. They might be successful, have some hobbies, and may have even enjoyed travel and other luxuries. Yet, no matter how wonderful things appear, or may actually be on the outside, they remain miserable, dissatisfied, and frustrated.

Why is this so? Are they unhappy on purpose? Do they enjoy being stressed and frustrated? Of course not. But these people feel they have no choice. They think they'd be happy "if only" things would change.

Unfortunately, there is no way to have a good enough life if your thinking tells you otherwise. You could have a beautiful body, but if you think of yourself as fat, you will be dissatisfied with yourself, as you would be were you to focus on any other perceived flaw. The world is full of beautiful young girls who feel terrible about the way they look. You could be a millionaire. Yet, insecure thoughts can erase all sense of security. There are plenty of people with lots of money who feel very poor. You could be popular and loved by your friends, but no amount of positive feedback can overcome taking one's doubting thoughts seriously. You could travel to hundreds of exotic locations around the world. Yet if you compare yourself to others, you might still feel unworldly.

One of the wisest people I know is a woman named Mavis Karn. Years ago she was one of the first people to encourage me to refer to thinking as a secret. Mavis teaches many people, among them teenagers, to live happier lives. One of the "secrets" she teaches young people is that it's impossible to feel badly about yourself without *thinking* badly about yourself. She wrote a beautiful letter which she calls "The Secret":

Dear Kids (and former kids),

I have a secret to tell you. Nobody meant to keep it from you . . . it's just been one of those things that's so obvious that people couldn't see it . . . like looking all over for the key that you have in your hand.

The secret is that you are already a completely whole, perfect person. You are not damaged goods, you are not incomplete, you are not flawed, you are not unfinished, you do not need remodeling, fixing, polishing, or major rehabilitation. You already have within you everything you need to live a wonderful life. You have common sense, wisdom, genius, creativity, humor, self-esteem . . . you are pure potential . . . you are missing nothing.

The only thing that can keep you from enjoying all that you already are is a thought. One thought. Your thought. Not someone else's thought. Your thought . . . whatever thought you are thinking at the moment that feels more important to think than feeling grateful, alive, content, joyful, optimistic, loving, and at peace . . . that's the only thing that's between you and happiness.

And guess who's in charge of your thinking . . . guess who gets to decide where your attention goes . . . guess who gets to write, produce, direct, and star in the moment you're in the middle of . . . you. Just you. Not your past (stored thought), not the future (did you ever notice that it never, ever shows up?), not your parents (they all think their own thoughts), or your friends (ditto), or school or television or situations or circumstances or anything else. Just you.

Thinking is an awesome capability. Like any capability, it can be used either as a tool or as a weapon against ourselves and others. And just like with any other tool, we can tell whether we're using it for or against ourselves by how it feels. When we think against ourselves or others, we get in trouble. When we don't, we usually stay out of trouble.

FEELINGS EXIST TO WARN US AWAY FROM USING OUR THINKING TO CREATE TROUBLE IN OUR LIVES AND TO GUIDE US BACK TO OUR NATURAL, HEALTHY ABILITY TO LIVE OUR LIVES TO THE FULLEST.

So . . . please remember that your thoughts are not always telling you the truth. When we're in low moods, feeling down, our thoughts are not to be trusted . . . our IQs drop. When our thoughts pass and we lighten up, our thinking is once again creative, positive . . . our IQs go up. The only way you can feel badly about yourself and your life is if you think badly about them . . . it's up to you, every single minute you are alive. It's always up to you! This is the best, most liberating secret I ever learned, and I want you to know it too.

With love,
Mavis

Consider the wisdom of those words, which are absolutely true. A student could have straight A's on their report card. They could be the top student in the class, acing every test. They might be advanced in every subject, receive a great deal of approval and attention, and be headed toward a top university, maybe even a scholarship. But they could, nevertheless, feel terrible about themselves. What would make them happy? Would it be better grades?

At some point, a person can no longer use that argument. Once you've achieved perfect grades and top scores, it becomes obvious that a sense of dissatisfaction or insecurity must come from somewhere else.

On the other side of the coin, there are students who, for a variety of reasons, struggle in school. It's possible that their scholastic ability is less than their straight-A colleagues, or that their IQ isn't as high. Or it may be that they have had fewer opportunities or encouragement. Perhaps they don't work as hard. Maybe their family lives in poverty, or they don't have the benefit of a healthy breakfast. But regardless of the circumstances, some of these students remain hopeful, grateful, happy, and lighthearted. How can this be? If performance is the key to happiness, these students should be depressed.

The secret, of course, is one's thought. There is nothing else that really matters. The reality of the situation—the opinion and/or the approval of others, how we compare to other students, our past grades and future outlook—is irrelevant in terms of determining how one feels about himself.

Our thinking has the power to bring to life that which we focus upon. Our thoughts can keep big things in perspective, or they can blow little things way out of proportion. They can magnify a flaw, or overlook an imperfection. Our thoughts can dismiss something as insignificant, or they can keep an argument or a feud going on, literally forever.

There are two distinct aspects of thinking to be aware of. The first, of course, is the content of our thoughts. This is the "what we think about" or "what's on our mind" part of the equation. Going back to how we feel about our appearance, for example, we might be focused at any given moment on the ten pounds we'd like to lose. Never mind that we might be perfectly healthy or even that our doctor says we are a perfect weight. Forget about the fact that much of the world suffers from starvation or that others tell us we "look great." At that moment nothing is as important to us as those ten pounds. As we think about it, we literally "feel fat." Logic doesn't matter. Nor does encouragement from others.

The content of our thinking is all over the map. Sometimes we're thinking of our problems or something we'd like to change. Other times we think about our plans and goals, things we'd like to do. Sometimes our thoughts are sad, other times they have to do with worries. But the one and only constant is that whatever we are thinking about is essentially what we are experiencing during that moment. Case in point: I was visiting a friend who was having a conflict with her neighbor. For the first ten minutes of my visit, her spirits were high. At some point, her attention shifted and she brought the conflict into the conversation. At that moment, she became concerned. I could see it in her eyes and hear it in her words. As she discussed the details, she became visibly angry.

The conflict itself had been there all along. Nothing had changed, not a single bit. One minute earlier, everything, including her sense of well-being, had been fine. But as she began to think about it, the event came back to life, including her resentment and concern.

We all bring to life conflicts and concerns many times a day. As our thoughts flow from one thing to the next, our experience of life changes as well. One minute we're laughing; the next, we're upset. We can talk with friends about our being upset, but as long as our thoughts remain on the event, we remain concerned. At some point, however, we will be distracted. The phone will ring. Or the topic will change. Or we will get bored and want to move on to something else.

Again, the event itself—the conflict, problem, situation, or whatever it is—may be real, or may have to be dealt with. It still happened, or will happen, or may happen. But it's our thinking that brings it to life and gives it significance. This is one of the most empowering facts you can ever be aware of because it enables you to step back and adjust the volume and tone of what's going on in your own mind. Very simply, if you don't like what you're experiencing— and you're aware of the significance of your thinking—you have the capacity to think differently, or less intensely.

Without this understanding you are, in effect, a victim of your own thoughts. Whatever happens to be on your mind will affect you greatly. You will lack perspective because you give significance to your thoughts, simply because they have come to mind. This is a very painful and confusing way to live.

The other aspect to our thinking is related, but slightly different. It's the actual awareness of the fact that we are, in fact, thinking.

Are you aware, right now, of your left knee? Unless it's hurting, you're probably not. But it's still there, and it's very important. The same is true with our thinking. The fact that we're not aware that we're thinking doesn't change the fact that we are. But not being aware that we are thinking can be, and usually is, disastrous.

Imagine this. You're out doing an errand. Out of nowhere, you're reminded of an ex-friend who has in some way wronged you. In a matter of seconds, you're thinking about the details. It's brought back to life, almost as though it's happening all over again. Although no one except you is aware of it, you're feeling rage toward that person.

The event itself could have happened yesterday or three years ago. But to you, in this moment, it's very real. It's happening right now.

The critical question is: "Are you aware, awake to the fact, that you're thinking?" Not of "what" you're thinking about, but actually the fact that you are engaged in thought? If someone were to ask you during a moment such as this, "Are you aware that you're thinking?" you would most certainly say yes. But chances are, on a more subtle level, you were not aware at all that you were thinking. Instead, as I have done so many thousands of times myself, you became temporarily lost in your thoughts. You quite literally forgot that you were thinking.

Becoming aware that you are thinking is not a philosophic exercise. In fact, it's one of the most, if not *the* most, practical mental tools you can possibly become aware of. Imagine how many times each hour we get caught up in or lost in our thoughts. Imagine the power you would have and the perspective you would enjoy were you able to step back during these moments and realize what was happening.

If you were aware that you were having resentful thoughts, for example, about your friend's betrayal, you would be able to say to yourself, "There they are again," or some other simple recognition of the fact that you were being haunted, once again, by the same old thoughts.

The betrayal still occurred. You're not attempting to deny any facts. You're not pretending to feel any differently. You're not making the betrayal okay. But the difference is that you now have a choice. Rather than automatically delving deeply into the content of those thoughts and almost certainly feeling badly because of it, you are aware of the mental dynamic taking place.

The implications and relevance of this awareness to the big stuff in our lives is endless and cannot be overstated. A divorce, for example, can be a new beginning, or it can be the beginning of an endless nightmare. When we are unaware of the power of our own thoughts, we can take a painful event and make it even worse. We imagine the worst, build a case in our mind about how we're never going to get through this one, and feel defeated. But when we tune into the "secret," we are able to recognize when we are creating even more pain for ourselves. We create internal options that would never exist otherwise.

I heard an athlete being interviewed who had made a serious, embarrassing error in his last game before retirement. It had cost his team the championship. Among the questions he was asked was, "Will you be able to live this down?" The question had to do with how he was going to internalize this event. Was he going to remember his fifteen-plus-year career in a positive light? Or was he going to feel dejected for the rest of his life?

To me, this is an extremely powerful real-life example. The

answer to how he will respond remains to be seen. The error was what it was. It's over, and may as well be ancient history at this point. That's not to say it wasn't unfortunate, that he wouldn't have preferred a different final game, that he didn't care, that it wasn't a little embarrassing, or that it didn't hurt. In the end, however, the only relevant determinant will be the athlete's own thinking. Some people would take something like this in stride and might even see humor in it. Others would feel like a complete failure and might even become depressed. How one responds to this and other major events is wholly determined by one's thoughts. There is nothing else that ultimately matters.

I was once having a conversation with two people who had lost family members in the Holocaust. One of them had remained hardened and angry. Her feeling was that it was impossible to feel any differently.

The other person, who had experienced remarkably similar pain, was quite gentle and peaceful. She said to me something so beautiful that I'd like to end this chapter with her words. She said, "My goal is to be an instrument of peace, and to be filled with kindness. I admit that there are many times when my head fills with thoughts of despair or anger. But I've learned that those thoughts are simply that—thoughts. I'm grateful to know that I have the capacity to live a life of love."

If I could share only one secret with you, it would be the "secret" of thought. I hope you'll reflect on the power of your own thinking, because if you do, your life will never be the same.

19. Soften

A dear friend of mine was moving his office from one location to another. I was helping him carry a piece of furniture down some stairs. I twisted the wrong way and damaged my back. Ouch!

My first reaction was somewhat typical and very understandable. I cried out in pain and tightened every muscle around it. I clenched my fists and my entire body, and curled up on the floor. The pain in my lower back throbbed for a few minutes.

My concerned friend came over to comfort me. But rather than offer a habitual overture such as "It will be all right" or even "Are you okay?" (both of which would have been appreciated and well received), he said something very different that dramatically changed the way I try to relate to any time of pain—during that moment and ever since. In a reassuring tone, he said, "Richard, soften around the pain and it will be okay."

It's funny because the same words, offered with a different feeling behind them, might have easily sounded shallow or even arrogant. Yet, it wasn't that way at all. Instead, his words offered hope, a "reverse psychology" of sorts, given our almost certain hardening to any type of pain, physical or emotional. It was as if I had something to do other than fight my suffering. I could let go.

Nothing, of course, will instantly remove intense physical or emotional pain. And softening around it is no exception. On the other hand, the intent of softening isn't really to get rid of the pain, but rather to relate to it differently.

Softening to our pain offers us an alternative from a lifetime of tightening, fighting, and running from that which we dislike and fear. We are so accustomed to—and in a way are programmed to—holding, cursing, squeezing, and tightening everything we associate with pain or grief.

Perhaps it was because the pain was so intense—or maybe it was because my friend was so confidently reassuring—but for whatever reasons, I was open to trying something new. I was able to take his words to heart and begin to let go, to soften. Like a tight fist releasing its hardened grip, I softened to the pain in my back. Instead of sending thoughts of hate and anger to the pain, I turned my thoughts to mercy and love. Instead of "being" the pain, I noticed the pain.

This was my first conscious experience of relating to pain with love instead of with fear and hatred. To this day, I remember noticing how the intensity of the pain shifted from unbearable to manageable. I remember the moment things began to change because I recall, so well, the specific thoughts I was having. My thoughts went from "Oh God" to "It's okay, it's okay." But the gentler thoughts were not intentional. Instead, they were a by-product of the softening.

Years later, the opportunities for practice continue. It could be the loss of a dear friend, family member, or colleague. It might be the disappointment of a lost opportunity, or the violation of being robbed. It might be a professional or financial setback, or a horrible stomachache. It could be practically anything.

Whether it has had to do with physical pain or discomfort, or emotional pain or hardship, I've found that when I'm able, the most effective antidote for any pain I've experienced is conscious softening.

A dramatic opportunity for me developed one day when someone was making some untrue, cruel comments about one of my children. Mentally, I dove quickly into an attacking defensive mode. My mind hardened and I became angry. I wanted to say something mean in retaliation.

While this was taking place, I happened to notice a bird drifting and gliding in the sky. It reminded me of the power of effortless motion. In an instant I shifted from relating *from* my pain and anger to relating *to* my pain and anger—and the experience became drastically different. It was as if I took a step back and could see my own reactivity. Instead of being submerged in a painful pit of anger, I noticed how painful it was to be entertaining such anger. I became the observer, noticing my mind's merciless activity. More than a twist of words, it was a shift of consciousness.

I began to soften around the experience of anger. In doing so, I started to feel compassion for myself. I realized how hard it can be to remain calm when feeling attacked, yet how important it was for one's sanity. I was noticing how painful it was to be angry.

This was a turning point in my life. Before this, my angry thoughts would be met with more angry thoughts and would tend to spiral. But this time was different. Instead of compounding the anger with increased mental activity, I treated it with love. I said to myself, "This anger hurts. I wouldn't wish it on anyone."

The difference sounds small, but it isn't. Imagine the difference between *being* an angry or disappointed child—versus *watching* an angry or disappointed child. In the latter, you are one step removed, slightly detached. It's easy to have compassion for a child who is in pain. So, too, is it easy to have compassion for yourself when you learn to soften, when you become the one who is noticing.

I had just finished a lecture to a large group of people when a wonderful man who had just lost his wife to cancer approached me.

I remember him so well because he was so full of life. He said that the most important thing he had learned was the importance of softening to his pain. He described it as being the opposite of fighting life and the painful events within it. This, he said, had allowed him to stay open to God's grace and open to "what is," even when he didn't like it.

He said that the softening to one's pain is what allows gratitude to fill one's heart. It made a great deal of sense to me, as I reflected on the losses I've experienced in recent years. Every time I soften, my heart opens. I'm reminded of the love I had felt and still feel for the people who had shared a part of their life with me.

Just as we naturally soften when we see a newborn baby, we can learn to soften to the painful parts of life as well. And when we do, we are rewarded, not with a pain-free life, but with a perspective that can help carry us through.

20. Finding Life after Death

When my dear friend Robert died in a car crash, I was totally unprepared, as everyone always is at an unexpected tragedy. It happened so suddenly. The timing couldn't have been worse either, as the accident occurred two nights before my wedding. I was tense already, but Robert would have been able to help make me laugh and keep things lighthearted. He was a warm, supportive, and loving friend—and we had always known we would be friends for decades to come. But it wasn't to be.

For a while, my world fell apart. It was the first time I couldn't "fix" a situation or even pretend that it was fixable. This time I couldn't run away. There was nowhere to go, nor was there anywhere to hide. I had been considered strong, even wise for my years, but I proved everyone wrong. My grief was too overwhelming for me to even pretend to put up any pretences.

The first time I "came up for air" was when I was able to spend a day sharing my grief with Stephen Levine in San Francisco. You may know Stephen for his landmark book, *Who Dies?* I thought of him as a remarkably loving being, and someone who was more comfortable with the subject of death than anyone I had every known. Had we not met that day, I do not know what would have happened to me. What he shared with me changed my outlook forever.

When our familiar world falls apart, especially through the pain of death—of losing someone we love—we are shaken at our very core. We realize, perhaps for the first time, that there is no easy or quick way out. We must go through the process, which will be a little different for each of us—the common thread being pain.

In the midst of that inner struggle, however, something begins to happen. There are the moments that are most resisted—and there is extreme pain. Simultaneously, however, there are voluntary or involuntary bursts of letting go. Perhaps the pain is too much for the moment—the mind takes a break, shuts down, or wakes up, I'm not really sure. But in those moments, there is a release from the pain; an acknowledgment that although we don't understand it, and it hurts like hell, the universe somehow knows what it's doing.

One of my favorite sayings comes from Seng-Ts'an. He said, "Our way is not difficult, save the picking and choosing." Entire books and weeklong courses could be developed around these words. The wisdom is simple, but extremely powerful and profound, particularly when dealing with loss. Although it's so much easier said than done, when we take a step back and a full breath, we can see loss from what I believe is the deepest perspective. We can see the seasons come and go. We can know that although God did not plan or cause the death of our loved one—or the pain we are going through—he is, nevertheless, there to comfort us.

God may speak to us directly, in line with our own faith and belief, as we quiet down and listen. Or he may show up cleverly disguised as a friend, neighbor, family member, minister, rabbi, spiritual teacher, emergency worker, or someone else whom you may never suspect. But however it happens and regardless of how God presents himself, you will experience his presence as hope, compassion, strength, and kindness.

One night, after speaking to an audience in Chicago, I went out for a quiet dinner, all alone. In the booth next to me was a man who told me an extraordinary story. He had experienced the unimaginable pain of the death of his only child. Already being a single dad, he had few places to turn for comfort.

One day, in the midst of his deepest grief, he met an angel, disguised as a waitress. His connection to her was spiritual, not physical. She had been through a similar experience herself and was able to give him a gentle push in a healing direction. He connected with a new church and a whole new group of friends. He said that he could trace his entire healing process back to that waitress, whom he had never seen again. There was no doubt in his mind that God had visited him that day.

When dealing with lesser things, it's easier to see that if we did not want these things to be different, then we would be free. Certainly if we didn't wish to control our world, the events and people in our lives, then we would be at peace. How much of our pain and suffering stems from our intense need for things to be different?

Our way through life should not be difficult—but it is. The fact is that our lives are filled mostly with picking and choosing. "I want this, but not that." And because things are not anything other than the way they really are, we suffer. Nowhere is this more apparent and painful than when we are trying to find life after death. We so desperately want things to be the way they were. But they are not. So the longing itself becomes an additional source of suffering.

After almost two decades of meditation and a personal lifetime commitment to truth, I have both good and bad news to report. The bad news is that there is no hiding from the painful thoughts that are the inevitable by-product of the death of a loved one. The comforting news is that it's possible to relate to our pain in a more compassionate manner.

As painful thoughts and feelings arise, we are tempted to go in one of two directions. Sometimes we indulge ourselves in painful memories or anticipate future pain. We become immersed and absorbed in the pain, and our thoughts frighten us. Or instead of thinking about our loss, or even talking about it to others, we repress or deny its existence. As thoughts come up, we push them away. We pretend they don't exist. We keep busy and distract ourselves. It's too painful to face—so we don't.

A third option is not a compromise. It's neither an indulgence, nor is it any form of denial. It's simply a compassionate acknowledgment of the truth. As thoughts arise, we don't push them away—or hate them. Nor do we run. We simply see them as they are: "There's pain, and there's loss. And now I'm missing my child, my partner, my lover, my friend." The thoughts are not judged or altered, nor is the pain minimized in any way.

But while this is going on we relate with compassion to whatever is arising. We send love and kindness to ourselves and to our thoughts. As we do, an openness and a spaciousness begin to emerge. In the absence of mental energy running toward the future— or the past—our pain begins to soften and dissolve. Healing begins. We become stronger.

We just keep giving our pain space, over and over again, for however long it takes. Days, months, years—or an entire lifetime. It doesn't matter. We keep allowing whatever is—to be there. Just as we would hold a child close to our heart to keep her feeling safe and comforted, so would we do the same for ourselves. Offer no resistance. Don't push it away. Instead be kind and compassionate to your pain, as you would be for that child, or for your best friend.

In 1989, the above-mentioned and admired Stephen Levine contributed to a book that I had coedited with my dear friend Benjamin Shield called *Healers on Healing*. He wrote about a woman he had worked with who was suffering from an excruciatingly painful bone metastasis—cancer. Up to that point, she had lived a life of anger and self-pity. She had never even met her grandchildren, and even in the

hospital she greeted every person with rage. She hated the world—
and it hated back.

One night, after weeks in the hospital, the pain became unbearable. A lifetime of withholding and resistance became too much, and
she could withhold no more. For the first time in her life, she opened
and surrendered to her pain. Instead of sending it hate and hardening her heart, she softened—finally. For the first time in her life, she
treated her pain with something other than anger and fear. She
treated it with loving-kindness. As this happened, she suddenly felt a
lifelong buildup of compassion for others. She said she knew, for the
first time, the suffering of others. She even described her pain not as
"my pain," but as "the pain."

In the next six weeks before her death, she experienced a complete turnaround and emotional healing. Her anger completely dis-
solved and turned to love. She continued to soften around her pain.
She begged her children for forgiveness, which she received. Within
days, the grandchildren she had never met were comforting her by
her side, stroking her hands. Unbelievably, she became one of the
most loved people in the hospital. Nurses and doctors would go out
of their way to visit her.

Hers was the most remarkable healing I have ever heard about. It
taught me several important things. First, that healing goes far
beyond the physical. This woman died as healed as anyone could
ever hope for. Secondly, it reinforced the incredible power of softening to one's pain. Whether our pain is physical or emotional—as
when we lose someone we love—the key to healing is a softening to
our pain.

Recently I read an extraordinary book, *How to Survive the Loss of
a Love* by Harold Bloomfield, M.D., Melba Colgrove, Ph.D., and Peter
McWilliams. If you are experiencing any type of loss, I recommend
this book above all others. If there was a single message that stood
out for me as I read and reread the book, it was that we *will* survive,

and that this is not in doubt. Healing from a loss is a natural process of life—just as healing from a broken bone is too. Knowing this in the midst of pain is of great comfort.

If it's at all possible, don't be alone. Seek out the comfort and help you need and deserve. This is not the time to be brave or strong. Instead it's the time to reach out to others and to be open to receive their kindness. It's your turn. Finding life after death is among the greatest challenges we face. But it is possible, and it will happen for you. I send you my love.

21. **Admit to Your Common Ground**

How much of life is filled with conflict with other people? This is especially true with people we "love" or "used to love." How many times have you heard someone in the midst of a crushed relationship, or during a bitter divorce, mutter the words, "We have nothing in common." We also insist this applies to our teenagers during hard times, as well as to virtually everyone with whom we engage in serious conflict.

I heard a line from a story that changed the way I looked at and dealt with conflict: It said that the way to "make God laugh was to tell him that bickering lovers had nothing in common." I don't know whether it makes God laugh or not, but it sure did make me laugh and gave me cause to reflect.

When you are angry, arguing, frustrated, and needing to prove yourself right, there is such pain in your heart. The drama and feelings of tension are intense. There is withholding, a sense of stubbornness. There is confusion in the mind and an urgency in the heart. There is an absence of peace, a sense of emergency.

Has there ever been an exception? Not in my experience. Indeed, I've never known anyone to say to me, "When I was bitter toward another, or extremely angry, I was experiencing great harmony and peace." Or, "Boy, I remember how good it felt to hate that person."

What I've learned is that if I'm arguing with or feeling resentment or bitterness toward another person, and they toward me, then ironically I have *everything* in common with that person and vice versa. Despite what either one of us would care to believe, we share the same closed heart, the same confusion and fear, and a very similar lack of peace.

This awareness has changed my life dramatically. I still experience conflict, more than I'd like to admit. And I still have issues with other people—again, more often than I'd like. But it's different from before. Recognizing my shared inner experience with others, despite its negative edge, has allowed my heart to remain open in the midst of pain or conflict. It allows me to have compassion for myself, for my own lack of peace, and for others—for the experience they are having with me. How can any of us remain hostile when we are aware of, and acknowledge, the fact that inner pain is the source of outer conflict?

No one. Neither you, nor I, nor anyone else wants to be unhappy. To the contrary, it can be said that all anyone really wants is to be happy and at peace. The fact that few, if any, of us know how to be happy doesn't change this essential fact of life. We believe, mistakenly, that we would be happier if others would behave differently or if the world would accommodate us with fewer demands. I witnessed a heated, but (I thought) rather humorous conflict between two drivers. They almost hit each other—I couldn't tell whose fault it was. One driver flipped off the other and threw him a look that I can only describe as arrogant. The recipient of that look blurted out a defensive, yet in some ways funny, comment. He yelled out, "I know, I know. If it weren't for people like me, your life would be so much better." You could cut the tension with a knife. Both drivers were in such obvious pain.

A few weeks later, I was nearly in an accident myself. Thinking about it objectively, I believe it probably was my fault, but I'm not sure. But when the driver raised both his fists toward me, as if to say, "I'd like to kill you," I responded differently than before. Instead of reacting with my own rage, I could sense our common ground. I remembered what it was like to feel such intense anger. To be so angry at another, regardless of how "justified" it may be, is painful. To carry such hostility means zero inner peace. I waved politely, as if to say, "I'm sorry." I meant it, and the event was over.

Derek hated his ex-wife. In his words, she had "betrayed" him. Despite having a son they needed to jointly raise in separate homes, they could barely communicate, except through lawyers. He couldn't even talk about her without feeling tense and bothered. He wanted revenge and couldn't imagine forgiveness.

When the pain of an angry heart became too much to handle, Derek began to investigate ways to calm down and reduce his stress. Some friends had studied meditation and suggested he give it a try. It was one of the hardest skills he had ever attempted. He became acutely aware of his angry and extremely busy mind. He said that at first things seemed even worse, and he almost quit. But somehow he was able to work through the learning process. He learned to witness, observe, and allow his thoughts to come and go, to present themselves and then to drift away. He was able to step back and observe his own angry, judgmental, and unforgiving thoughts. He learned to observe rather than to react to them; to detach rather than jump in. In time, he became much more peaceful.

He shared with me that the greatest insight he received through a quieter mind was his ability to see what I'm calling "common ground." It was as if he began to experience "his pain" as "the pain" instead. Far from being an Eastern philosophical notion, he was simply tuning into the reality that the prerequisite to being in extreme conflict with another person is pain. What he realized, of course, was that this also applied to his ex-wife, as well as to everyone else he had hated over the years.

I doubt that Derek has become friends with his ex-wife. On the other hand, I'd be very surprised if he weren't friendly and forgiving toward her. When I saw him, it was absolutely clear that he had worked through the worst of his anger and had become very accepting toward her, not in any self-important sort of way, but rather through genuine wisdom.

Seeing, understanding, or experiencing our common ground is not about pretending to accept someone or some situation. It's not about denying anything that has happened or about pretending there is no pain or that we like someone. It's all about shedding our hostility toward others so that our lives can be experienced with fullness and with love. There is no need to pretend. Many of us have people in our lives whom we would never choose to see again, or work with, and that's fine. We may have neighbors whom we will not invite into our homes, and that's fine too. There is great peace, however, in not needing to be angry with these people ever again. It's time to let it go and move on.

The notion of our common ground, our shared experience, allows us to let go of our hostility and our intense focus on our dislike for others. Regardless of what has happened or what someone has done to us, we have the capacity to see our common ground and to let it go, whatever "it" was or is. As you reflect on your life and attempt to put this into practice, I hope you'll share the "common" experience of our common ground.

22. **Let Go of Your Past**

Imagine this scene: It's the bottom of the ninth inning and there are two outs in the final game of the World Series. Your favorite star comes to bat with the bases loaded. Your team is behind by one run. If he gets a hit, your team wins. If not, they lose. The count is three balls and two strikes. The next pitch decides the outcome of the game. All fifty thousand fans are on their feet, along with millions watching on television.

There's a sudden, unexpected time-out in the action.

A man runs out onto the field and pulls the batter aside. It seems he's reviewing the star's personal history.

He reminds the batter that he has been in four previous nerve-wracking sports scenarios. The first time, he was only a tot in the peewee league. He had struck out and let his entire team down. The next time, he was in Little League. The pressure was on, and again, he struck out. His parents had expressed their disappointment, and the girl he had a crush on walked away with someone else. The next incident was in high school. He wasn't batting that time but attempting to catch a routine fly ball. The sun got in his eyes and he dropped it. His team lost, and he was the laughingstock of the entire school. A few years later, in college, he was again on the spot. He tried to steal a base but was thrown out by the catcher. His team lost the game, as well as their first-place standing in the division. As a result of his team losing, his best friend ended up losing his scholarship. The man reviewing the star's personal history reminded him that some people had speculated that it was his fault.

The statistician then encouraged the star to attach himself to and focus on the facts from his past. Furthermore, he insisted they were of primary importance.

The question is, "Does the star hit the ball and win the game?"

I'll leave that up to you. I would say, however, that the odds are slim. With so much attention riveted to one's personal history (especially the most select negative parts), and so little attention on the present moment, it's unlikely that the result will be very positive.

God knows, as we all do, that life can be very difficult. Dealing with big things is hard. But add to that the burden of a nagging personal history, and it's all but impossible. Imagine our poor sports star in the above example. He's already facing a world-class pitcher, fifty thousand screaming fans, a national television audience, and an excellent opponent. But now he has filled his head with negative memories, which creates additional anxiety and imagined pressure.

Our lives are like that too. All of us have had hard times and have had bad things happen; some obviously are worse than others. No doubt our individual personal histories are very complex and multifaceted. In many instances, they are quite painful.

And although our past helped to shape who we are today, one of the keys to effective living is to let go of our past so that our present and future experiences are not adversely tainted. We can honor and appreciate our past, and we can certainly learn from it. As the saying goes, we don't want to forget the past. Yet if we label ourselves based on our past successes, failures, and disappointments, and if we are overly attached to our own history, we severely limit our capacity for joy as well as our ability to solve problems and maneuver through life.

This is not a simple task, and perhaps a healthy balance is the best we can hope for. I met a woman who shared the following story with me. As a child she had been physically and emotionally abused, and both of her parents were alcoholics. As an adult, she had wisely entered therapy, as well as some very nurturing support groups.

Although she claimed that the group and individual therapy had been extremely necessary and helpful, she remained unhappy and insecure. Her therapists had encouraged her never to forget what had happened, but she had taken that advice too far. In fact she had learned to label herself a "survivor." She thought of herself as a victim, and came across that way in all she did.

Her support groups had encouraged her to reexamine her personal history. She had been instructed to "reframe" the past, which she took to mean that she should look at it differently. Though this exercise was undoubtedly helpful and healing, clearly in her case, its ability to help her move on was limited.

Her life-changing shift occurred when a close friend suggested she was riveted and overidentified with her personal history in an unhealthy way. She began to pay attention to the number of times each day she would refer to her past, and how often she thought about it. She realized that the past wasn't ever going to be different from the way it was. So if she didn't develop a healthier relationship to it, she would never be able to live effectively, joyfully, or successfully. Over time, she was able to let go of her past enough so she could move on, which is a spiritual step beyond reexamining the past. She seemed to me to have developed a healthy attitude toward her present life. She certainly wasn't denying any part of her past, but instead was releasing its grip. Her change was the result of her willingness to let go of the past and step fully into the now.

In *Don't Sweat the Small Stuff at Work*, I wrote a chapter called "Don't Live in an Imagined Future." I discussed our collective tendency to imagine how much better or worse our lives would be in the future if certain conditions are met. Very often we also have a tendency to anticipate how awful or stressful something is going to be, well before it happens. I've met tax accountants, for example, who are exhausted in early March, not because they are overworked, but because they are anticipating the tax season rush.

Letting go of your past addresses the other side of the same problem. Rather than being stressed by circumstances yet to come, we have a tendency to be held back by the events of our past. A person may have had a bad experience, for example, during an interview. He may then rationalize his lack of drive by thinking, "I'm not equipped for this job." In reality, there may be no relationship between one event and the other, but the memories from the past interfere with a clear and responsive vision.

Notice that I titled this strategy "Let Go of Your Past" instead of "Get Rid of It." The suggestion is this: Your past certainly affected you and helped create both your strengths as well as your weaknesses. Your personal biography, family tree, painful and joyful events, and list of accomplishments are important. Yet, by giving our personal history less significance, we are able to fully enter the present moment. As we become less attached to and dependent upon who we were or the circumstances we faced, we become much more equipped to make appropriate and wise adjustments today.

The person who nervously recalls the embarrassing interview would benefit by acknowledging the thought, then reminding himself that his memory is, in fact, just that—a thought. It's not "real," but imagined. One of my favorite ways to illustrate this is to have you think back to when you were a child. There was probably a time when you imagined there was a monster (or some other scary thing) in the closet or under the bed. You may have been quite frightened, despite your mom and dad's assurance that there was nothing to fear. Then one day you have the necessary insight. "Oh, it's not real, it's just my imagination." From that moment on, most people are never again frightened about the lurking monster. Even if a scary thought arises, you can relate to it in such a way that it doesn't scare you anymore.

A similar insight is helpful when relating to memories. I remember being really nervous about speaking to a group of five thousand people. About ten minutes before I was about to start, I remembered the time I fainted while speaking in public. Luckily, I was able to take a deep breath and remind myself, "It's just a thought, it's not now," and I dismissed it. As is usually the case for me, doing so took the edge off of the fear. It added that tiny bit of perspective, which can be the difference between getting lost in a memory and moving beyond it.

I can only imagine how differently things might have evolved if, instead of reminding myself that my thoughts were memory and not reality, I had instead continued to think about the fainting incident. I'll never know for sure, but I can certainly imagine that the same thought might have spiraled and paralyzed me with fear. After all, it was a "real" memory, based on real facts. By acknowledging a thought, however, then quickly dismissing it as merely a thought, you can often avoid the snowball problem, which is when a harmless thought reinforces itself and gets bigger in direct proportion to the amount of attention we give it.

But some social reinforcers can encourage the tendency to hang on to our personal history, for example whenever someone says, "But you've always done it that way," or "You've always been a businessperson," or "You've never taken that position." Taken to heart, these types of statements can encourage us to feel guilty or afraid to make a change or to step into the unknown. As I see it, the key is to consciously and continuously distinguish between who you were then, and who you want to be now. Keep differentiating between memories, which are thoughts, and the present moment, which is real.

Be aware that others referencing your past can be a trap of sorts, and be aware of your own similar thoughts. As your mind drifts toward "There's only one way" or "I've never been able to do that before," notice the thoughts and release them. Like a shadow, our history follows us everywhere we go. And that's okay, and harmless, as long as we keep it in proper perspective.

23. Survive Those Financial Setbacks

What goes up almost always comes down. And what comes down often goes back up. But not always. Financially, there are good times and bad, secure and insecure. The wisest people seem to take most of it, including the lows, in stride.

During the 1980s, real estate seemed like a brilliant investment in many parts of the country. Ironically, however, a few of the people I knew who were making a fortune in real estate took this perceived wisdom completely with a grain of salt. At the time, I didn't fully realize how much knowledge these people possessed, nor how much I would use this wisdom during my lifetime. These wise few had no arrogance about having "the magic touch," nor any assumption that the good times would last forever. Instead, they had the wisdom to know that while they were very good at many aspects of the business, many other factors outside their control were working in their favor—mostly timing. While they enjoyed the success they were having, and certainly didn't minimize it, they had no doubt in their minds that times would change. And they did.

When real estate values declined, in some cases dramatically, those who had anticipated it had hedged their bets. These people, even those who lost most (or in select cases, all) of their earlier gains, did so with a great deal of perspective.

As a witness to what was happening, I was more impressed with the way people lost money than I was with how much money had been made. I was, and still am, in awe of the power of perspective.

There was a similar but even more dramatic and visible "mania" surrounding the United States stock market in the mid-to-late 1990s. It seemed like almost anyone "in the game" was coming out a winner. Even the most modest investors were, in many cases, looking like geniuses! At times, college-age kids (sometimes even younger) were making a fortune with their ideas, and investment returns were soaring.

Then the bottom fell out! Million-dollar portfolios were wiped out, estates were cut in half—or worse. In many cases, even the most sophisticated investors were brought back to earth. Personally, my own retirement plan is down 30 to 40 percent from its high as I write this piece. Others fared much worse.

Financial perspective, as I'm defining it, means being able to take a great big step back and see (and accept) the long-term picture as it's likely to be—without tainting it with fear, on the one hand, or arrogance, on the other. With the correct vantage point and a crystal clear mind (not a crystal ball), panic *or* irrational enthusiasm is replaced with calm wisdom. It's precisely such wisdom that allows people to do everything possible to put the odds in their favor without being immobilized if the results aren't what they hoped for.

One of my earlier books, *Don't Sweat the Small Stuff About Money,* had a lot to do with keeping your financial and creative bearings, and realizing that any success we enjoy is usually despite our worry, not because of it. There is an inner wisdom that can take over and run our lives, which flows and adjusts to life rather than simply reacting to it. When we are tuned into this natural rhythm, we maximize our competence and effectiveness, as well as our chances for success. At the same time, however, we become surprisingly lighthearted and accepting of the way our finances play themselves out.

This inner wisdom I speak about can be easily and naturally accessed when our mind is clear and calm and when we learn to trust in the process. It's an intelligence that guides us and helps us make clear decisions. It gives us the confidence to keep learning and to take wise, calculated risks when appropriate. It's an intelligence that makes allowances for our weaknesses and makes adjustments as needed. It tells us when we need to ask for help, how to identify and move beyond our fears, how hard we need to work, and what courses of action are necessary and appropriate for our success.

This inner "knowing" is also very practical. It helps to keep you from duplicating mistakes. It also alerts you to danger signals such as when you're spending too much money, or when you're in need of some sort of change.

When you are down on your luck, out of a job, or suffering financially, it's critical to be in touch with this inner source. From my perspective it's the best, and in many instances the only, way to get back on track. It's the opposite of panic and reactiveness.

Assume (or better yet, know) that a calm state of well-being is your most natural, as well as your most effective, state of mind. While in this state of mind, you are wise and responsive to the moment. During these times, it's as if your thoughts "think for you." In other words, instead of searching or grasping for ideas and solutions, those ideas flow to you.

You can be confident that this is where you'd be—and how you would feel unless and until you drift away from it. In other words, this is your homeostasis, or "home base." We've all had moments like this when a perfect idea or solution arises. "That's what I need to do," we say to ourselves. The solution seems obvious, even though it may have evaded you for years.

All that is required to make this seemingly coincidental, or what appears to be "random," wisdom become more consistently available "on demand," is to have faith that it, in fact, exists. When you develop this trust, or confidence, you begin to notice that the wisdom is always there, no matter what. Mostly we just need to be quiet and listen.

The problem is that we engage in mental processes that interfere with it—they pull us away. It's no more complicated than that. For example, we jump on various trains of thought that take us away from this source. They might be self-doubting, fearful, or cynical thoughts. Or we might get carried away by plans or memories. We remember a past failure and say to ourselves, "I can't do this" or "I'm not qualified." The more attention we give to thoughts like these, the more they take hold of us.

The way you know this is happening to you is, very simply, by the way you're feeling. Go back for a moment to the concept of having a "home base," a feeling of calm. Ideas and solutions are percolating and flowing. There is an ease in your thinking. You are centered and have a sense of well-being. Despite whatever is going on around you, you feel confident.

Of course, the more time you spend in this state of mind, the more your wisdom has a chance to deepen and to present itself in creative ways. This doesn't mean you never have doubts. The difference is that you treat them as passing thoughts instead of entertaining them for extended periods. You factor into your answers your strengths, weaknesses, talents, *and* fears, but you don't get lost in any of them.

It can be helpful to think of this natural wisdom as a bank account. When you are calm and "present" in the process, the account fills up—with ideas, solutions, creativity, and confidence. On the other hand, when your mind spins, churns, and worries, your "account" gets depleted. It's easy to tell when you're in touch with your wisdom because your responses will seem relatively effortless and calm. Decisions and actions will flow easily and gracefully.

Like a flashing bright light on the dashboard of a car, your feelings are your indication that you've drifted away from the source. All this means is that you've moved away from your center. Instead of feeling confident, you'll feel agitated, angry, nervous, frightened, or resentful. Simple as it sounds, all you have to do is recognize what's happening. When you notice yourself drifting (or zooming away, as the case may be), simply let go of the thoughts that are taking you in one or more of these directions. Allow yourself to come back. It's a self-adjusting system. When you drift away, it's no big deal.

Over time, you'll make a connection between gently allowing yourself to come back and having great ideas and solutions. You'll see that when your mind is spinning and churning, good ideas will be scarce. But when you are centered and trust in your inner wisdom, ideas will pop up all over the place, and your creativity will flow. You may have an insight about how to talk to people differently, how to ask for a raise, how to create a less defensive atmosphere, or whatever. Maybe you'll think of a way to overcome an obstacle or a nagging fear. Or perhaps you'll think of someone who can help you solve a problem. Who knows? You might even come up with a million-dollar idea! It has happened before, and it can happen to you. The specifics of what occurs will depend on your needs. Your wisdom is tailored to you.

I encourage you to try this for yourself in the coming days and not to dismiss it as too simplistic. Go about your ordinary business with one slight difference: Keep your mind as empty and quiet as possible, free of worry and irritation. Rather than struggling or trying to force answers, see if you can relax instead, as situations come up. Instead of being reactive, be patient and know that a solution, answer, or idea will present itself when needed and when you allow it to emerge.

Imagine the thousands of thoughts floating in your mind as silt settling in a pond. Rather than trying to make sense of anything during the confusion, allow the silt to settle. Allow your thoughts to be still. Don't be concerned that you're *not* thinking, because you *are* still thinking. You're just doing so in a different, gentler way. Your mind is operating more like the back burner on a stove instead of being fired up to full capacity. Remember, however, that some of the best, most complicated meals are cooked on very low heat!

Not long ago, I met a man who had been recently laid off from his job. Despite the fact that his wife was panicked, he had kids to feed, and a mortgage to pay, he had remained confident in this source of wisdom. Specifically, he said, "I didn't know what I was going to do, but I did know that I would know!" While it's a funny play on words, that's precisely how I would say it!

Most of the people he spoke to wanted to commiserate with him. Not one person was a calming influence, which was what he knew he needed most. He sensed that what was necessary was a clear head, free from distraction and worry.

While driving in his car, he heard a radio advertisement for a technical seminar that was coming up a few days later. Previously, he'd had no interest (or skill) whatsoever in high tech. He said that in the past, regardless of any financial need, his mind would have rejected anything having to do with technology. But this time his mind was completely open. He thought to himself, "That sounds interesting. I wonder if there might be something in it for me."

His mind was clear and his wisdom was receptive. He loved the seminar and quickly found a new job with even greater potential than his previous work had offered.

The important thing to remember is that the magic wasn't the seminar. It was the fact that his mind was open and that he was receptive to answers. If it hadn't been *this* solution, there would have been another, right around the corner. Had he been wallowing in or zeroed in on his bad luck and fear, listening to his friends and ex-coworkers instead of his own wisdom, it's possible he would still be out of work.

His calm demeanor reminded me of my friends who had thrived in the real estate market years ago. Like them, he knew that there were factors at play beyond his control. In this instance those financial realities had worked against him when he lost his job. Knowing this helped him to avoid blaming himself or being too hard on himself. It helped him to relax, despite the seriousness of his situation. Once again, I was in awe of the power of perspective, which he demonstrated so beautifully. In a way, he was a great teacher of happiness. He knew that the secret of happiness isn't necessarily getting what you want, but being able to get what you want—or not get what you want—and still be at peace. The ironic part about it is that when you are at peace, chances are you will end up thriving in all you do.

One of the things that begins to happen as we develop more trust in ourselves is that we intuitively begin to focus more on what we want to see happen—and less on what we don't want to see happen. In this man's case, his mind was clearly on the solution instead of on the problem. There was no question in his mind that an answer was "out there" (meaning "in there"). As he saw it, it was his job to allow the answer to unfold.

All of us have the same capacity. We have a powerful inner wisdom that can guide us toward the ideal financial solutions in our lives, irrespective of our circumstances. Regardless of what has happened in the past or how difficult the circumstances we face today, there is a solution. Believe in yourself and in this process, and you will know what to do.

24. Catch and Release

It would be a huge stretch to call myself a fisherman. However, on those rare occasions when I do go fishing, I practice what is known as "catch and release." This means that if and when you catch a fish, you gently release it back into the water. The idea is that the person doing the fishing gets the enjoyment of the activity, but the fish, other than during extremely rare exceptions when the hook is too engaged, swims away unharmed.

I love the metaphor of "catch and release" as it applies to our mental lives. I'd estimate that I've taught more people this technique over the course of my career than perhaps any other. It's simple, easy to learn, and unbelievably effective at disarming internal stress and angst.

It's amazing to think about all the aspects of life that we associate with stress. We think about our finances, relationships, taxes, and health. How about the Democrats or Republicans? There are pesky neighbors, political enemies, social and fairness issues. Then there are family and work-related issues, to name just a few.

But how often, when we think of the stress and pain in our lives, do we blame it on our own attitude and thinking? Or how often do we even consider these to be contributing factors? If you're like most people, practically never. Virtually everything except ourselves is seen as a source of stress in one way or another.

But think about it. Our own thoughts, attitudes, and perceptions are far and away the most important ingredients that determine our level of contentment and peace of mind. To me, that's not even in question. But beyond that, for the most part, it's the only aspect of life over which we have virtually *any* amount of control! In my book, not to make attitude a top priority is not only a huge mistake, but it's also practically emotional suicide!

In my opinion, most of us vastly underestimate the harm we do to ourselves with our own thinking. The way we think becomes so invisible to us, and so "normal," that we don't even know it's happening. Yet hundreds of times a day we engage in everything from stray negativity to outright trains of thought that, over time, beat us up. The physical equivalent might be something like taking tiny poison pills that wear down your body. Imagine being not so sick that you couldn't function, but sick enough so that you felt terrible most of the time. In a way, that's how many of us live our lives on an emotional level. We surely function, yet we are stressed and miserable. Most of us are unhappy and lack contentment and fulfillment. Yet time and time again, we ignore the mental aspects of life and focus exclusively on external factors. It makes no sense, and it's completely ineffective.

The concept of "catch and release" is remarkably simple. Most of us are aware of and probably fear weapons of mass destruction. The premise of catch and release is that negative thoughts are like weapons of *self*-destruction. They are firing all the time, almost non-stop. But unlike real weapons, no matter where they are directed, how many times they are fired, or how precisely they are aimed, negative thoughts, like a boomerang, *always* return to their original source. And that source is the person doing the firing—you! There is never an exception. There is no way for the thoughts to harm others or to end up at their target. It doesn't matter how evil the target might be or how justified the attempt. There are no hidden escape routes and, to continue with my war analogy, no "secret forces" that can help. Technology is irrelevant.

The first step in mastering the process of "catch and release" is to be totally and completely convinced, beyond any shadow of a doubt, that harboring negative thoughts is self-destructive. We only do it because it's familiar and because no one has taught us otherwise.

The next step is to begin to pay closer attention to the thoughts that run through your mind. It would be nice if you could simply read this paragraph, and that would be the end of it. Unfortunately, while this is a simple process, it's not quite that easy. Your intention may be to keep track and pay closer attention to your thoughts, but you'll be shocked at how quickly you'll forget.

I'll give you a personal example of this. When I first started practicing this technique, I would wake up and say to myself, "Today I'm going to pay close attention to my own thoughts." Inevitably within a minute or two I would get distracted or the phone would ring—or whatever. Believe it or not, sometimes it would be a day or two later before I even remembered what I was trying to do!

The best way that I know to combat this tendency to forget is to narrowly define the period of time you're working with. For example, try it for half an hour. It's a good idea to jot down your intent on a piece of paper and have it with you, where you can see it while you're practicing.

Once you have the intent, a defined period of time, and a reminder card, you simply do whatever you're doing. You might be driving alone or with the kids, sitting at a desk, talking on the phone, or watching a soccer game. It makes no difference what you are doing as long as you are paying attention to what's going on inside your head.

Along with all the normal and necessary thoughts, plans, memories, and so forth, notice how negativity sneaks in as well. A memory, for example, might come up out of nowhere about a painful event from the past. Or a worry might creep in about a deadline or some concern. This will happen as you're sitting on the bus or in the office.

Just yesterday I was on the phone with someone who had started to experiment with this process. In his words, "It's absolutely amazing to me. In the course of five minutes, twenty demanding, self-effacing, critical, or judgmental thoughts will stream through my mind. Sometimes the same thought or thoughts will come back again and again." Prior to this, he had no knowledge of the extent of or how to determine his own negativity. And he's not alone. Many people have told me that it's as if the negativity has a life of its own. At times it's relentless. One of the reasons we feel so stressed, scattered, anxious, bothered, and confused is that all this mental activity is going on without our awareness. We're so accustomed to it, we don't even realize it's having an impact on us.

Just as in fishing, the final component of the process is the release. And like fishing, this is the part that brings relief. For the fish, it's more than relief, of course; it's the difference between life and death. For us, it can be the difference between feeling resentful or peaceful; anxious or secure. It's one of the best ways I know of to bring peace to our lives.

The release itself is very straightforward. After noticing (or catching) a thought or series of thoughts that are negative, angry, critical, or stressful, you let them go. You give them less attention. Some people like to experiment with mental images such as gently holding the thought in the palm of your hand and blowing it into the sky. Whatever works best for you is the way to go. It's simply a matter of getting used to the idea of letting a thought go instead of allowing it to snowball.

The idea isn't to deny the thoughts you are having, or to pretend they are not there. Nor is the idea to push them away. All you have to do is notice what's happening (that's the "catch" part of the equation). And once you catch the thoughts, you simply release them. Let them go.

Most people report feeling lighter right away. Your sense of urgency may diminish, and the number of things that bother you will lessen. A woman recently told me that for years it drove her crazy when her desk was cluttered with papers and notes. She started to notice her thoughts, like "Damnit, I hate messes! No one ever helps around here. I've got way more than I can handle," and so forth. Every time she would see her desk in any shape other than perfectly organized, her mind would flood with anger and disappointment.

Then she began to notice her thoughts. She would "catch" her thoughts in action—and then release them. She would, in effect, say to herself, "There's another one," and she would drop it (release it). "Whoops, there's another one," and so forth.

The result was that the edge was taken off. She still vastly prefers an organized desk over one that is messy, but it's no longer the same emergency. She walks in and sees the desk. If her mind starts to spin in her old familiar direction, she catches herself—and lets it go. She then spends a few minutes cleaning up the desk so that she can feel more organized.

Catch and release works wonders on big stuff as well. I met a man who had been sued by a former friend. He was furious. He told me that had he not learned this or some similar process, he believes he would have had a stress-related heart attack.

He realized that he was thinking about the incident and his ex-friend many times every day. In his mind, he was justifying his anger and hostility. He would think of all the ways he'd been taken advantage of, and he would plot his revenge. He wished the person ill health and bad luck. He was obsessed by the event.

The conclusion he came to is the same one that I've realized. We certainly "have the right" to our own thoughts and can always justify why we should keep thinking them. But the reality is that we are not getting anywhere by doing so. Just as a child only cheats himself when he cheats in school, we only hurt ourselves when we continue to harbor resentful thoughts.

This man reported a freedom he never even knew existed. He said that the same thoughts try to sneak in every now and then, but most of the time he catches them—and releases them. Rather than becoming obsessions, they are now nothing more than passing thoughts. Instead of spending his life being angry about something in his past, he has learned to be happy again—despite what happened.

It's difficult to quantify, but my experience has been that the same dynamic applies to every scenario in life, regardless of how painful it may be. As far as I'm concerned, anger, disappointment, grief, jealousy, anxiety, envy, and most other painful feelings are inevitable for all of us. But even the most severe feelings are compounded and exacerbated by the way in which we think. As we learn to catch and then release the painful thoughts that enter our minds, an undeniable inner glow and a sense of peace fills our hearts. I hope this technique is as helpful to you as it has been to me.

25. Reflect on What You're Going to Want to Say— Before You Need to Say It

I can think of so many instances in my life when I was totally unprepared to speak. The moments were so significant, yet I was caught off guard. Deep down, I knew that what I needed and wanted to say was important. Yet because I hadn't reflected on such moments, what came out of my mouth was less than I would have hoped for.

There were times when a relationship was ending and I didn't know what to say—so I didn't. There were times when friends or associates died unexpectedly. I was totally and completely unprepared to speak to grieving parents, family, and friends. I didn't know where to start.

A few years ago, I was speaking to a hospice worker. She suggested that knowing what to say in a difficult moment was like many things—we're better off prepared than not. As a result of that conversation, I set out to "prepare" myself. Over the course of the next few months, I spent a little time each day reflecting on responses to various "big" things. I asked myself some important questions. Among them:

- What would I say to a seemingly happily married friend who suddenly announced his divorce?

- What would I say to a parent who lost her child—or to a child who loses her parents?

- What if a friend, colleague, or even a neighbor shares with me that he or she has a terminal disease?

- What would be an appropriate response to a major disappointment (an effort has failed, something has been taken away)?

There were probably thirty such questions ranging from the serious to the unthinkable.

What I discovered was that the specific answers to these types of questions were not nearly as important as the process of asking the questions themselves, and then reflecting on them. In other words, it's not possible or even desirable to "rehearse" what you're going to say—that's not at all the point. In fact, what's needed in most instances is a heartfelt, genuine, loving, and spontaneous response.

Like many aspects of life, this type of preparation isn't meant to be treated like a spelling test. We're not memorizing material or facts, or creating an outline. Instead we're simply planting seeds of wisdom and compassion that will emerge spontaneously when the time is right.

One of the best analogies that comes to mind in my life is preparing for a lecture. Before I speak to a large group, I always prepare. It seems, however, that I almost never stick to my original plan. In fact, I seldom use any notes that I have created. At the same time, however, without the preparation, it's more difficult for spontaneous wisdom to surface. In an unquantifiable yet undeniable way, reflection and preparation make the subject matter more interesting, and even the jokes are funnier.

To me, the ideal preparation is to reflect on the subject matter and then to completely let go of the preparation. You put it on your "back burner" and trust that it's there when and if you should need it. Again, to be sure, you're not memorizing any material—you're not saying to yourself, "Exactly what do I say in this situation?" Instead you spend time thinking deeply about your responses to your own questions. You imagine certain scenarios and take plenty of time thinking about various responses. If something confuses or frightens you, you make a note to discuss the issue with a friend or an expert. Perhaps you'll read a book on a related topic. Then when you have more information, you'll come back to the topic and reflect again. The preparation isn't a one-time venture. It might be spread over several weeks or even months. The idea is to develop thought-out responses that replace what would be uninformed reactions.

What seems to happen as a result of prolonged preparation is this: The best parts of our compassionate and appropriate responses are in there (in our minds)—somewhere—while the rest is filtered out. Once something has been reflected upon, it's as if the wisdom is waiting at the starting gate. Then at the moment it's needed, often at the most critical time, some part—however small—of that wisdom will come to mind. You'll intuitively know how to respond and what to say—or what not to say.

Here's an example. I asked myself the question, "What would I say if told by a grieving parent about the death of their only child?" Since I can't imagine anything more painful than the experience of that parent, it was difficult to even think about a response.

Over the next month or two, I reflected on what I have been taught by hospice and hospital workers and by parents who had lost children. I also thought about some of the most helpful books I have read, and I tried to put myself in that horrible position. I kept coming back to the question, over and over again.

Two things kept coming to mind. First was the importance of

knowing what *not* to say. I reflected on the wisdom of *not* trying to be a teacher during a painful encounter, and of not dishing out advice. I remember reading about and witnessing the importance of *not* trying to talk someone out of their grief—and of not trying to make sense out of or rationalize the situation to that person.

The other theme that emerged was the importance of being a source of love, of being "empty," attentive, and highly present—of just being there. Without the shallowness and distraction of having an agenda or trying to be helpful, it's possible to be in the right mind-set that allows a grieving person to be what he or she needs to be.

Then it happened. I was introduced to a woman who had lost her only child to a freak accident. I absolutely didn't feel that I was helpful—but I also know that I didn't inflame or exacerbate her pain by reacting as if I had never considered the subject. Sometimes it seems that the best we can do is to be sure we're not making a bad situation even worse. In this case, that was the value of reflecting in advance. What would you say in a similar situation?

I was deeply touched by a voice mail message I received from her a few weeks later. All she said was, "It was really nice to meet you. Thanks for listening." It was very simple but very sincere. As I hung up the phone, I realized how many times I *hadn't* listened in the past because I was too busy trying to give advice or cheer someone up. I also realized how helpful it is to spend at least a tiny bit of time reflecting on big and painful topics—and our potential responses to them. After all, if we react to someone cutting in front of us in line or to a slow-moving grocery clerk, how will we be able to offer someone comfort in their time of need? If we haven't spent any time thinking about it, I don't think it's very likely.

One of the by-products of this practice is that by preparing and thinking about responses to "big stuff," we are automatically preparing ourselves for many other things—small, medium, and large. For example, by reflecting on what you would (or might) say to a friend who was fired from her job, you are also preparing yourself—without trying—to relate to a coworker who is going through a messy divorce. Although the situations and details are drastically different, your imagined responses would overlap—your listening skills, attention, compassion, and empathy, for example.

Something else I discovered, particularly after meeting the woman who had lost her child, is that there are many things for which you can't fully prepare. While preparation sounds good in theory, the reality is that many life situations are too complex, confusing, or painful to put into any box. Emotions run high. Circumstances are unpredictable and change quickly. There are so many factors we can't ever anticipate, including our own feelings and those of others.

This again became obvious to me when a friend opened up to me about her decision to leave a relationship. During my initial questioning period, I had thought a great deal about this issue. I imagined a similar scenario and how I might respond in order to be supportive. When it actually happened, however, it was still very difficult and awkward. But despite the awkwardness, it was still worth every second I had spent thinking about it. In defense of preparation, what did stick with me was, again, what *not* to say. Because I had spent some time considering the subject, I didn't jump in and offer advice, as would have been my tendency. I didn't blurt out, "It's going to be okay," and I didn't automatically bad-mouth her ex-boyfriend. Had I not prepared for this type of encounter, it's quite possible that my response would have been far more reactive and may have had unintended consequences.

Going through this process of reflecting on what to say—before it's necessary—was extremely valuable to me in ways other than any real or imagined preparation. In particular, thinking about serious questions heightened my awareness of two important aspects of life: compassion and gratitude.

As I reflect on these types of questions, they remind me of how difficult life is at times for all of us. At some point, everyone is going to be touched by illness, divorce, death, and separation, among other "big" things. How can we not be compassionate toward others, knowing that every human being has a story, and every story has at least some hardship, pain, and grief? When you look into the eyes of another person, or even think of him in this context, it's much easier to be kind and gentle. It's easier to be forgiving. And it's easier to be compassionate.

Take a moment, even right now as you're reading this, to think about someone who annoys you—or someone with whom you are angry. Step back and know that this person has pain in his or her life. As much as this person may have irritated or hurt you, or been misguided, remind yourself that deep down, what this person is really looking for is happiness. The fact that they are off the track and don't go about it in the right way doesn't change this basic truth. Be assured that his or her life either is, or will be, filled with big issues, including pain.

When you think about someone in this light, isn't it easier to let go of any harbored resentment? I'm not suggesting you invite that person to dinner, or even that you necessarily invite them back into your life. I'm only suggesting that it's easier than you might think to have compassion for others—even when they don't seem to deserve it. When your heart fills with compassion, you are the primary beneficiary. Anger, frustration, hostility, and stress are replaced with inner peace. More than a nice theory, this is the actual result of compassion in everyday life.

I'm also filled with genuine gratitude as I ponder these questions. Inherent in every one of them is a reminder of someone or something important in our lives. For example, when I ask the question, "What would I say to a parent who has just lost her child?", I'm instantly reminded of how blessed I am to have two beautiful children. Or when I ask, "What would I say to someone who has just lost their job?", I'm reminded of how fortunate I am to have work that I enjoy.

Reflecting on what you're going to say before you need to say it is an exercise of enormous proportion. It gives you a powerful opportunity to deepen your acknowledgment of the pain of others, as well as the pain in your own life. When you spend a little time preparing for what is ultimately inevitable, you'll be more available to others when you are called to do so. You'll also be reunited with an awareness of the joy that exists in everyday life. I hope this exercise is as valuable to you as it has been to me. My hope is that you will learn a great deal about yourself in the process.

26. Straighten Your Patience

The other day I heard the following riddle: What's the definition of a millisecond? Give up? The answer is: It's the time in between a red light turning green and the honking of the horn coming from the car behind you!

Whether you think it's funny or not, you must agree that we live in an almost unbelievably impatient culture. The other day I brought one of my kids and a friend of hers to a fast-food restaurant. The person in front of us in line had ordered enough food for eight or nine people. She was incredibly annoyed that it took almost five minutes to prepare and hand her the meal! She was pacing the floor, glaring at her watch and talking under her breath. She tried to convince me, in the midst of her frustration, that the employees were incompetent and should be fired. I'm not kidding.

You see it everywhere. Whether it's in traffic, at the airport, in the office, at home, while shopping, on vacation, wherever—people are impatient. Collectively, we are annoyed when anything takes longer than planned or expected. But rather than looking at our own impatience or even our expectations, we zero in on what we believe to be the problem—the waiter, the salesclerk, the computer, our kids, the person we're doing business with—whatever or whomever.

"If only people were more efficient—or computers were," we argue, we'd be happier and wouldn't be so impatient.

I don't buy it! If efficiency were really connected to our happiness, most of us would be euphoric. When you consider how convenient life has become, it's pretty amazing. It seems we take everything for granted—computers, instant banking, fast food, Laundromats, cars, trains, and airplanes. Speaking of airplanes, I've often been amazed as a passenger. On a recent trip between San Francisco and New York, for example, two businessmen were commiserating with each other about the "hassle" of air travel. They were particularly annoyed that the plane took off thirty minutes late, and about how long the trip was going to take. The entire trip, including the delay, was around five and a half hours. That's about 2,500 miles in less than six hours! Imagine the inconvenience!

For as long as I can remember, I've heard people suggest that it's important to develop patience. But it wasn't until a few years ago that I made the absolute connection in my mind between patience and the ability to get through things, small *and* big.

The manifestation of impatience over "small stuff" catches up to us later on when we have to deal with bigger things. One of the most dramatic examples I've ever seen was when a man was actually impatient about how long it was taking his elderly father to pass away. But he wasn't angry at his father, which made his behavior seem even more dramatic and bizarre. At least this would have offered some sort of explanation. Further, he wasn't particularly desperate about the costs of his father's illness.

The only explanation was that he had made such a habit out of being impatient—it was such an automatic response—that he felt he needed to "get on with his life." He was a victim of his own impatience. He hadn't spent any time or effort developing his patience. Instead, he was waiting for the world to "come around" and to become more accommodating.

Luckily, most of us aren't nearly as unconscious as that. However, it's been my observation that most of us aren't aware of, or even particularly concerned about, our own impatience. Despite the rampant levels of impatience in our world, rarely do I hear someone say, "I really need to work on developing my patience." There seems to be a complete disconnect between patience and quality of life.

But the connection is there, it's real, and it's substantial.

The opposite of having something come back to haunt us is practicing something, and then having it pay off later on. If we can strengthen our patience during day-to-day life, this is precisely what will happen. We get to enjoy not only the current benefits of patience but the long-term aspects, as well. By building on the strength and power of patience, we become wiser and more resilient as time passes. So as the stakes get higher, we are more prepared to deal with them.

There's no question that patience is one of those qualities that requires resolve. It's been my experience that it's not possible to become more patient unless one sees it as a virtue and it becomes a priority. In order to experience patience, we must first convince ourselves that it's a good idea. I've found that it's helpful to ask yourself the question (and to reflect on it regularly), "Would my life be served if I could become more patient?" My guess is that if you think about it, it would.

Imagine not being annoyed by the fact that someone is running a little behind schedule. Wouldn't it be nice to relax while waiting in line instead of pacing the floor or getting upset? What if, instead of anticipating what's next, you were able to enjoy "what is"? What if everything didn't have to be perfect—or even go according to plan—in order for you to enjoy it and to be happy?

Patience adds a very real dimension of quality to our experience. It allows us to be fully where we are instead of constantly wishing we were somewhere else. It allows us to experience something without the mental distraction of being in a constant hurry. Patience allows us to experience life in a calm, unrushed manner. We become more responsive to the events of our lives rather than just reacting in habitual or routine ways.

Being patient pays off in many different ways. It helps a businessperson determine the ideal course of action. I've been told by real estate professionals and other negotiators that by taking the "I can wait" or "I'm willing to walk away" approach, and not being in a hurry, they have saved and/or made up to hundreds of thousands of dollars in a single transaction.

It's exciting to watch a sports superstar demonstrate patience. Often while the fans are screaming, "Hurry up—time is running out," the athlete will patiently wait until the perfect opportunity, and with that extra instant of patience, which might be less than a second's difference, he or she will win the game—or sink the putt—or hit the basket—or throw the pass, or whatever.

There are, of course, hundreds of daily opportunities to practice becoming more patient. Anytime we're waiting for someone or something is a great place to start—whether it's waiting for our child or our spouse to get ready to leave the house, or waiting for a return phone call or E-mail from someone at work. I heard a story of a meditation teacher who was picked up at the airport and brought to a class he was teaching. On the way, he and his driver were caught in an enormous, ugly traffic jam. While the driver was complaining and apologizing for the traffic, the teacher calmly suggested that traffic was a wonderful opportunity to practice being patient.

Admittedly, it's difficult to remain this calm in the midst of chaos and delays. However, it's important to acknowledge our less desirable options. If we *don't* prioritize and practice, it's absolutely predictable that we will spend a great deal of our lives being upset and frustrated. The reality is that life rarely goes according to our plans. I'm reminded of the joke, "If you want to make God laugh, just tell him about your plans."

A woman told me about her terrifying experience of witnessing her friend having a heart attack in her apartment. She called the ambulance and was given instructions on what to do. She had been studying yoga and meditation for several years, with plenty of emphasis on patience and staying centered in the moment instead of rushing ahead. She told me that had she not developed her patience, she would have surely panicked, and her friend may have died.

Who knows for certain if that would have happened? Her story did, however, remind me of the obvious importance of having patience during critical moments. Whether it's staying calm during a crisis, which enables us to hear instructions and to be of assistance to others in need, or whether it's having the wisdom to see a financial plan unfold over many years, patience is a key element to success and in some instances to survival.

The secret is to start small, but to start today. Remind yourself that someday, your practice will pay off. It might be that you avoid an unnecessary confrontation at work or with your teenager. Or it could be that you assist someone in a real emergency. In any case, use your everyday experiences—waiting in line or traffic, dealing with other people and delays—as opportunities to practice.

When you feel the impulse to react with impatience, try to notice it before it spins out of control. Feel yourself ready to jump into familiar territory. But before your mind has a chance to reinforce your impatience with memories of past experiences ("this is the tenth time this year this has happened") or defeatist thoughts of the future ("I'll never make it on time"), bring yourself back to the moment. Take a deep breath and remind yourself of the importance of patience.

For many, it's that initial hump that's so difficult to get over—the initial impulse to react or become impatient when something or someone pushes your buttons. But it gets much easier over time and with positive reinforcement. If you have the resolve to become more patient and you continue to practice, you'll be rewarded with a richer experience of life—and the security that comes with a calm mind. Give it a try—but whatever you do, be patient with yourself.

27. **Be All You Can Be**

I've always loved this tag line, but I give it a slightly different twist. I'd say, "Be as effective as you can be." To do so puts you in charge of your own life, strapped right in the driver's seat. It keeps you from scrambling throughout the day, putting out those fires and postponing the things that, deep down, you really want to do.

I felt that it would be irresponsible not to include a strategy on effectiveness in a book about big, important things! I felt that way for several reasons. First of all, both big and bad things can happen to anyone, regardless of how prepared or effective you might be. You can call it luck, timing, karma, or whatever. The point is, none of us is exempt. However, when we are living an effective life, we are living the life we have chosen for ourselves. We are navigating our own ship, making our own decisions, and rarely feeling like a victim of circumstance. Because of this, we have few regrets. If life were to end tomorrow, we would have peace in knowing that we lived as we wanted to live.

Those of us who live effective lives have the courage to back up our convictions and to focus on our priorities. We also have the discipline to work hard, postpone some of our gratification in order to get things done, and focus on what's really important.

Effective living enables you to prioritize well, which often means leaving certain things undone. Effective people know the difference between what's really important and what can wait. The more effective you are in living your life, the easier it is for you to see the bigger picture—which includes, of course, solutions to the problems and issues that come up for all of us. So whether it's a work-related problem, a heath-related issue or accident, a financial crisis or big decision, a relationship issue, a personal emergency, or the need to step in and take charge of a situation, effectiveness is the key that pulls it all together. Without it, it's nearly impossible.

Whenever we're dealing with something really significant, it's critical that we have our emotional bearings and are able to have a plan of action. These two ingredients are a natural by-product of effective day-to-day living. In other words, the act of practicing an effective life, day to day and moment to moment, increases the odds dramatically that, as big things come up, you'll be more equipped to deal with them. You'll be familiar with how to prioritize a solution and how to implement a plan. You'll also be familiar with how to make quick adjustments to your plans, which are almost always necessary when dealing with a crisis or significant event. Being effective doesn't guarantee that it will always work out the way you want, but it sure puts the odds in your favor. On the flip side, when you're not living as effectively as you could be, it's extremely difficult to navigate through life, especially as big issues come up. Being preoccupied and frustrated with getting through "small stuff," and reacting to life instead of responding to it, make small things seem big, and big things, insurmountable.

It's important to know that without effectiveness, we stumble. We're so busy putting out fires and reacting to life as it comes at us, that we become victims of our circumstances, to one degree or another. A lack of effectiveness implies a certain lack of organization, foresight, discipline, and follow-through skills. Thus it becomes easy to feel as if you're not in charge of your own life.

A simple example would be a person who had two extremely important phone calls to make on a certain day. However, when he arrived at the office, there were twelve less important calls that needed to be returned that seemed necessary, as well as a stack of papers on his desk to go through. You already know the end of this story: By the time he got around to the really important calls, it was too late. He had lost his opportunity. His boss was furious at him for not doing what was most important, and he ended up feeling resentful and victimized by his life. He wasn't able to see that he was the sole creator of the experience.

I realize this is a very simplistic example and that usually other factors are involved. Yet for illustrative purposes, allow me to make this comparison because, in many ways, it really is this simple. An effective worker would have come to the office and taken a moment to evaluate what was most important. And regardless of how inconvenient or uncomfortable they might have been, he or she would have made those calls first—or at least at the first realistic opportunity. That person would have realized that those two phone calls were far more important than everything else combined. They were the engine that allowed everything else to happen. That person would have left his or her office, regardless of what else didn't get done, feeling as though he did what was necessary. This example shows the connection between effectiveness and self-esteem.

The process of becoming a bit more effective is easier than you might think. In fact, most people I've spoken to who have made the attempt have told me that the learning curve is very sharp, and that the slightest improvements make an enormous difference. I've heard people say they have learned to stop wasting time and have stopped procrastinating. Others have reported spinning their wheels less often and making more money. Still others have found the time to put first things first and to spend more time with their families. In all cases, people have found that life can be much calmer than it used to be. This has to do with that old cliché: Work smarter, not harder!

I've spent a lot of time exchanging ideas with very effective people. There are different schools of thought on effectiveness, but after discussions with many different people, the following consistent themes seem to emerge.

From my perspective, the three keys to becoming more effective are: (1) having a clear mind each day; (2) using that clear mind to prioritize and keep from being distracted by the hundreds of other things grabbing at your attention; and (3) following through on that which is most important. These are all, of course, very closely related. It has been my experience that if I do nothing else except these three things, then my entire life flows easily and effortlessly. All the other important as well as the mundane responsibilities still get done, and I have plenty of time left over! To be certain, there are days when I forget to take these steps or when I get distracted by something that is cleverly disguised as an emergency! And when I "take the bait," my life is just as chaotic as anyone else's!

Having a clear, undistracted mind is critical. Several times a day, it's critical to clear your mind and see things freshly. Some people can do this by closing their eyes, taking some deep breaths, and emptying the contents of their thoughts. They allow their mind to relax for a few minutes. This allows the "dust to settle." Without effort, it allows your mind the opportunity to reorganize and "reset." By the time you're finished, say five minutes later, your "to do" list will be carefully constructed with the most important things standing out.

Going backward for a moment, think of all the times you had important things to do but were flustered with the demands coming at you from all directions. When you're overwhelmed and off balance, the best you can do is react to what's going on around you. You end up moving very quickly, but not necessarily getting very much done!

Years ago I shared this idea of taking a moment to clear your mind with a mother with six children. Although she was trying hard and was a loving mother, she was very ineffective. In fact she looked as if she was about ready to have a nervous breakdown. She was scrambling here and there, always in a hurry, and always running late. She was constantly disappointing others due to her consistent lateness, followed up by her defensive reactions. She felt completely victimized. She would say to people, "Don't you realize that I have six children?", as if that were an adequate blanket excuse!

Her turnaround was one of the simplest and most beautiful I've ever seen. She could immediately see the logic of a few "mental resets," as she called them. They were her chance to regroup, make adjustments, and set new priorities. She discovered that for her, the most important time to do this was first thing in the morning before the chaos started, and then to "check in" a few times a day to see if any adjustments were needed. It was that simple. She would close her eyes and empty her mind of all preconceived ideas. She wouldn't think about yesterday's chaos or anticipate today's chaos. Instead, she would simply clear her mind and allow everything to fall away.

She would then ask herself, while still in a calm state of mind, "What are the most critical things that need to be done this day?" She also asked, regularly, if there were any adjustments that she could make that would make her life easier and calmer. In other words, were there things she could do differently?

To her surprise, the answers were pretty simple. While in a hurried state of chaos, the best she could do was scramble from one activity to the next. But in a calmer state of mind, it was easy for her to see that there were tasks she could delegate, carpools she could organize, and other things she could drop altogether. By taking steps toward becoming more effective rather than simply moving faster, she was able to transform her life almost overnight from a state of frenetic frustration to one of relative peace.

I didn't know her long enough to see how she did during a crisis. I can speculate, however, that by being calmer, more organized, and less reactive, she was far more prepared to deal with anything that might have come up—an emergency with one of the kids, for example.

Like this mother of six children, all of us have the capacity to become more effective, almost immediately, regardless of our starting point.

All of us have different lives, responsibilities, priorities, and goals. Therefore it's an individual process for each of us. My primary goal at this time, for example, is to prioritize working on this book. Each morning I get up early, and after a cup of coffee, I have my first "clear my mind" session. What generally happens is that I'm reminded that this book is my top priority until it's finished. My best plan of action is to start working on the book before anything else. I'm also reminded that there will be dozens of potential distractions during the morning: phone calls, E-mails, bills, projects that need to be organized, other work-related things, stacks of paper on my desk, requests for help, and so forth. All of these things are important to me, and it's tempting (and often much easier) to focus on them instead of on my top priority.

What the "clearing" session does for me, however, is to give me the resolve and the reminder I need to follow through on what's most important—instead of convincing myself that I'll get to it later. The "I'll get to the important stuff later" argument is the antithesis of effectiveness. It's nothing more than an attempt to fool ourselves.

As I mentioned above, when I do stick to my top priorities, my effectiveness stays with me throughout the day. When my writing time is done, I can feel good knowing that I've done what I set out to do. Then it's usually time for another clearing session. From a calm state of mind, I again ask the question: "What's most important from this point on?"

The answer will be different for each of us, but the point is that the answer will be clear. For some, it might be time to switch gears and work on something else. For another person, it might be time to take a five-minute break and get right back to what he or she was doing before. The key is to identify that which is most important—which will vary from day to day—and then have the courage and conviction to follow through on the important things. Remember to put first things first!

Effectiveness isn't a science; it's an art. But it's really fun and sat-isfying to become more effective. It's like a dance, in that it's impor-tant to go with the flow and to make adjustments. When you prioritize and practice effectiveness, it's pretty difficult to get into a rut because you're constantly looking at what's most important—which will, of course, change from time to time.

We all have plenty of room for improvement. I hope you'll join me in attempting to become the most effective person you can be. It will pay off in all areas of your life. Good luck!

28. Treat Others As If They Were Going to Die— Tonight

I have always been an admirer of Og Mandino. One of his many wise ideas was this: "Treat others as if they were going to be dead by midnight. Extend to them all the care, kindness and understanding you can muster, and do so with no thought of any reward. Your life will never be the same again."

If you've ever lost someone you love, especially suddenly, you can relate to this important wisdom. When you realize and then acknowledge how fragile life can be, and how short it is, it's much easier to extend loving-kindness in someone else's direction.

In my opinion, one of the main reasons we remain angry, bitter, or resentful toward someone else, and one of the primary reasons it's so difficult to keep our perspective and forgive, is because we forget that whomever we are angry with could, quite literally, die tonight.

Not long ago, I was really angry at someone and couldn't seem to let go of it. A friend suggested I apply this philosophy to my feelings toward this person. Sure enough, within a short time, I was able to completely let go of my hostility. If you think about it, it makes sense. When we are angry or hostile toward someone else, we are the one who suffers. We're the one who carries around the anger. We have to live with it, feel it, and either hold on to it or express it.

When you look at (or even think about) another person and realize that he or she could, quite literally, be dead tonight, it puts things into a different perspective. It makes it difficult to stay mad or to fill your mind with all the reasons for remaining resentful. I remember being in a huge room full of thousands of people for a seminar. One of the first things the speaker said was something like this: "Take a look around you. Within a year, some of you will be dead." It wasn't at all meant to depress the audience, but rather to put things into perspective; to wake us up. And that's exactly what it did.

It's easy to stay hooked into our gripes and dissatisfactions, and to believe that if certain things or people would change, then we'd be able to be happy. We keep postponing living because there is always something that must be taken care of—there's one more person who has to change or "shape up." "If only they would behave differently, then we'd be happy," or so we imagine. Even though it has never worked before, we keep giving it one more try.

One of my all-time favorite books is *A Path with Heart* by Jack Kornfield. To live a life where "heart" is prioritized is a magnificent way to approach one's life. It puts difficulties into a different perspective and makes it easier to forgive and move on. When "heart" isn't our top priority, it's tempting to live our lives believing that the goal is to "set it up right" and to manipulate the world and our circumstances so that we can be happy. We imagine, consciously or unconsciously, that it's possible to have a life that is set up so perfectly that there are no frustrations, and no one who will bother or disappoint us.

To me, living a path with heart means that even though I can't always do it, my goal is to face my life—including my problems and frustrations—with grace and equanimity. I want to keep my heart open, even when those around me aren't willing or able to do so. I want to know, beyond any shadow of a doubt, that when anger is in my heart, it's me who holds the key to releasing that anger. It's my anger, not theirs. When I'm frustrated or resentful, it's me who must forgive. By recognizing this, I become the captain of my own ship. My life belongs to me. I realize that ultimately it's not my circumstances that need to change, but my reactions to them. I no longer have to wait for others to change so that I may be happy. And neither do you.

One of the keys to having a fulfilling life is to begin to see our difficulties not as a series of "curses," but instead as opportunities to grow and let go. The idea of treating someone as if he or she were going to die tonight is a practical way to make this transition. Implementing this strategy isn't about being frightened of death, but rather about being open to life. It's about being willing to confront our frustrations, not with stubbornness, hatred, or rigidity, but with a sense of openness and humility. There's a freedom that comes with this openness. Instead of being bogged down and burdened by our annoyances and frustrations, we are able to become much more accepting and therefore much more joyful and peaceful. As situations arise, we are less inclined to run from them, deny them, or act defensively.

I met a woman who had fallen into a very negative and destructive pattern with her teenager. Her child would rebel, and she would feel scared, disappointed, and angry. The teen felt her mom's disappointment and responded with more resentment. They were fighting each other at every turn, and their relationship had evolved into a battle. Neither of them felt listened to or understood. The parent had read many books on raising teenagers and had spoken to numerous "experts." They had tried counseling. Nothing helped. Eventually both the parent and the teen literally gave up. They were told by their friends that this state of affairs was "normal." Apparently, most people do simply give up.

I'm the first to admit that raising kids is an extremely difficult job. There are times when you get so frustrated you can hardly see straight. And it seems our kids are usually frustrated with us, too! What's more, they can justify and rationalize their disappointment just as articulately as we can ours. Yet when someone shared this "dead by midnight" idea with this particular woman, things started to change. It wasn't a magic pill, but it was an important dose of perspective.

When any of us are locked into frustration, it's easy to feel as though it's going to last forever. Furthermore, it's easy to understand why, if something were indeed going to last forever, it would be difficult to let go of angry thoughts and resentful feelings. When you live with a teenager and you're sparring back and forth, and you're dealing with all the issues of growing up, it seems like a long process. It's different, however, when you acknowledge the reality of life and death.

Last summer we were driving across part of the country. On one stretch we passed a series of roadside "In Memory Of" crosses. The dates suggested that most of the fatalities were teenagers. What a blessing it is to be reminded. Suddenly I had more compassion and understanding for the two young ladies in the backseat.

If you reread the opening quote from Og Mandino in this strategy, take note of the final two sentences. They also play a critical role in a quality life. "Extend to them all the care, kindness and understanding you can muster, and do so with no thought of any reward." In the original *Don't Sweat the Small Stuff . . . and It's All Small Stuff*, I wrote a chapter called "Do Something Nice for Someone Else and Don't Tell Anyone About It." The point was that while many of us often do nice things for other people, we almost always expect—consciously or unconsciously—something in return: praise, a return favor, credit, a thank-you note, or some type of acknowledgment. It might be very subtle, but it's usually there.

However, there is something truly magical and powerful about doing something thoughtful—a favor, an act of kindness, an anonymous gift, or whatever—but never even mentioning it to anyone, nor expecting anything in return. There's an old saying, "Giving is its own reward." And this is so true. If you can extend loving-kindness to others, even when they don't deserve it, you'll be richly rewarded by the feelings that come with unconditional kindness and compassion.

I'd go so far as to say that when you expect, anticipate, or demand reciprocation, you lose out and dilute the value of your kindness. You'll be more focused on the response to your kindness than on the kindness itself. By keeping the loving attitude pure and the kindness unconditional, you are doing what the world needs most—spreading love.

Of course, you can extend this wisdom to anyone with whom you are having a problem. Whether it's your spouse, partner, child, colleague at work, neighbor, friend, or even stranger, it really helps to put things in perspective.

Once when I was sharing with a group of people the idea of treating others as if they were going to die tonight, a woman made a good point. She said, "The problem is, we can't live our lives always assuming that each person we have a conflict with is going to die. That's not practical. It's almost a cop-out." And from a certain perspective, I found myself agreeing with her thoughts—which led us to further discussion. In the end, the group decided that the idea isn't to walk around assuming everyone is going to die tonight, but rather to be aware that it's always a possibility. This way, we can return to the ancient wisdoms about love. For example, never go to sleep angry with another person. And take a few extra moments to say "I love you" and "Good-bye" as someone you love walks out the door. Finally, when you're mad at someone and neither of you is willing to budge an inch, take a step back and remember how quickly it all passes. This might give you that extra bit of perspective, which will allow you to forgive and move on.

29. A New Look at Stress

If I had to guess, I'd say that most of today's stress management professionals would tell you that they have "stressful" jobs! Most people that I speak to say the same thing. Everyone seems to believe that they are under enormous stress, personal and professional. Stress is blamed for many things, including overeating, smoking, drinking, unhappiness, and poor marriages.

I've spoken to many groups where it seems as if stress in the workplace is worn as a badge of honor. People will commiserate and compare their levels of stress, as if it's some sort of contest. One person will say, "I haven't had a vacation in five years." Then the person standing next to him will say, "Yeah, but I spent eighteen hours at the office today." Many of these claims seem exaggerated, but it's clear that often people are proud of the fact that they are under enormous stress. Sometimes people are even offended if you don't seem stressed out. They act as if something is wrong with you—that you're out of touch with reality, or that you're lazy.

Stress is an interesting subject. On the one hand, as I just said, people are drawn to it, even proud of it. On the other hand, most people, when asked, will say that they wish they had less of it in their lives. I've given the subject a great deal of thought and believe that,

through looking at stress a little differently, we can begin to dismantle its grip upon us.

As hard as it sometimes can be to accept, stress is not something
that is happening to us, but rather it's something that is manufac-
tured from within our own thinking. Our own thoughts tell us what
is "stressful" and what isn't. Examples of this abound. A friend of
mine, for instance, loves snowboarding. To him, this is the ultimate
way to relax! To me, it seems like an incredibly stressful way to spend
your time. My doctor said my chances of getting a knee injury from
snowboarding are great, particularly after my recent basketball
injury. Plus it seems like other boarders are always coming up from
behind and whizzing by the others, particularly beginners! It looks
difficult and dangerous. So who's right—my friend or me? Is snowboarding stressful, or isn't it?

I was talking to a man the other day about the need for silence. I
told him that one of my greatest joys is spending multiple days all
alone in total silence. I experience this time as peaceful and joyful.
He told me that doing so would cause him a nervous breakdown. In
his own words, he would "go insane" with the lack of stimulation. He
seemed like a normal guy to me. So the question is, "Why is the same
event stressful for one person and de-stressing for the other?"

Another example is the size of one's family. I've met many people
who absolutely love having a large family—five, six, even seven children. They thrive and have fun. It works for them; they have plenty
of patience and love for one another. Other people claim that children cause them enormous stress. To them, having even one child in
the room makes them anxious. The question here becomes, "Do children cause stress?" Many insist that they do! If so, why are some people so much more stressed than others?

A similar question can be asked about income. I've met some
people who are perfectly happy and claim to have virtually no financial stress on very little income. Others with more than a hundred

times the same amount of money have told me that "too little money" is their greatest cause of stress. I've met many people with a lot of money, but very few seem secure. Again you have to ask yourself, "Where is the stress coming from?" If a certain amount of income were required for a sense of well-being, then wouldn't everyone, by definition, below that level be under enormous stress? Using the same logic, wouldn't individuals with income levels above that amount be free from financial stress?

What about time spent on the job? Some people seem to thrive on those twelve-hour days, and subscribe to the TGIM club (Thank God It's Monday). Others are completely overwhelmed working four hours a day, three days a week, and stay dedicated to the TGIF club (Thank God It's Friday). One person recently told me, "I don't know how I do it." Although she had a part-time job and no children, she was completely overwhelmed by her level of responsibility. Where was her sense of being overwhelmed coming from?

It goes on and on. Moving, for one person, is cause for a celebration. To someone else, it's cause for concern, or even a nervous breakdown. Plenty of studies will suggest that the act of moving is inherently stressful. How can this be?

Here's one for you. I absolutely love the rain. I feel very peaceful when it's raining, and really look forward to it. I enjoy the sound, the smell, and the overall feeling. I would be thrilled with thirty straight days of rain. On the other hand, I've been told by numerous people that rain causes them to be depressed! I've even known people who after having moved from California to Oregon, became depressed enough to move back to California because of the amount of rain!

The more you think about it, the more clear it becomes: Ultimately, it's our thinking, not our circumstances, that creates much of our stress.

It's critical to understand this distinction because, without it, "big stuff" can become overwhelming. After all, even small stuff is blown out of proportion when we believe that external events are responsible for our sanity. A minor inconvenience such as traffic or a slow waiter becomes a major emergency in the mind of someone who believes "outside factors" determine internal peace of mind.

Just this morning, I witnessed a great example of this. After dropping off my kids at school, I arrived at the post office just as they were scheduled to open. A line was forming outside the door, and for whatever reasons, the employees were running a few minutes late and failed to open the doors on time. Most of the people in line took the five- or six-minute delay pretty much in stride. One man, however, thought it was an emergency and became angry. He stomped around, asking everyone to sign a petition. He was complaining about the employees' "incompetence" and even wanted to contact the local newspaper and have a story written. To be honest, he seemed like he was going to have a heart attack! He stormed away from the door about a minute before a very nice person opened it, apologized, and in a very professional manner explained that they were having a computer problem.

You might rationalize this incident by thinking that he was the only person who was in a genuine hurry—and *that* was why he freaked out. But that logic doesn't seem to pan out. Several people in the same line were running late to other appointments and were clearly short of time. But their response was very different. After looking at their watches and noticing the delays, they calmly walked away. They probably weren't thrilled about being inconvenienced, as I surely wasn't, but it was just one of those daily hassles, not a full-blown emergency.

It's fun to tell stories about small stuff. But when the stakes are high, it's particularly important to be aware when we are on the verge of using our own thinking against ourselves in some way. To do so exacerbates our feelings of stress and ultimately makes us less effective.

The predicament is this: As soon as we describe and think about stress as coming from somewhere other than from our own thinking, we automatically set ourselves up to experience more of that stress. After all, we have just confirmed its existence and are now thinking of ways to "cope." Usually, when we define stress as coming from an external source, we then have to find equally external ways to deal with it. Suppose, for example, someone feels that they are experiencing great stress due to the way their employer speaks to them—perhaps the aggressive tone of her voice.

There could be several typical responses to this perceived source of stress. A person might, for example, spend time complaining and commiserating with friends or coworkers. They might also spend a great deal of time and energy thinking about it in private. He or she might seek counseling or read any number of books geared toward this problem. The person might also consider confronting their boss or bringing it to their attention. The problem may consume that person, and as long as the assumption is that all of the stress is coming from the boss, it can seem pretty hopeless.

What if the problem (the tone of the employer's voice) doesn't change? As long as you insist that this is the actual source of stress, you're stuck. If you can't get the result you want, how are you going to achieve inner peace?

Please know that I'm not minimizing the problem of having a difficult boss, particularly if that person is at all abusive. Nor am I minimizing any problem we might have. I'm also not suggesting that using reasonable attempts to get what you want, which in this instance, would entail confronting the employer, might not be a good idea. In fact it sounds like a wise thing to do. Instead, what I'm pointing out is that the way we *define* stress and the way we think about it have a great deal of influence over how we deal with it, whatever the perceived source happens to be.

In this example, suppose the employee knew that her stress originated and "brewed" within her own thinking. She would have the advantage of knowing that if she weren't careful, she would blow up the "problem" in her mind, which would lead to an even greater source of stress. This would make her even more frustrated, and her responses, as well as her judgment, would be severely limited. This would reduce her options. She would be disempowered.

If she knew that her thinking had the potential to make things worse, she would also know that by being "present" and staying calm, she could keep the number of thoughts firing through her mind to a minimum. She would be sensitive and would be paying attention to the quality and content of her thoughts, so as not to allow them to spiral out of control. She would sense which thoughts to pay attention to—and respond accordingly. Just as importantly, she would know which thoughts deserved less significance, and even which ones to dismiss. She would experience quiet wisdom, and this wisdom would tell her exactly what to do. It could mean anything from reporting the employer or confronting him—to dropping it.

If you've read some of my other work, you might know that I often use the term "thought attack" to describe the way our thinking feeds on itself. One thought leads to another, then another. As our attention is riveted on something, the object of that attention will grow and seem more significant. As a result, our stressful feelings will tend to seem even more justified. Again it's super important to make the distinction between "having the right" to be upset (which you certainly do) versus compounding existing feelings of being upset by the way we are using our thinking (such as engaging in a thought attack)!

Thought attacks are like dramas playing out in our minds. They start small and then grow. The more detail and attention we provide, and the more we dwell on the subject, the more "real" it will seem. Here's an example.

I heard a story about a woman whose sister had "betrayed" her by telling someone one of her deepest secrets. The actual event, the betrayal, had occurred almost a year earlier. The problem was that she was experiencing it as if it were happening now. She would think about how many times she had pleaded with her sister not to tell anybody. She remembered how her sister assured her that she would never tell and how she could trust her. Every detail of the forbidden conversation was imagined, over and over again. When she would think of her sister, she would think of revenge and wish her ill will.

To me, this example demonstrates how powerful our thoughts are in keeping our stress alive. Without them, it couldn't exist. The only way that I'm aware of to dismantle this type of stress is to first acknowledge where it's coming from (thoughts). After all, there's no way to go back and change what has happened, and we certainly don't want to spend our lives suffering over disappointments.

To be sure, it's absolutely true that what happened was a disappointment, as are so many other things. Our disappointments can certainly teach us and help us make appropriate adjustments. There is no discounting the pain that exists in life. But at this point, in terms of dealing with it in the here and now, it's helpful to acknowledge that the pain we experience stems, to a large degree, from our own thoughts.

It's helpful to think of stress as a warning signal, which alerts us that we're at it again—thinking! It's not bad or wrong, or our fault, that we're thinking. We're all thinking creatures. It's a natural part of us. It's not necessary to stop thinking. It's only necessary to *notice* that we're thinking. Our stress is the feeling that helps us with this recognition.

In my view, the key to this woman being able to move on would be for her to notice when she was feeling resentful, angry, or disappointed. Those feelings would remind her that she was "getting back in her head" again. And just as we're taught in meditation, all that would be necessary would be a very gentle dismissal of those thoughts, which would bring her back, again, to the present moment. The earlier she is able to notice what is happening, the easier it would be to make such a dismissal.

When you think about stress in this way (as a signal), it no longer has to be your enemy. It's more like a friend. Just as a sprained ankle lets you know that it's time to back off of your jogging, our stressful feelings can also bring us important spiritual and emotional information.

Years ago I learned an important lesson: be easy on yourself. Like many other people, my own thoughts bombard me on occasion. Like the woman in the previous example, I'll be reminded of a painful past event—or will begin to overanticipate something in the future. What I have learned, however, is that this doesn't necessarily have to be a problem. As long as I'm aware of what's happening, and as long as I notice it early enough, I'm usually able to realize what's going on inside myself. I can then ever so gently bring my attention back to the present moment, the only place where it's possible to experience genuine peace.

30. **Rely on Optimism**

For as long as I can remember, I've been interested in the healing power of optimism. Depending on the situation, it's usually a far better option than the alternatives—pessimism or cynicism. To me, optimism is synonymous with hope and effectiveness. When you are optimistic, you see the possibilities as well as the steps to get there. You feel that things will, or at least may, get better.

When someone you love is sick or injured, optimism carries you through and gives you strength. Even when a loved one dies, eternal hope brings you peace. Likewise, if you lose your job or are struggling financially, optimism inspires you to keep going, to continue searching for new opportunities. During or after a divorce, optimism is what leads you to believe that you're going to be okay and that you'll love again. When you're sick or hurt, optimism plays a role in your power to heal and/or get stronger. There is even evidence suggesting that optimistic people live longer than their cynical counterparts.

Historically, it's been proven wise to be an optimist most of the time, depending on the circumstances. There have always been many who have believed that the world was coming to an end, for one reason or another. But they have always been wrong. Despite our troubles and hardships, here we are. Human beings are highly resilient and resourceful as long as we think something can be done. And as long as we are appropriately optimistic, that something usually does get done somehow.

To become more optimistic, it's helpful to see the compelling logic of becoming more so. Once you're convinced that it's a wise way to live, the path becomes clear. After all, there have always been those who argued "it can't be done," whatever "it" happens to be. Yet whether it has had to do with making technological advances, traveling through space, performing amazing athletic endeavors, overcoming major obstacles, curing diseases and making other medical breakthroughs, or achieving so many other things, the naysayers have usually been wrong, or will be.

Becoming familiar with optimism, reflecting on it, and making it a priority to become more optimistic are powerful life tools. Seeing optimism as a possibility, instead of dismissing it as a sign of naïveté, gives you more options. It allows you to know that very often you have a clear choice about how to respond to or think about something in your life. Optimism is an attitude or outlook about something, and as such it nudges your perception one way or the other. Consciously choosing optimism over pessimism can sometimes make the difference between success and failure, winning and losing, being neutral and getting depressed, moving forward or giving up.

It's even more. Optimism isn't just about predicting the future with an "it can be done" attitude. It's also about present-moment responses to ordinary, day-to-day events that shape the fabric of our lives.

Take a look at the following conversation between two women who were directly in front of me at the grocery store. I'll call them Betty and April. Betty had just completed her transaction and was now waiting for April to pay for her groceries.

Betty: "How's it going? How are Dan and the
kids?"

April: "Okay, I guess. There's not much time
these days, we're always running."

Betty: "I heard you guys went away for the holidays. How was that?"

April: "Kind of disappointing. We had thought
we could get away for a couple of weeks, but
there was too much to do. We ended up taking
a few days in the motor home instead. That's
always a hassle, you know?"

Betty: "Hey, I love that wine you've picked out.
Are you having a party?"

April: "We are if you count having Dan's corporate group coming over. Actually, I can't stand
it when they come. They stay too late, and
we're always tired the next day."

At about that point, I tuned them out. April was a classic pessimist.
Every response was negative in some way. I didn't know for sure if
she was just in a bad mood, but it seemed as if she was the type of
person who absolutely couldn't be pleased. Whatever "life stuff" she
was presented with would be thought about in a negative, pessimistic way. It would never be good enough because she was so
skilled at finding fault. Her family was too rushed, so she couldn't
enjoy them. Having a recreation vehicle was taken for granted and
considered a burden. Even throwing a party was looked at in a negative way. It was as though her mind was determined to find some way
to look at everything in a negative light. You can only imagine how
she would think of her physical appearance, the size of her bank
account, and everything else.

The question becomes, "How can a person like April ever be happy?" On the surface, it would seem that you couldn't really set up her life much better than it already was. And even if you could, it would be irrelevant. As long as any of us are in the habit of thinking about life from a cynical or pessimistic outlook, we can't become satisfied with daily living.

Even more important, how is this type of attitude going to fare when the stakes get big? If we can't find ways to be optimistic about even the positive, fun aspects of life, how in the world are we going to be able to handle any future pain? How will we be there for others when they are in pain?

Without being fake, or pretending to be happy, April could learn to have a nicer experience of life simply by thinking about things more optimistically. Rather than focusing on the one aspect of a scenario that is problematic or less than perfect, she could just as easily focus on the brighter spots. Rather than characterize the holidays as negative—and anticipate a horrible, fatiguing evening—she could focus on the parts of her holiday that were a blessing. She could also learn to anticipate an enjoyable corporate evening. Since she's going to be putting the party together anyway, she could learn to make the best of it. Who knows, she might even have fun! Since she knows the parts of the party she doesn't like, she could decide to make a few adjustments and set it up in a way that would practically ensure a richer experience for herself, and probably the guests, as well.

I'm not suggesting that's it's *always* appropriate, realistic, wise, or even desirable to be optimistic. Far from it. There are endless, obvious examples of times when it would be downright stupid or foolish to be an optimist. Once, while at a party, a friend of mine drank way too much. As I grabbed his keys to prevent him from driving, he yelled at me, "Don't worry about it—I'll be fine." It would have been foolish and irresponsible of me to be "optimistic" that he was right.

Similarly, it would be ridiculous to think you could manage a long hike in the desert without any water. Or imagine being optimistic that you'll retire in comfort without having saved any money. Think about the relative wisdom of being blindly optimistic about your marriage after your spouse has had multiple affairs.

Think about business matters for a moment. How would you like your accountant or financial advisor to be optimistic about taking foolish financial risks or unethical or illegal deductions? What about the treasurer, banker, controller, and other typically conservative-oriented people in a business? Should they switch to being overly optimistic? I don't think so. I could go on and on and even share with you horror stories of people whose lives were ruined because of uncalled-for and foolish "optimism."

Perhaps the least appropriate, even cruel thing you can do to someone when they have experienced a tragedy or personal loss is to encourage them to "be happy" or to "know that everything is going to be okay." Although that's the ultimate message you will want to share, to do so at the wrong time is, in my opinion, worse than nothing.

These examples are not what I'm talking about. What I'm advocating is optimism when there is a clear and rational choice between two ways of looking at a situation. For example, no one in their right mind would suggest you be blindly optimistic that you'll have enough money to retire—the old "just don't worry about it" attitude. On the other hand, if you are fifty years old and are just now thinking about saving money, you have one of two choices. You could think, "It's not worth it. I've never been able to save before. Why bother?" Or you could think, "There's no better time than right now to start. I can do this."

The same principle is involved in whatever we happen to be dealing with. If your teenager is hooked on drugs, you could easily convince yourself, "It's hopeless." Or you can tell yourself and believe that you and your child can and will do whatever is necessary to solve this problem.

One of the interesting and hopeful aspects to optimism is that the more you think about it and learn about it, the more obvious it is that you can learn to be more optimistic. It's my belief that you can become a healthy optimist, even if it's not in your nature to be one. I've met many people over the years who described themselves as "extremely pessimistic" who have since become more optimistic. Interestingly, these transformations from pessimist to optimist are internally self-generated. In other words, there was not a particular "good reason" for someone to suddenly become an optimist. They didn't win the lottery, inherit a fortune from a distant relative, or become the beneficiary of some other extraordinary good luck. Instead, something switched inside themselves. They had an insight about the age-old adage of "putting the cart before the horse." In other words, they realized that how they framed certain situations in their minds, how they thought about them and perceived them, was going to play a large role in the outcome.

Helen lost everything in a huge fire. I mean everything. Since the fire occurred in her home office, it also destroyed her home-based business, including all of her records. All of her photos were lost. Her pets were killed.

She was devastated, although not destroyed.

As with all painful life events, her mind was at a fork in the road. It would have been easy for her thoughts to drift toward and focus on the near-impossible predicament she was facing. It certainly seemed justified.

But she took another route instead. She decided that she would not be defeated. She made a commitment to herself to not become despondent, but not to bury her feelings or pretend that everything was okay. She realized that she was lucky that she wasn't in her home while it happened. Every day she woke up and reminded herself that she was lucky to be alive and that she was going to make *that* day the best day it could be. Her strategy was to take it one optimistic day at a time. I think it was a brilliant strategy that can be applied to so many other circumstances.

I heard a great quote the other day: "Circumstances don't make a person; they reveal him or her." It seems to me that optimists either intuitively, or through training their minds, understand this. When something happens that they don't like, or something painful occurs, they apply this general philosophy the best they can. Pessimists, on the other hand, surely without knowing it, turn this philosophy around to say, "Circumstances are what it's all about." When something bad happens, they use it as evidence of what they have believed all along—that things aren't likely to work out.

Other than the weak argument, "I'm being realistic," I've always wondered what the advantages are of being pessimistic. What good does it do? Pessimism keeps you heavyhearted and focused on defeat. It saps your energy and takes away hope. Because it's difficult to be around pessimistic people, they end up pushing others away. The final argument against pessimistic thinking is that, to a large degree, your thoughts determine the way you feel. So if your thinking is cynical and pessimistic, it's almost as though you're trying to convince yourself that it's a good idea to feel bad!

Although you may be accustomed to thinking about things (big and small) in a negative way, I'm convinced that we are all capable of changing the ways we look at life. Take a look at the following three steps, which I believe are some important keys to making this transition.

First of all, *Recognize that you tend to think pessimistically*. It's widely understood that the first step in overcoming any problem is to recognize and admit that you have one. Whether it's alcohol, tobacco, anger, overeating, or being too critical, one must acknowledge a problem before attempting to solve it. It can take some humility, but it's really worth it.

Thinking "the glass is half empty" is really nothing more than a mental habit reinforced thousands of times over a lifetime. Remember April from the earlier example. Like her, we can just as easily learn to think more positively, if we set our minds to it. Start paying attention to the thoughts that run through your mind, and particularly to the automatic responses you have to the things that happen in your life, and to the things people say. When you catch yourself thinking pessimistically, challenge yourself to look at it differently. You can even say to yourself, "There's that habit again." Then try something new, a more positive response. You may be amazed at how quickly you can reverse this habit and how much brighter life will immediately seem.

A second step is to *Remind yourself that you are the thinker of your own thoughts*. The pessimistic thoughts and responses that run through your mind are created by you—the thought-maker! When I tell myself, "I can't do that," it's me, Richard, who has done the thinking. Or if I point out the flaw of someone's argument, simply to be "right," then again, it's my own thoughts that have produced that negativity. Simple as this sounds, it's true. If I am the one who created the thought, I'm also the one capable of challenging it. I can give it less significance, even dismiss it. If I can create negative thoughts, I can also create more optimistic ones. I'm not saying it's never appropriate to "correct" someone or find the faults, just that when we do so out of habit, it's self-destructive.

A third step is to *Be easy on yourself*. My guess is that very few of us do things purposely to harm ourselves. Pessimistic thinking would certainly fall into this category. It's very understandable, when we look around us, how anyone could become cynical. After all, there is plenty of pain in the world and in our own lives. It's easy to get into the habit of picking things apart and looking at "what's wrong." But we don't get into that habit because we're determined to be miserable. We simply fall into it very innocently.

It's important to remember that there is also plenty of beauty in the world. There is much to be grateful for—and hopeful about. The bottom line is this: Generally speaking, you'll find what you're looking for. If you're looking for validation or proof of the ugliness in the world, you'll find it because it's there. On the other hand, if you're determined to see the beauty and the blessings, you'll see that too. Because it's there as well.

If you find yourself thinking pessimistically, even after you've decided to become more optimistic, it's okay. See the innocence in negative thinking. Learn to have a sense of humor about it by seeing yourself as a character! That way, when pessimism creeps into your thinking and into your conversations, you can say, "Caught you again." Then, very gently, let it go and see if you can come up with a more optimistic way of looking at the same thing. You'll find it's not very difficult if you give it a try! It doesn't have to be a big deal, but rather a process that over time will become second nature to you. I don't know about you, but I'm optimistic that you can become more optimistic—if you choose to do so!

31. Cultivate Your Compassionate Heart

Sometimes it's tempting to minimize the impact of compassion. It sounds like a good idea, but it can be hard to quantify, and sometimes difficult to put into practice. I've heard many people say things like, "I'd like to be more compassionate, but what can I do?" Others have asked, "Can my actions really make a difference?"

My experience has been that nothing prepares us for big stuff more than cultivating compassion. Much more than a beautiful ideal, it's actually a practical way to help ourselves become stronger, wiser, more self-confident, and more resilient. Developing our compassion also ensures that when those we love need our help the most, we will be ready and able to give. Compassion helps us to face the most difficult, frightening, and painful parts of life with courage, kindness, and love. Even if you were to discount the kind and humanitarian aspects of compassion, and your only goal was to selfishly prepare yourself for difficult times, I'd still say that the best thing you could do would be to cultivate your sense of compassion. It's that powerful.

While attending a meditation retreat, I heard a beautiful story about a meditation student. It seems he wanted to make compassion more a part of his everyday life. He lived in an apartment in a major city. At the bottom of his stairs, on the sidewalk, there lived a man who was homeless.

For a long time, like most others, he walked right past the homeless man, never making eye contact. He had given the man some spare change a few times, mostly out of guilt. Other than that, he didn't give the man a second thought. He wasn't mean or cruel, just indifferent.

The meditation student realized that he needed to open his heart to his fellow human beings—not in the abstract, but in real, day-to-day life. He decided that a great place to start was with this particular man.

One day he walked out the door and looked the man in the eye as if he were a close friend. The homeless man was uncomfortable and looked down immediately. However, the door of compassion had been opened.

Weeks and weeks went by, and every day the meditation student would walk by the man, gently trying to make eye contact. Each morning on his way out the door, he would politely say, "Good morning. How are you today?" And, each evening, on his way home from work, he would say, "How was your day?"

Eventually, his kindness paid off. Little by little, the man came out of his shell and starting glancing back, even smiling on occasion. Finally, after quite some time, he began to respond to the questions. He would say, "I'm doing pretty good this morning. How about you?" In the evening, he would say, "I'm doing even better than I was this morning. Thank you very much." His confidence was growing.

It became a ritual that the student really enjoyed. He would genuinely look forward to seeing his "friend," and he found it easier to be friendlier with other strangers as well.

One day, the man disappeared without a trace. The student found himself saddened by this and wondered what could have happened. As the days and weeks went by, he continued to miss the man. Eventually, however, his memory faded and he went on with his life as usual.

One day, months later, the student approached his steps as he was returning from work. There was a strange man sitting there who immediately stood up to greet him. He didn't know the stranger, who did look vaguely familiar.

The man held out his hand and said, "I'm sorry to bother you, sir, but I just had to come back and thank you."

"Thank me?" the student responded. "Thank me for what?"

"You see," said the stranger, "I used to live right here, under these steps. I was so ashamed of myself and had so little self-respect, that no one really knew me." He went on to say, "For as long as I can remember, no one was nice to me. No one would look at me or give me the time of day. I had no friends and no self-respect. But then you started to be nice to me. Eventually I realized that if you could be nice to me and show me some respect, then maybe I could show myself some respect too. So I went and found myself a job and a place to live. I got some new clothes. My life has changed. And you know what? It's because of you. Your kindness and willingness to respect me and be nice to me changed my life. I just wanted to say thank you."

After this story was told, there was a beautiful silence in the room and more than a few tears in the eyes of the audience. It's a wonderful story for several reasons. First, it shows how incredibly easy it is to bring compassion into daily life. When it becomes a part of our nature, deep meaning is brought to even the most basic aspects of life; in this instance, simply speaking to another human being. Of course, that human being doesn't have to be homeless. It could be anybody.

Secondly, the story shows how much difference one simple act of kindness can make in the life of another person. In *Don't Sweat the Small Stuff for Teens*, I shared a story about a teenage girl who worked in an animal shelter. She worked there because she loved animals, and she would regularly go the extra mile to find homes for them. Unfortunately, like most animal shelters, if homes could not be found, the animals were destroyed.

One day a friend of this teenager came by the shelter to pick her up at the end of her shift. The two of them were off to a party.

Although her friend was restless and in a hurry, the teen insisted that she had to make one more call. A woman had come into the shelter the previous day who was considering adopting Charlie, a sweet older dog who had no other chance to find a home. The next day would be his last. The teen's friend yelled out, "Come on, we're late already!" But the teen replied, "Be patient, I have to do this for Charlie."

A few minutes later, the friend had lost all patience and practically screamed, "Hurry up already! Forget about it. There are too many animals in here for you to make any difference." At that moment, the girl's friend overheard her saying, "Thank you so much, Mrs. Wright. Sure, I'll meet you down here at the shelter tomorrow so you can pick him up." As she hung up the phone, she smiled at her friend and said, "Why don't you tell Charlie that I can't make a difference."

Over the years, I have heard dozens of similar stories about one person making a tremendous difference without altering his or her life at all. I'm sure you can remember special times in your life when you made someone happy, or helped in some meaningful way just by doing the right thing. And as a result, you felt peaceful and secure. You grew as a human being, and I would argue that you prepared yourself for something in the future.

Compassion is one of my favorite subjects, so it's no coincidence that I talk about it a lot to other people. I've noticed something very touching. When I've asked people to share with me some of their most memorable moments, their responses are often very similar.

When reflecting on their favorite memories, most people have told me about some ordinary act of kindness, or patience, just like the previous two stories about the meditation student and the teenager.

People will smile when they think about the time they gave up their seat on an airplane. They did it so that a total stranger, who would have otherwise been bumped from the flight, could get home to his daughter's birthday party. I've seen tears in the eyes of a parent when she found out that her daughter shared her lunch with someone who had forgotten theirs and was hungry. (I had the same reaction when my daughter did the same thing!)

One person told me that his favorite memory was the time he stood up for a salesclerk in a department store. She was an older woman who was being yelled at and verbally abused by a bunch of impatient customers. That's when he stepped in to defuse the situation. She was so grateful that she started to cry. Although this man ran a large business and probably had lots of great memories, this was the event he was most proud of. Over and over again, we discover that it's the little compassionate things, all added up, that make the most difference.

We make a difference—every single day. The way we drive in traffic and behave in the grocery store make a difference. Every time we smile at someone who is having a bad day (or a good day), we make a difference. Each time we make an ethical business decision, or donate our time, energy, or money, we make a difference. When we demonstrate and model loving-kindness, that makes a difference, too.

Compassion also includes things like becoming a better listener and becoming less judgmental. As we quiet down our judgmental and critical minds, we're able to allow others to be who they need to be. Just by listening, we help them to be their best. This is important, not just because it's polite and kind, but it also prepares us for bigger things. Imagine how valuable it is to be an excellent listener, particularly when there is an emergency or when the stakes are high. Think about how valuable it is to be able to see and hear clearly, without judgment. How much more effective will you be when you can see things the way they really are? You'll have an incredible and powerful perspective. But it takes practice to get there in the form of daily compassion.

One of the most noticeable forms of daily compassion is patience. When someone is struggling, for example, are you able to be patient? When someone makes a mistake or proves to be human, can you make allowances? Most of us long for and love to be around patient people. They are wise and nonreactive. But did you ever consider how necessary it is to be patient when you're dealing with really big things? Have you ever stood by someone who was very ill for a long period of time? It takes loving patience.

Imagine how much patience it would take if you were to become ill. Have you ever taught someone with a learning disability? That takes patience too. What if you have to learn a new skill someday? Patience is the key. Have you ever had to deal with logistics or bureaucracy after a tragedy such as a fire or earthquake? Better be patient. These and almost all other difficult tasks in life require tremendous patience. By being patiently compassionate toward other people and the world at large, we are, literally, preparing ourselves for life. There are hundreds of daily opportunities to practice patience. Imagine being interrupted right now. Can you remember to be patient?

Compassion is contagious. As we model compassion, it rubs off on others. After I heard the story about the meditation student, for example, I found myself being kinder and making eye contact more often with strangers. I discovered a shared humanity that exists between us. I'm not talking about running up to people and hugging them. Rather, it's simply about being kind and respectful.

One of the most dramatic by-products of compassion is the inner strength that almost always develops. When you talk to hospice workers, for example, many will tell you that working with dying people has helped them to face their own pain and fear. When confronted with their own death, or the death of a loved one, they have had more inner strength to carry them through. When you ask people who work for many wonderful causes—whether it's with the homeless and the poor, for animal rights or the environment, or with children or the elderly—you often hear that spending time doing valuable work is even more beneficial to themselves than it is to the people and causes they are attempting to help.

This is because there is, inherent within compassion, a series of inner rewards. Giving is its own reward. It always comes back to us, with interest. Sometimes it comes back as a feeling of peace and satisfaction. Other times, it comes back in the form of increased wisdom or confidence.

One of the things that accompanies compassion is a sense of ease within oneself. If you ever have the privilege of seeing the Dalai Lama, one of the first things you'll notice, in addition to his almost constant gentle smile, is his obvious sense of comfort with himself. He is able to deal with even the most painful aspects of life with grace and equanimity. He is able to keep his bearings, even a sense of humor, during difficult times. You sense absolute kindness.

Many accounts of Mother Teresa were much the same. She had a peaceful self-confidence that allowed her to be of incredible service to humanity without weakening or falling apart. Despite being a very small person physically, she had an enormous heart and tremendous resolve. She worked tirelessly with some of the poorest people in the entire world, but she treated each and every person with the same respect and kindness she would use interacting with heads of state.

I'm not advocating that we try to become like the Dalai Lama or Mother Teresa. They are (and were) two extraordinary people who developed their own ways of bringing compassion to daily life. They are, however, great examples of what is possible.

All most of us have to do to cultivate a more compassionate heart is to keep on doing exactly what we're doing now, only slightly more consciously. We need to remember our humanity and remind ourselves that the most peaceful feelings stem from acts of kindness and patience. In virtually every action, there is the potential for compassion and kindness. All we have to do is add a tiny dose of "intention" to be more compassionate, and the rest will take care of itself. It's part of our nature. When we foster this part of ourselves, we feel complete and nourished, peaceful and calm.

When we look back on our lives, two of the most important questions we will ask will be: "Was I kind?" and "Did I make a difference?" In my opinion, these are the greatest achievements we can make on this earth. Luckily, everyone has the potential to become more compassionate, once they decide to. Everyone has it in them to be kind. Everyone can find someone, or something, to love. And everyone can be helpful and, therefore, make a difference on this planet.

There are so many ways to incorporate compassion into our daily lives. It's endless. The goal is to make compassion such an automatic response to everyday living and such a part of ourselves that we can't help but be that way. It doesn't take much effort, and we don't have to do too much. As Mother Teresa said, "We can't do great things on this earth. We can only do small things with great love." Those small things, however, are the ways we prepare ourselves to face the really big things in life.

32. Listen to Your World

I'd like to share with you one of my fondest, most healing mem-ories. I was a teenager and had broken up with my girlfriend. My heart was aching. I was devastated, depressed, and confused. It was a rainy day, and I was sitting outside, not caring that I was getting soaked.

My mother, Barbara, sensed what was happening and came outside to sit beside me in the pouring-down rain. She put her arm around me and told me she loved me. At that point, I did most of the talking. She listened and listened and listened.

It was only a matter of time before I began to feel better. The healing power of listening had taken effect. The healing that took place had very little to do with what she said. It had everything to do with the way she listened.

At that painful moment of my life, I could have spoken to any of the world's greatest experts on relationships—and it wouldn't have done any good. No amount of reassurance, lecturing, optimism, encouragement, or anything else would have had the slightest bene-fit. The same would have been true regarding counseling, discussions, support groups, or friendships. Nothing was going to help me because what I needed was to be listened to. I was, and it helped.

From that moment I had an even greater respect, love, and

appreciation for my mother than ever before. I've tried to remember this important lesson ever since. I've found that when someone is in pain, usually the best thing to do is to simply listen. Since that memorable experience with my mom, I've witnessed and have been involved in hundreds of examples that reinforced this same lesson. One in particular stands out.

Well before the events of September 11, 2001, I was waiting in line to board an aircraft. The person in front of me was extremely angry. The flight had been delayed several hours, and allegedly this man had experienced similar lengthy delays during each of his last few flights.

It didn't matter to this particular man, however, that the reason for the delay was a mechanical concern. There were mechanics working on the problem.

While standing in line, he started talking under his breath to the ticket agent. His voice was angry, agitated, and quite frankly, a bit frightening to myself and a few of the other passengers. He mumbled something about suing the airline, then started verbally assaulting the people he hated in the airline industry. He was tense and visibly shaking with rage. Although he didn't specifically threaten anyone, he did use foul, violent, and offensive language. Several of the other people in line picked up their things and moved away, obviously disgusted and frightened. I don't know how "air rage" is defined, but this certainly seemed to be the "on ground" version, or at least close to it.

Rather than tell him to shut up, which I felt would have inflamed him even further, or confront him in any way, I looked him calmly in the eye and listened. I tried to be as soft-spoken and nonjudgmental as possible. "Sounds like you've had a tough couple of days in the air," I said. "It's tough being a frequent flyer, isn't it?"

Initially his response was nothing more than increased agitation and certainly not what I had hoped for. In a mean-spirited and unwelcoming tone he said, "What's it to you?"

In as nondefensive a manner as I could muster, I answered, "I've had a ton of delays lately too." I then asked him, "Where are you headed?"

It turned out that a flight delay had caused him to miss his son's birthday. To compound his frustration, his boss gave him an additional assignment to fill in for someone who was ill and couldn't travel. He had a host of other complaints as well.

Time passed rather quickly as he shared with me a good portion of his "life story." It wasn't too long before he released his briefcase from his clenched fist and put it down. His body language became less aggressive, and the volume of his voice softened.

I think this is a powerful story because I'm not a professional negotiator, nor was I trying to be a hero or a healer. There are plenty of times when I overreact as much, or more, than the next person. In this instance, I was just an average person waiting my turn to get on an airplane. All that happened was that my instincts were telling me that the best thing to do, given the circumstances, was to be still and listen.

I'm not excusing this man's behavior, and regardless of his personal problems, he had no right to take out his frustration as he did. His conduct was inexcusable and I'm not calling it "small stuff." Sometimes, however, heated confrontation, physical strength, whispers of disgust, talking behind someone's back, or even judgmental thinking only serve to fuel an already ugly circumstance.

Every situation is different, of course. After the terrorist attacks, I may have turned this same passenger over to a security person. In any event, I'm pretty sure that if I didn't, one of the other passengers would have done so. As it turned out, however, all he needed was to be listened to.

I wonder how many people just need to be heard. When your spouse or boy/girl friend is complaining, does he or she really need a solution—or do they simply need to share their frustration with someone who will listen—without judgment? I remember one specific instance in my own marriage when I felt very unhappy and frustrated. I had a number of complaints that I had been stewing about for a while. It seemed very serious, and I wasn't sure what was going to happen.

Kris asked me to tell her what was going on. It felt so good to talk about it that I started to cry. I must have talked for fifteen or twenty minutes before she said a word. Then all she said was, "It seems like it feels good to talk about it." There was no edge to her voice. She wasn't defensive or argumentative. She simply allowed me to voice my concerns—and to be heard.

My mind was eased and my fears quickly subsided. My anger, frustration, and confusion faded away as my love for Kris became even stronger. It was her listening, not her words, that reassured me that she loved me.

I couldn't help but think about all the people I've known who have yearned for a similar conversation with their spouse or partner. Yet in most cases, rather than an honest heart-to-heart stemming from deep listening, the listening never happens. Defensiveness and overreactions invariably prevail.

I have no way of knowing for sure, but I suspect that a large percentage of the human-created problems we face have at least something to do with a person not feeling as though he or she was listened to. So many times adults, teens, and children have told me, "No one ever listens to me." When someone "acts out" in deviant or violent ways, I often wonder how differently things would have unfolded for that person had he or she felt listened to.

I heard someone say, "God gave us two ears and one mouth, so we should be listening at least twice as much as we talk." Yet how many of us follow these guidelines?

How much more effective would we be as parents if we would spend more time listening and less time lecturing? It's much easier to talk about than to do—but the end result would be better communication between parents and kids. There would be less built-up resentment, which would be replaced with laughter and a lot more openness. In my entire lifetime, I've never heard a child say, "My parents listened to me too much!" It's always the other way around.

The same "wisdom of listening" applies at work. I'm always amazed when an employee really listens to what I want. Unfortunately, it's the exception rather than the rule. When customers are listened to, they want to buy your products and services. It makes you trust them. When employees and colleagues are listened to, they get along better and work better as a team.

Listening gives you insights about the world around you. In addition to helping you "read" people better, get along with others, and resolve conflict, listening allows you to see the bigger picture. It gives you perspective into whatever you're doing.

Listening is the opposite of reacting. It gives you a chance to take in all of the information and to reflect on it. Thus you can respond to a situation in the most appropriate manner possible, after having a chance to digest honestly and completely what's going on. Suppose, for example, your eight-year-old child comes home from school with a major complaint. She storms in the door, crying. The first words out of her mouth are, "Tammy shoved me and the teacher didn't do anything about it."

You've heard enough. You pick up the phone and call the teacher. Your intent is to get to the bottom of the situation and to have words with Tammy's mother!

After more than an hour of discussion with your daughter's

teacher and Tammy's mom, the conclusion is that there were two sides of the story. The "shove" wasn't really a shove—but a tiny push. There was some question about who pushed whom first, and which of the kids started the shouting match.

Rather than immediately reacting and coming to the rescue, might it have been more effective to spend some time listening to your daughter? I can tell you (unfortunately!) from firsthand, personal experience that often your time is better spent simply listening.

What would have happened if, when your daughter stormed in the door, you quieted your mind and simply listened. What if you were able to stay calm and centered and could have dismissed your own thoughts long enough to listen to hers? What if, as a result, she felt she was being heard?

The more time you spent listening, the more data, insight, and perspective you would have into the situation. With each passing minute, the sense of emergency would lessen. The need to react would diminish, if not disappear entirely.

Two positive things would almost certainly have happened. First, you would have saved time, frustration, and energy. It would have taken substantially less energy to sit calmly on the couch and listen than it did to make two heated phone calls. Second, you would have demonstrated to your daughter that not every conflict needs to be dealt with as an emergency. Hopefully your example would help her deal with future conflicts in a healthier way.

Wisdom comes from a quiet, patient mind that is listening to what's going on instead of judging or reacting to it. The only way to be able to absorb something in its entirety—and to see it clearly—is to listen.

Listening and patience go hand in hand. As we allow ourselves to absorb and listen to what's going on around us—openly and fully—we train ourselves to become more patient. We start to see that if we can get beyond that initial knee-jerk need to react, the next level is far more interesting, as well as less threatening. That was clearly the case, for example, with the man in the airport. My initial reaction was revulsion, and my thoughts were judgmental. Had I not wanted to save my place in line, I might have walked away! However, once the process of listening took over, the situation quickly became less intense; in fact, it became harmless.

Listening involves more than our ears. We can also listen with our intuition. The key is to be as silent and "interested" as possible.

Have you ever seen a movie focused around a competitive sporting event? It seems like they are usually about football, base-ball, or basketball. During the last scene, the film is shown in slow motion. You watch the final play develop while the suspense builds. Usually the very last part is someone diving over the goal line, or shooting a basketball, or some equally exciting climax. You wait to see the outcome.

Have you ever noticed what happens to the sound during those scenes? Often, despite hundreds or even thousands of screaming fans, there is total silence as you watch the action. It's as if you become that athlete, or at least you can hear what he or she hears.

These scenes have always been fascinating to me because they show how easy it is to concentrate when the mind is quiet. The ath-lete tunes out everything except that moment. She is intently listen-ing to her surroundings and knows exactly what is going on all around her.

Sometimes "real" champion athletes will report a similar experi-ence. During the most intense moments—at the free throw line, for example—with the game riding on one shot, he reports hearing nothing! Somehow he is able to get his concentration to a level beneath the roar of the spectators and of his own mind. Can you imagine how effective he would be if he were listening to his own self-doubting thoughts? He'd miss for sure!

There is no question that the rewards for becoming a better listener are great. They include having better, more fulfilling relationships and a more effective work life, being a better parent, and dealing with far fewer conflicts.

The way to become a better listener is surprisingly easy. Once it's a valued priority, all it takes is observation and a lot of practice. As you face a situation or sit with another person, try to clear your mind and listen. Then watch as your mind quickly fills up with all sorts of things. You'll notice "solutions," "reactions," "fears," "plans," as well as many other types of thoughts. It's not that they are bad—it's just that they occur so automatically. Rather than deeply listening, you'll find yourself waiting your turn to talk. Before you know all the facts—or before someone is even finished talking—your thoughts will be formulating a response of some kind. It's like a sprinter at the starting gate anxiously awaiting the gun! If you're feeling threatened, your thoughts may be defensive. If you're feeling compassionate, your thoughts may be comforting.

Try not to judge your inner chatter. Rather, simply notice it and gently let it all go. Instead of planning or rehearsing a response, remain quiet and still for a few additional moments. That's where the healing power of listening resides—in those few quiet moments. Give that inner wisdom, stemming from stillness, a little extra time to develop.

You may notice something quite remarkable happening. With your extra attention geared toward listening, being present, gathering information, and being inwardly still, better, wiser answers will begin to surface. The reason this happens is because you're allowing the full brilliance of your mind to operate. It's not your intellect I'm talking about, but rather the deeper, wiser, healing intelligence that exists independent of your thinking mind.

Listening is an incredible gift that you can give to yourself, as well as to others. You can create this gift at will and develop it over time. It will make seemingly difficult decisions easier to make as a new sense of calm and clarity emerges within you. As others feel your new sense of presence and patience, it will help nourish your professional and personal relationships. It will also make complicated issues much easier to understand, as your perspective is heightened and as you see more options. Finally, I believe that it will make all the big stuff in your life much more manageable as your habitual reactions turn into wise responses.

33. Turn Toward Your Religion

In 1981, I attended Pepperdine, a university committed to the highest standards of academic excellence and Christian values. As an athlete, my primary intention was to go to college, get my degree, and play on the men's tennis team. Like many new students who didn't know anyone, I was a bit nervous. I felt enormous pressure to achieve both academically and in sports.

The first day I arrived, however, a member of the faculty introduced himself to me. He said, "From my perspective, in this school, God is our top priority. Academics, sports, achievement, and community service are highly emphasized, and we are among the best." He then added, "But without God, nothing would exist; with him, everything will fall into place. So you can relax and let God take over."

I didn't know it at the time, but that was an important moment in my life. There was a quiet "knowing" in his voice. Because of the humble resolve in which they were said, his words were comforting and seemed to put things into perspective. His philosophy matched my own: "Without kindness, gratitude, and faith in something bigger than ourselves, nothing really matters." I have always believed that the most important things in life are not things! To me, they are God—along with family, love, kindness, compassion, friendship, creativity, tolerance, and gratitude—all of which are invisible but magical.

As the years have gone by, I've noticed that most people who have faith in God, a higher power, or a deeper intelligence—whatever their religion happens to be—seem to have a healthy and loving perspective toward life. They appreciate the gift of being here, and they handle difficulties—even pain and anguish—with courage and dignity.

The decision to turn toward your religion and to make spirituality an even deeper, more important part of your life is not easy, but the rewards are great. It involves sacrifice, honesty with one's self, reflection, time, commitment, and honor. Putting your religion or spirituality first means doing the right thing, being committed to truth, and sticking up for your values, even when they are not popular. It means letting go of the ego in order to allow God to work within you, and tapping into the universal intelligence that flows through all of us. To me, more than anything else, it means choosing love over hate, and kindness over proving yourself "right."

During college, when things went well, we were encouraged to give thanks. When things didn't go so well, and when there were problems, we were encouraged to go inward to ask for help, strength, guidance, and wisdom. Many students practiced daily prayer, giving thanks for the opportunity to be in such a beautiful and stimulating environment. It was during college that I first started to meditate and first attempted to deepen my relationship with God. The people I was around and the friends I met, including my wife, Kris, encouraged me to "go inside," get quiet, and listen for answers.

My learning to trust in God resulted in many things. Among them, I became a Big Brother for the Big Brothers of America program. Almost everyone I knew supported this decision, and it turned out to be one of the most meaningful experiences of my life. The quieter I became on the inside, the more clearly I could see the path I was to follow. I was then able to see the cause-and-effect connection between compassion for others, and one's own happiness and peace of mind.

One of the other major revelations that came to me at that time was that it became clear it was time to give up my competitive tennis career. Other factors were pointing in this direction already—injuries and not being quite good enough, to name a few! But it was really Kris's encouragement to trust in the inner messages I was receiving that gave me the confidence to move in a new direction. I was learning to trust that God was within me and that, if I was quiet and willing to listen, I would know what to do. I would be guided by an inner intelligence, which was a tremendous source of wisdom and comfort. That guidance, which I rely on to this day, is there during ordinary living, as well as when I need a shoulder to lean on when the stakes are high.

As time has passed, I've met many people who trust in God—and in their own ability to hear the wisdom that results in this listening. I've known other people who didn't have this faith, and who were uncomfortable going inside themselves. What I have observed is that those with an inner faith travel through life with more confidence and less struggle. They know that the directions they take and the choices they make do indeed matter. Their lives have a sense of purpose.

Another observation I've made is that people who turn toward God, those who feel his presence, have confidence in the bigger picture. They know that even though they can't always see or understand something, the universe is perfect—in its own imperfection. More than a wishy-washy "wanting this to be true" philosophy, it's knowing that everything will be okay. There is a sense of order within the chaos.

Having genuine faith in God helps us to celebrate the gift of life. It also comforts us during difficult and confusing times. I've had friends and acquaintances who belonged to many of the world's religions, including Christianity, Judaism, Buddhism, Hinduism, Taoism, Islam, Confucianism, and others. All of them have told me that they turn to and trust in their religion to guide them in their lives and to help them find answers to the toughest questions.

In addition to being a top-notch school in every sense of the word, Pepperdine University is one of the most beautiful college campuses on earth. It overlooks the Pacific Ocean in Southern California. What made it even more beautiful than the physical environment, however, was the unifying connection that many of the students had with God. When you are a student away from home, it's easy to become lonely. You are part of a large tapestry, comprised mostly of people you don't know. However, if there is a common thread among people, it's easier to feel connected, strong, and happy, as though each of you has a purpose.

The love of God was ever present there, and when I was quiet, it could be felt. That love was expressed not only inwardly but also externally in practical ways. It encouraged people to do everything from picking up litter on campus to opening their hearts to new students trying to meet friends. The faith that students had in God enabled them to help others during a crisis or a particularly difficult time. It was very comforting during such an important and impressionable part of my young life.

Kris's dorm once caught on fire, and everything she owned was destroyed. Rather than freaking out over the destruction, however, many of the people involved, including Kris, were genuinely praising God for keeping the students safe. That was the first time I saw Kris's true character emerge during a crisis. Her first instinct was to make sure that everyone else was safe. Once that was established, her attitude became one of gratitude, looking only at the bright side. There was, after all, plenty of "brightness" to look at. Consider these facts: No one was hurt. Most material things can, eventually, be replaced. The fire wasn't worse. It didn't spread. The people who put out the fire were brave and kind, as were the students who rushed into the dorm to help. It was good to be alive. In some ways, the fire actually brought the students even closer together. I could go on and on listing the bright spots of what could have been seen as a tragedy.

The emphasis on faith and spirituality enabled people to see the good instead of focusing on the bad. Without a spiritual life, this same event could (and probably would) have been seen quite differently. It's easy to imagine feeling victimized, or as though life isn't fair. After all, Kris and some of her friends in the dorm lost practically everything other than the clothes they were wearing. To make matters worse, Kris had very little money to replace any of her things. But faith kept her strong, hopeful, and optimistic.

As people turn toward God or a higher power, a sense of fear and uncertainty is replaced with faith. Over time and with practice, this faith extends well beyond believing that there is life after death. You start to "know," at a deep level, that there is an intelligence that runs through all of life—including each and every one of us. By trusting in this intelligence we can, quite literally, take the pressure off of ourselves and our stressful lives. We turn our lives, decisions, and problems over to a higher power, or God.

Like many people, I've grappled with the question, "If there is a God, why is there so much destruction and suffering?" For years, I've reflected on this question, and the answer I've come up with is in alignment with my overall optimistic attitude toward life. I believe that God doesn't create the pain and suffering in life. He does, however, share with us and provide the strength and tools for healing. God shows up in many ways. He's there in the form of a fellow human being, an insight or idea—or as an act of love. If you have an inspirational idea to be helpful, it's because you've tapped into the universal intelligence, which is God. This intelligence is always available to us, and the more we trust in it, the more it will show up in our lives. The more you look for it, the more evidence you'll see.

The terrorist attacks of September 11, 2001, are one of the best examples of the role of God in the history of our world. God didn't create that pain, of course; people did. Yet God was there immediately, to help ease the pain. He was there in the form of rescue workers, firefighters, police, and other courageous and selfless people. He was there giving strength and perspective to our government and military personnel. He encouraged a generosity in the average citizen, the degree to which had never been seen before. From the moments immediately following the attacks, I could see God everywhere I looked. And everyone I talked to saw the very same thing I did.

The most helpful book I've ever read about dealing with extraordinarily difficult times is Harold Kushner's *When Bad Things Happen to Good People*. Since all people will eventually suffer, or will be with others who will be suffering, I wish this book were required reading. It's hard to pinpoint a central lesson from such an important book. If I had to, however, it would be this quote: "God, who neither causes nor prevents tragedies, helps by inspiring people to help." He goes on to say, "God shows his opposition to cancer and birth defects, not by eliminating them or making them happen only to bad people (He can't do that), but by summoning forth friends and neighbors to ease the burden and to fill the emptiness."

In my opinion, all loving religions point to God. Whatever your religious background or spiritual practice, I encourage you to delve deeply into your faith. Use your religion, not to separate, but to join together in the heart of humanity. Love your God with all your heart. If you do, you'll never be alone. Together you can get through even the biggest stuff of life.

34. Retirement

One of the great ironies of life is that the best way to live it seems to contradict itself. On the one hand, you want to live as if you have forever. This attitude enables you to be lighthearted and carefree. It helps you to be able to take risks, be adventuresome, and seek a wide variety of experiences. You have nothing to lose, so "go for it." On the other hand, you also want to live as if this is your last day on the planet. This attitude reminds you to take nothing for granted. It reminds you of the preciousness of life, and of the importance of telling those you love how you feel. You don't have a moment to lose.

I think of retirement in a similar way. I try to simultaneously convince myself that retirement is going to be the best thing that could ever happen to me—AND I try to be indifferent about it, all at the same time. I say this because retirement, like every other aspect of life, is totally in the eyes of the beholder. Your expectations will determine whether or not you look forward to retirement. Your moment-to-moment thinking is, or will be, responsible for whether or not you enjoy it. You definitely want to think of retirement as a great part of life—but at the same time, you want to enjoy every step that leads toward it.

Donna bought into the notion hook, line, and sinker of "preparing" for a comfortable and happy retirement. When she turned fifty, she met with a financial planner. He took her aside and said, "Look, Donna, assuming you want to retire at age sixty, you have ten years to get your financial house in order." He went on to say, "Now is the time to worry and to sacrifice."

Unfortunately, she took him literally and spent the next ten years doing just that. She saved as much as she could and worried every step of the way. "Looking back," she said, "it was as though I felt it was my duty to worry." Rather than enjoy and appreciate her life as it unfolded, she fretted and planned. She became paranoid and convinced herself that she would only be able to relax when she retired.

At sixty-one, Donna was diagnosed with breast cancer and was told she might not live more than one year. Suddenly she realized that the most important thing isn't to prepare in a conventional sense for life, but to live it—right now. The same set of circumstances, including the identical "balance sheet" and bank balance, looked very different. It wasn't as though her finances were no longer seen as relevant. That would have been ridiculous. Instead she realized that its importance was relative.

It took an illness to teach Donna what everyone needs—perspective. Every single day is a gift and no moment, past or future—and no period of time, retired or otherwise—is more important than any other. What's obvious but often overlooked is that this isn't going to be more or less true ten years from now. The only variable will be the extent to which each and every one of us realizes it.

I'm not suggesting for a moment that it's unimportant to plan for the future. On the contrary, I think that's a great idea. If you have the capacity and discipline to plan ahead, by all means do it. I'd even go so far as to say that if you don't have the discipline, try to develop it. Get some good advice and develop a solid plan.

But planning is no substitute for living. While feeling financially secure may be preferable to being financially insecure, it's not essential to one's happiness. If it were, you would see very few happily retired people, and that is certainly not the case. Here's another one of those ironies: Though you want to put the odds in your favor, the last thing you want to do is convince yourself that you can only be happy or feel secure if certain financial milestones are met.

The only actual requirement for a contented retirement is presence. This is the ability to "be here now," not superficially, but deeply on a day-to-day, moment-to-moment basis. The present, of course, is the only time there is. It's now. This is true whether you're sixteen or ninety-six. The past only exists in the form of thoughts and memories. It would be foolish and incorrect to say "the past didn't exist" or that "the past didn't matter." It did exist and it did matter. It's equally foolish, however, to long for the past, or to have regrets about what you did or didn't do. And perhaps more than anything, it'll make you crazy to wish you were younger!

The other side of the coin is the future, which exists only in our imaginations. We can dream about it if we want to, or anticipate what it will be like. We can fantasize that it will be wonderful, better than today, or we can worry that it will be dreadful. Either way, it's still just our thinking, appearing to be reality. It's a mirage. It's interesting because, if you stop to think about it, the "future" never actually arrives. It's always now. A year from now, on this day, it will be another "now." When you retire, it will be "now."

This simple wisdom, as common and clichéd as it might be, is extremely powerful. Being in tune with the present moment allows us to be happy, curious, and lighthearted. We become open-minded and comfortable with the unknown and with new possibilities. When we're present, we're okay with being a beginner again, and learning new skills. We're not busy comparing our experience with other things. What a perfect mind-set for retirement—or planning for retirement!

Richard Carlson, Ph.D.

The absence of being present, however, is guaranteed to cause misery. We're so busy judging our experience, or comparing it to other things, that it's impossible to enjoy it. That's why the best actual "preparation" for retirement—and the best antidote to an unhappy or unfulfilling retirement—is one and the same: to learn the art of presence. It's crazy to think that if you can't be present right now, you'll magically be able to be present and satisfied ten years from now. You'll be faced with the same dilemma. You will be in a moment, and you'll either embrace it—or wish it were different. You've probably seen this dynamic in action. Someone spends his or her entire life looking forward to retirement. They convince themselves that life isn't that great now—but it will be later on. Then when retirement arrives, they long for their younger days. There never is a time when it's okay for things to simply be as they are.

Being present is a gift you can give yourself and share with others. It's also something you can work on. The easiest way to practice presence is to notice its absence. When you find yourself longing for retirement—or dreading it—it simply means you have temporarily removed yourself from the present. You're here, but you're thinking of there. If you've already retired, the same logic applies. If you're here, now, you have the capacity to enjoy this day to its fullest potential. One day after another, retirement will be joyful and will be filled with the deepening of wisdom.

One of my favorite exercises is this: Stop what you're doing right now. Ask yourself this question: "What am I doing with this moment?" It can be an eye-opening experience to discover that, often, we aren't here at all. Instead we're tainting the now with memories of the past or thoughts of the future.

Life is a series of moments, one after another after another. Have you ever seen a sign that says Enter at Your Discretion? This means you can enter—or not. The sign doesn't care! We have the same capacity to enter any moment, at any time, to be fully alive, right here, right now.

Being attentive to just this much, this single moment, is the breeding ground for brand-new options. Being aware or mindful of this moment—how we're feeling, what we're thinking—is what allows us to see our own habits in action. We're able to see how compulsively we "don't like" something, or how habitually reactive we are to certain things. I once met a man who said to me, "Since retiring, I've become far more reflective about myself. I realized how boring it was to get mad and frustrated at the same old things, over and over again." By paying attention to his own thinking, moment to moment, he could see his judgmental mind in action. He said it was amazing how his mind "in sixty short years" had become stuck and predictable! He could watch his own thoughts drifting toward self-pity, longing, and frustration. He was, quite literally, relearning how to relate to life. This time, however, he was getting it right!

He claimed that a simple daily meditation practice had greatly enhanced his wisdom. By being quiet and still for a short period of time each day, he was able to see how the mind creates conflicting thoughts, with total disregard for the well-being of the thinker. It's only by learning to relate *to* one's thoughts rather than from them, that freedom is discovered. He told me that many of the same thoughts such as "It's not the same," or "I miss my work and responsibility," still travel through his mind. The difference is that instead of reacting to them with fear or loathing, he simply allows them to float by in his consciousness. Rather than inviting them in for dinner and letting them upset him, he acknowledges them and lets them go—giving them the limited significance they deserve.

Imagine your own thoughts for a moment. Which ones haunt you and prevent you from creating the retirement most people could only dream about? If those thoughts could be taken less seriously, you'd be left with an open mind and unlimited possibilities. Pay close attention to which ones dominate your thinking and which ones taunt you with disappointment. Notice them, but relate to them differently. Instead of being a victim of those thoughts, remember that you are the master thinker. You hold all the cards! As you observe those thoughts, you can pick and choose which ones to explore, which ones are relevant, and which ones are no longer welcome. To me, this is the essence of meditation in action, and it's the secret key to having the retirement of your dreams.

A former schoolteacher told me that she used her retirement as an excuse to becoming more childlike again. She said that over the years she had seen hundreds of kids grow up and become overly serious. Along with their innocence, they lost their sense of wonder. Almost without exception, she witnessed kids learning to take their thoughts too seriously—not just the ones that served them, but the ones that darkened their spirits as well.

There is so much we can learn from kids. One of the best-kept, yet easiest to understand secrets of happiness is: To live a happy life—whatever stage you're in—stay in the present moment and be grateful for that moment. Amazingly simple, but that's really it! Watching kids is proof that, whenever you can be totally absorbed in what you are doing, that activity is a potential source of enjoyment. There's nothing inherently interesting in many of the things young kids do—collecting rocks, stacking leaves, climbing a tree, talking to themselves, or whatever—yet they are usually fascinated with life. To them, ordinary things are experienced as being extraordinary. The reason this is true for them is simple: They aren't comparing these experiences to other things. They aren't thinking, "My job will be more interesting than this someday."

The moment a child begins to think, "Collecting leaves is boring," is the exact moment when that activity becomes boring. It's not a coincidence! When a child starts to believe that stacking leaves is a waste of time, her mind will long for something more interesting.

So many times, I've seen this precise mental dynamic either destroy or delight a person's retirement. When activities are thought of as being "less significant" than whatever that person was doing before, he feels let down, bored, and discouraged. On the other hand, when a person believes that every day is special and equally important, his or her world is a book waiting to be read.

The most interesting aspect of all of this to me is that being satisfied in retirement isn't just about "positive thinking." It's both much deeper—and much simpler—than that. In other words, you don't have to force yourself to think "I love volunteering" (collecting stamps, bird-watching, traveling, spending time with my grandchildren, or whatever) if you don't like it. The trick isn't to pretend that you like things, or to force yourself to think in certain ways. The idea is to simply step back and observe your thinking. It's fascinating to watch how your own mind sabotages your potential for enjoyment. When you pay attention to what's really going on inside, it's actually quite a show!

I fall into the same trap once in a while. Last night, for example, I tried to go for a jog for the first time since injuring my knees a few months ago. I got about a hundred yards when they started to ache. I limped home.

Almost immediately, my mind took over and convinced me I was getting too old to jog. All sorts of negativity crept into my thoughts. As I sat there, I became sad and started feeling sorry for myself.

All of a sudden, I woke up and realized what I was doing to myself. I had temporarily forgotten that I was the one creating those thoughts that were swimming around in there! As I detached myself, I began to think of my mind as a movie theater. There was this very sad drama appearing on the screen. By making it less personal, I could see how innocently this process takes place, and how easy it is to create an inner world full of pain and disappointment. Luckily for me, this time I was able to step back and gain some perspective. My feelings of self-pity turned to gratitude. After all, I can still walk just fine.

Waking up to our thinking is identical to waking up from a bad dream. The only difference is that in one instance you're asleep, and in the other, you're awake. Imagine having a dream one night that you turned into a real loser. You were a mean-spirited person who took advantage of others. When you woke up in the morning, you'd probably be relieved that it was only a dream. It's unlikely you'd start feeling depressed about the bad person you had become.

It's really the same dynamic. Had I not awakened to the daydream going on in my head after my jog, there's no telling how far I could have taken it. As long as I continued to give significance to those thoughts, I was giving my authorization to allow myself to feel bad.

One of my fondest memories is of talking to a one-hundred-year-old man when I was a teenager. I asked him, "Why are you so happy?" I'll never forget the genuine joy in his voice when he answered, with a chuckle, "It's so much better than the alternative." He was referring, of course, to the fact that he had two choices. He could, as he was doing, choose to delight in the fact that he was alive and well. He could laugh, smile, and share his wisdom with others. He could enjoy and make the most of each and every day he was given.

Or he could have just as easily convinced himself that his best days had come and gone. He could sulk, feel sorry for himself, and think about where he would rather be—and what age he would rather be. He could have easily felt really old. All it would have taken is for him to have taken seriously a few thoughts in that direction.

Ironically, almost to the day that I wrote this strategy, one of my good and most trusted friends told me she was retiring. She shared with me some practical advice to consider. Since she was a happy, effective person when she was working and was equally happy to be retiring, I listened carefully to what she had to say!

She suggested that when you retire (and if you have already retired, the same advice applies), you should think back to all the things you *would* have done if that darn job weren't in the way. There were so many things you could and would have done—traveled, learned to meditate, started that new hobby, driven across the country, gotten into better physical shape, learned how to play golf, relaxed, volunteered, read more books, or whatever. You never had the time, of course, but now you do!

The advice is simple: Take advantage of your time. Whether you retired twenty years ago, or will do so next week, now is the time. Take advantage of the fact that you have fewer responsibilities that are nonnegotiable. Free time can be a blessing or a curse. It all depends on how you look at it.

There are some special things to consider if you are in a relationship with someone *else* who is retiring. It's important to respect the fact that things are going to be different—not better or worse, just different. Just like being a newlywed, it's going to take some adjustment. If you respect that fact and keep your perspective and sense of humor, in all likelihood it will work out.

Keep in mind that your partner is going to behave differently than he or she did when working. It's going to seem strange. Your partner may go to one extreme, acting clingy, or to the other and seem indifferent. In either case, try to remember that this is a brand-new experience for your partner as well as for you.

One of my favorite expressions is this: "Instead of cursing the darkness, light a candle." I can think of no situation where this wisdom is more appropriate than when retiring. Rather than belittling your partner, or discouraging him or her by complaining, be as patient, encouraging, and enthusiastic as possible. Without being demanding, do everything you can to get your partner to see the experience of retirement as a unique opportunity to live life to its fullest. If he or she is having a tough time adjusting, gently guide him or her toward new options.

However, you may want to set some loving limits with your partner so that you don't drive each other nuts! There's no reason for you to give up your own scheduled activities simply because your partner suddenly has more time on his hands. While you want to be as loving and supportive as possible, it's not your responsibility to create your partner's new life. If you're used to seeing each other only during evenings and weekends, it's going to seem like a lot of togetherness if you don't have a life of your own.

The bottom line is that retirement is an exciting time for both of you. It's a chance, not only for your partner, but also for you to develop new interests and passions. My advice to both of you is quite simple: Embrace and celebrate today whatever age you happen to be. If you are planning to retire soon, or if you have already done so, congratulations! Make today the best day of your life. You are, literally, one thought away from making that happen.

35. Big Stuff and Moods

A few years ago, a man sat down next to me on an airplane.
Ironically, we had met once before on that same flight, so it was sort
of as if we already knew each other. About a half hour after the flight
took off, he told me that he wanted to divorce his wife. He had been
thinking about it for weeks, and his decision was final.

I remembered this man as being much happier the last time we
had met. My instincts told me that he was in a horrible mood. Rather
than jump immediately on his divorce bandwagon and agree with
his decision, I simply listened to what he had to say. After a while, I
tried to steer the conversation to happier topics. I didn't say or do
anything special. Mostly I just listened.

Over the next hour or so, the strangest thing started to happen.
His spirits started to lift and he became more lighthearted. He even
told me a couple of jokes (and he wasn't drinking alcohol!).

Without trying to be "therapeutic," I simply asked him what was
going on with him and his wife. In his better mood, he was far more
philosophical. He talked about a few of their personal issues and, all
of a sudden, became reflective about his own contribution to the
problems he was having in his marriage. It was as if he were a different person.

By the time the flight landed, he had changed his mind about filing for divorce. He told me something that put all big decisions and, in fact, all big stuff into a little better perspective for me. He said, "Thank God I didn't act on my low-mood thinking."

The definition of *mood* in the *Webster's College Dictionary* is: "A person's emotional state or outlook at a particular time." I think this is one of the single most important definitions we can work with to enhance perspective.

Let's think about the deeper meaning of this definition. To me, the key words are *at a particular time*. This suggests that moods are constantly shifting and changing. They are fluctuations in the quality of our thinking and our perceptions. This certainly rings true for me. How about you?

I'll define a "good" mood to mean that you feel secure and reasonably peaceful. You're not agitated, defensive, and stressed. In general, how do you perceive life under these conditions? I don't want to put words in your mouth, but I'd guess that, in general, you have a healthy perspective. Overall when you're in a good mood, life looks fine. You probably have a sense of gratitude for your family and friends. Your job or career seems meaningful. You feel hopeful. If you're criticized, you take it in stride. If you're delivered some bad news, you deal with it effectively. If you have to make an important decision, you do so wisely. I'm not suggesting you're blind to the facts or that you're unrealistically optimistic or happy—only that you're on solid ground.

I'll define a bad mood as the way you feel when you "wake up on the wrong side of the bed." For no apparent reason, you simply feel negative, cynical, and pessimistic. You're lacking perspective and wisdom.

Here's an interesting thing to think about. The same life, the same set of circumstances, the same problems, issues, challenges, and hurdles exist—but everything looks so different! Our moods can literally "trick us" into thinking that things are worse than they really are! It's quite fascinating when you step back and consider it. Our life can seem as if it has changed—but it hasn't. Think about the man I was talking to on the airplane. He had the same wife that he'd had an hour earlier. He had the same history with her. But he developed a totally different perception—influenced, as far as I could tell, by nothing other than his mood. In his low mood, he wanted a divorce. In a higher mood, he wanted his marriage to get better.

Does this mean that things are never as bad as they seem when we are in a low mood? Absolutely not. There are many instances when our mood makes no difference, and our perception will be identical. Our country's response to terrorism, for example, had nothing to do with the mood we were in! Similarly and obviously, not everyone is going to change his or her mind about divorce simply because their mood rises. The point isn't to overstate the importance of moods, but rather to be aware of their potential influence.

I once spent time with a recently retired man on two consecutive days. On the first day, he was glowing about the benefits of retirement. He spoke about the freedom, the ability to travel, and how much fun it was going to be. He was in a great mood.

The very next day, however, was an entirely different story. When he spoke, it was as if he had forgotten that we had discussed retirement the previous day. This time, he was feeling very badly about retirement. It meant that he didn't have enough responsibility—he was bored. It meant he had gotten old and insignificant. I couldn't resist asking, "But what about yesterday? I thought you were really looking forward to retirement." Here is what he had to say: "I was delusional and not seeing things clearly." The only thing that was clear to me was that he was in a rotten mood!

Suppose you need to talk to your teenager about drugs. If either one of you (or worse yet, both of you) are in bad moods, what are the chances of having an effective conversation? I'd say close to zero. The reason is this: When most people are in a bad mood, they are far more defensive and stubborn than when in a higher state of mind. Being aware of this is a tremendous gift. It gives you an enormous edge in all aspects of life. When you take into consideration another person's mood—or your own—you are able to make allowances for overreactions. You can anticipate defensiveness—someone else's or even your own. You can take comments less personally. It gives you that little bit of perspective that is almost always helpful.

From my own personal experience of having a teenager I can tell you that timing is everything. The same conversation about the same topic can be loving and effective—or bitter and useless. It largely depends on the mood of the parent and the child.

The same principle applies to your spouse or partner, the people you work with, even your friends. Being aware of your own mood—and being sensitive to the moods of others—makes communication a much easier task. Quite frankly, having an important conversation with someone who's in a low mood—or when you're in one—is a risky business unless you're aware of what's likely to happen.

Obviously, there are going to be many times when there's nothing you can do about the fact that you, or someone else you're talking to, is in a low mood. That doesn't really matter if you're fully respectful of the influence moods can have, and you can learn to take what you hear with a grain of salt.

My wife, Kris, for example, is one of the most skilled people I've ever met in handling someone else's low moods—especially mine. She senses when I'm in a bad mood, and quite literally, she doesn't take me very seriously during those times. Don't get me wrong: She doesn't mock or ignore me, and she certainly doesn't like it when I'm low. She simply doesn't overreact to my mood.

Kris is wise enough to know that all people—not just me—will say and do things when they are low that would never enter their minds if they were in a higher mood. She knows that I'll be more defensive, unreasonable, and reactive when I'm low than I will be when I'm in a better place. She makes allowances for this fact, and as a result, she usually doesn't take it too personally. She gives me space to feel low, and is confident that I'll eventually come out of it. So far she's always been right!

The opposite of this wisdom would be to take a person's low mood to heart on an ongoing basis. Imagine how painful this can be. If you've had young children, you already know that when they get into a bad mood, they will say all sorts of mean things. If you're wise, you know they don't really mean what they're saying—they are just venting. Since you know it's just their mood talking, it can actually be sort of cute—to a point.

All I'm suggesting is that we should give all people—not just kids—a little space for their moods. If someone you work with is in a low mood, try to see it as just that—a low mood. It will probably pass quickly. Rather than reading into it or making it a big deal, just let them be in the mood. In the meantime, don't take their negativity personally. If they snap at you or are a little short, just let it be. There's no need to fuel the mood by overreacting or trying to figure it out.

As an experiment, try giving yourself the same type of emotional space. If you're low, just allow it to be. Like a passing rainstorm, it will usually go away if you don't overanalyze all the reasons why you feel the way you do. Keep in mind that when you're low, you'll always come up with what seem to be valid reasons. You'll blame your job, your family, your personal history, the economy, the politicians, and whatever else seems reasonable at the time. But again, those same things will look very different to you as your mood rises.

When you recognize that you're in a low mood, the most important thing is to make the proper allowances and have compassion for yourself. Whenever possible, factor the state of your mood into your decisions. If you can, postpone making important—especially life-changing—decisions until you have a better perspective. If you can't wait, at least remind yourself that you're going to be more defensive, reactive, and prone to negativity than usual. By anticipating your own negativity, you can often overcome the effects of the mood.

Recently, for example, I was asked to participate in a certain event. I was in a horrible mood and my impulse was to turn down the offer immediately. My only saving grace was that I was fully aware of how negative I was feeling, so I was able to remind myself that this might look very different on another day. In this instance, I was right. A few days later, when I didn't feel so overwhelmed and irritated, it seemed like a fun thing to do. Had I not had respect for the power of moods, I would have surely picked up the phone immediately and turned down the opportunity.

Sometimes people object to this way of viewing moods because they think it's about excusing a person's behavior. I can assure you that's not the case. In other words, when someone does something wrong, the idea isn't to say, "Oh well, he was just in a low mood." If you're being abused in any way, for example, throw this material out the window and get some help. I'm also not talking about serious mood problems that could require medical help.

What we're talking about here, of course, is quite different—the day-to-day, normal moods that affect us all. We're talking about learning to make adjustments in our thinking and our responses, by taking into consideration the power of moods. Doing so gives us enhanced perspective in almost any situation.

I once received a nice letter from a reader who told me the simplest story—but one that changed her life. Her teenaged son would storm into the house after school. She had never thought about moods very much and had not taken them into consideration. She would take her son's behavior very personally and yell out things like, "What's the matter with you today?" She would say these types of things with a harsh, bitter tone. In turn, he would become defensive and say something like, "Get out of my life." This pattern continued off and on for months.

When she learned about moods, everything began to change. One day her son stormed into the house as usual. Rather than taking it personally, however, she became quietly compassionate. Instead of yelling at him, she smiled and kept her heart open. She knew that he was just in a horrible mood, and she now realized that no one gets into low moods on purpose. They are no fun. For the first time ever, she thought to herself, "There but for the grace of God go I."

There was a dramatic shift in his attitude. He felt her acceptance and love. He even stopped at the top of the stairs and looked down at his mother. With a tiny little tear in his eye, he said, "Hi, Mom. I'll be okay."

The implications of being respectful of moods are as vast as your imagination. A man recently told me that he had to fire someone at work. He did so, however, taking his and the other person's mood into consideration. He said it was still hard to do, but he was able to pick a moment when the person losing his job was in the best possible frame of mind. All things considered, he said that it went as well as that kind of thing can go. Rather than panicking or getting angry, the person who was fired asked the boss if he had any suggestions. He said they planned on having lunch to discuss it further. That's a great example of making the best of a painful situation. Had he chosen a different time to deliver the bad news, there could very well have been a different, less productive result.

Moods are funny things. We've all had thousands of them. It's comforting to know that most of them are only temporary. They will come and go like the tides of the ocean. My experience has been that most of them pass fairly quickly if we simply recognize them, respect their influence, and leave them alone. By factoring the influence of moods into your life, your wisdom and patience will be enhanced in many ways. As a result, dealing with the big stuff may become slightly more manageable.

36. **Meditation**

As with all of my writing, before sitting down to begin this strategy, I spent twenty minutes in quiet meditation. It was a very peaceful time. To me this is the most important optional twenty minutes of my day. Although it's not absolutely necessary that I meditate every day (and there are certainly many days when I don't), I prefer to make this choice more often than not. Usually, it sets a nice tone for the rest of my day. It slows me down and helps to put me in an emotionally calmer mind-set. After meditating, I'm noticibly less reactive to the events of the day. I have a heightened sense of perspective. It's also easier for me to remain present—focused on what I'm doing or who I'm talking to—which helps me get along better with others.

When my mind is quiet, I'm a better listener, which translates into a sharper learning curve. There's no question that when my mind is quiet, I can think more clearly. My decision-making process is thereby enhanced, and I tend to make fewer mistakes.

Another advantage of meditation is the opening and deepening of creativity. I'm certainly not the only author who relies on a "different" kind of intelligence, which I call upon to write my material. Many writers, artists, songwriters, poets, businesspeople, and other creative people agree that new or original thoughts rarely come from our memories. Instead, our insights come to us from a deeper, quieter place that is beyond our intellect. Memory, in fact, is nothing more than old, recycled thinking. In other words, most thoughts have already been "thought of" before. Therefore, they aren't very interesting and certainly not very original.

Creative insights emerge from a source beyond us; a source often referred to as universal intelligence. The way to connect with this type of intelligence isn't to try, or to fill up our minds. Rather, the idea is to empty and quiet down our minds—and to listen. When we are quiet enough, we realize that the insights are there for the taking. The hardest part is learning to listen.

This is made difficult because we are usually accustomed to following virtually every train of thought that happens to enter our minds. It's there—so we think about it. The result of our busymindedness is that many people get frustrated when they first attempt to meditate. They have never realized how busy and noisy the mind can be. The intent to quiet down may be met with a flurry of thoughts, plans, ideas, and worries.

To access new thinking, however—to think outside of the box— *requires* a quiet mind, uncluttered by memory. It's out of a quiet, deep place within that new ideas emerge, as if from out of the blue. There is no question in my mind that this wisdom or deeper intelligence exists within all of us. It's fascinating to watch and observe what happens to people when they first experience this new type of thinking. Suddenly, even the most complicated situations seem relatively simple.

I was once asked to intervene with a family that was having a lot of problems. Not knowing quite what to do or where to start, I asked the five of them to close their eyes and breathe. This was difficult for all of them because their every instinct was to argue, fuss, and fight. Each in his own way felt that it was important to prove to the others that he or she was "right." Individually and as a family, they were highly defensive. The only thing that was familiar to them was talking over one another and making noise. None of them knew how to listen. It was stressful just being with them, and I could only imagine how hard it would have been to be in that family environment.

I led them through a very simple meditation exercise and tried to help them to relax and quiet down. Then, one by one, I had them open their eyes while the other family members kept their eyes shut. While they looked at the others, I asked them to send imaginary love in their direction. To my pleasant surprise, this suggestion wasn't met with cynicism or sarcasm.

When they opened their eyes, I asked each of them to keep their minds as quiet and still as possible and their hearts wide open. I suggested to them that when aggressive, blaming, and accusatory thoughts reentered their minds, they treat these thoughts with kindness instead of hate, and dismiss them.

Next I asked each of them to write down, on a sheet of paper, what they felt in their hearts was the best way to proceed as a family. When I gathered the responses to read them out loud, I was awestruck at what I saw. All five people had written down pretty much the same words. Essentially, it was this: "What we need to do is to see the innocence in one another, to stop blaming, and to find a good family counselor." After the responses were read, there was a group hug and even a few tears!

I knew from personal experience that meditation was a powerful tool, but I had no idea it could have such a profound effect on an entire family. The simple act of quieting down, even for ten minutes, allowed their natural compassion and love for one another to emerge. Since that time, I have learned that stories like this are far from unique. The simple truth is, meditation works if you give it a chance!

I heard about a study in which CEOs of large and small companies alike were asked to describe the times during which they had their best ideas. The top three answers, in no particular order, were: in the shower, in the car, and on vacation. If you think about it, all three of these answers refer to places where the mind is relatively clear. In other words, the best ideas didn't come to mind while the CEOs were sitting in meetings, racking their brains. If the quiet of a shower can generate inner brilliance, I can imagine the depth of ideas that would develop in the corporate world through the practice of meditation.

But perhaps the most significant advantage I feel from my meditation practice is that it enables me to deal with and respond to adversity in a way that was completely foreign to me prior to this internal commitment. I've learned that there's a fine line between seeing and experiencing something as being an absolute emergency, and seeing it as "tough but manageable." Meditation has the effect of nudging our vision in this more hopeful direction.

As fate would have it, a dear friend of mine lost his father while I was working on this very strategy. He told me that one of the ways he was dealing with it was to quiet his mind through meditation. He told me that meditation had the effect of softening his pain while at the same time keeping his compassionate heart wide open. It allowed him to feel freely and fully. Meditation helped him to receive the love he needs from his friends and family, and, in fact, it helped him to stay lovingly connected to his father, even after his passing.

I have certainly had a similar experience. When I'm going through a difficult or painful time, meditation has had the effect of allowing me to receive love and support from my family and friends. Instead of pushing people away in my greatest time of need, I'm able to feel the love they are sharing. Ordinarily, I tend to keep to myself and socialize regularly with only a few close friends and family. Yet I know that when I'm in any kind of pain, one of the things that helps me the most is keeping my heart open to all those who care about me. Meditation is the tool that has helped me the most in this regard. It has had the effect of connecting me to others and to all of humanity.

I knew someone who was in desperate need of forgiving her father. The pain of resentment had taken its toll, and all attempts to get rid of it had failed. She had tried various types of therapy and had read every book she could find on the subject. Once again, meditation came to the rescue. As with the family I mentioned earlier, meditation had the effect of softening her defenses and helped her see the innocence. "Seeing innocence," of course, is not the same as pretending something didn't happen or excusing bad behavior. Instead, it's the ability to soften your heart enough to see the humanity in someone—even when you never saw it before. As your defenses are softened, so too is the pain of holding on too tightly.

Meditation is a gift you give to yourself, and I cannot recommend it highly enough. It's a period of time, removed from the busyness, confusion, chaos, noise, and stimulation of the day. It's a time to be quiet and still, tune in, listen, and watch—as the mind does its thing.

The way I look at it is this: There are 1,440 minutes in a day. If you assume roughly eight hours are taken up in sleep, that leaves most of us just under 1,000 minutes of waking time each day. It's awesome to consider the amount of stimulation most of us cram into those minutes. There's radio, television, newspapers, and computers. There's voice mail, E-mail, telephones, and other communication devices to deal with. There's planning, running around, driving in traffic, and of course, work. There are children, along with all the commitments and responsibilities that come with them. There are social and spiritual commitments. There's homework. There's cooking and cleaning and doing people favors. There are bills to pay and decisions to make; things to remember and endless chores to perform. There are people relying on us, and others who are probably disappointed with us. The requests and noise come at us from all directions. It's relentless and ongoing. All this stuff and so much more is coming at us—from the external world.

Meditation is a brief time out from all the madness and noise. It's a time to reflect, without effort and without trying. Some would argue that meditation is an attempt to escape from the outside world. But it's not that at all. It's really the opposite of escape. What meditation does instead is to allow us to enter into the world more fully. It's designed to wake us up. We train our minds to be able to see clearly what is happening while it's happening, and to make peace with this. Rather than judging life as it unfolds, we learn to embrace it, moment to moment.

In meditation, we are able to see, firsthand, how our thoughts are formed—what they do, where they go, and how they create enormous confusion within us. In meditation, we are able to step back and witness how tiny thoughts grow into monsters that want to convince us that there is much to fear and be angry about. As conflicting thoughts compete for our attention, our minds can turn what could be a beautiful life into an overblown emergency. My goal in meditation is to observe these thoughts and to let them go, allowing them to float away—like a log floats down a river.

The word *insight* can be broken down into its two syllables—*in* and *sight*. Insight comes from turning inward to find out what's behind all this thinking. It helps you "see" the driving force behind the confusion, hurry, frustration, fear, and anger.

Edgar Cayce said, "Prayer is like talking to God; meditation is a way of listening to God." That has been my experience exactly. When I meditate, I feel connected to God, as if I can hear the subtle whispers of insight and direction. It's very comforting and makes me feel as though I'm never alone.

I could spend pages trying to teach you the art of meditation.

However, my intention in this strategy is simply to pique your interest. There are many great books on meditation. One of my current favorites is *The Best Guide to Meditation* by Victor N. Davich. You can find many others in your local bookstore or library. There are also classes all over the place. If you're lucky, your local recreation department or gym may have an inexpensive class so that you can experience it firsthand. I've even seen classes advertised on bulletin boards at coffee shops!

However you do it, I hope you'll give meditation some serious consideration. If you do, be sure to stick to it for a while because, although it's simple, it takes a little patience to get the hang of it. The benefits, however, are enormous. If you give it a fair shot, you'll be more equipped to deal with all types of big stuff!

37. Experience Calm Resolve

While struggling for an answer in the midst of a personal challenge, I was consulting with a wise friend of mine. She made a suggestion to me that, in many ways, changed the way I look at serious problems. Specifically, she said, "Richard, what you really need is calm resolve." It hit me like a ton of (soft) bricks! Since that time, I have applied these words—and this wisdom—to a variety of sticky issues.

The word *resolve* means to come to a definite or earnest decision about something. Spiritually, I associate it with "coming to peace" with an issue. When something has been resolved, you can put it behind you and move on. For example, I knew two people who had been dating for a long time. Both of them struggled with the question of whether or not they should get married. Eventually they decided against it. For better or worse, they had resolved the issue! Any perceived mental burden about the decision disappeared.

The problem with resolution, however, or resolving something—a business conflict, a personal issue, a big decision, or whatever—isn't always the resolution itself but the manner in which we approach it. When we are insecure about what we are dealing with, we can get defensive and aggressive, or end up flailing for an answer. As we rush and struggle for a solution, it's easy to get frightened or timid on the one hand, or too stubborn on the other. Because of our insecurities, our wisdom doesn't get its chance to jump into high gear. Instead we get caught up in our own thinking—often banging our heads against a wall. We approach the issue from a place of desperation and confusion, sometimes accepting *any* resolution instead of the *ideal* resolution.

By aiming for a genuine sense of calm, however, you create a powerful force of wise determination that is destined to lead you in the right direction. It doesn't necessarily mean that you know what the answer is, but rather that you are confident that you will know, in due time.

It's interesting to consider that when you are *only* calm (without the resolve), it can be helpful or unhelpful, depending on the situation and on how you look at it.

I've met a number of people who were "calm" about retiring. Their attitude was, "I'm not worried. It will all work out." Unfortunately, it didn't work out. What was lacking was the "resolve." There needed to be a plan, a commitment to do whatever was necessary to secure a comfortable retirement. I'm convinced that if they had both components—the calm and the resolve—the result would have been different.

Likewise, having resolve can be a starting point, but in the absence of clear-headed wisdom, your own resolution can be setting you up for a mistake, or even more frustration and confusion.

Three sisters who were engaged in a family business were struggling on an interpersonal level. It seemed to me that what they really needed was a good family counselor or a skilled business mediator to step in and help. One of the sisters, however, was impatient and demanded that they come to a resolution by Friday of that week. She rolled up her sleeves and applied pressure. She already had the reputation among the other sisters as being "the pushy one," and her aggressive attitude only reinforced their feelings. They were no match for her persistence.

Friday arrived and the three of them reluctantly signed a "compromise" that none of them, including the one who pushed for it, were very happy with. The negotiation was unnecessarily rushed and the result was an unhappy "resolution." There were harsh feelings among the women, and as an outsider, it was easy to tell that moving forward was going to be a continuous struggle.

There are times when, deep down, we know what we need to do. Yet because we are uncomfortable or we listen to our doubting thoughts (or someone else's doubts), we beat around the bush, procrastinate, or we look the other way and pretend not to know what to do. A perfect example of this dilemma often exists in parenting.

Suppose your child has broken a serious rule and has disregarded your authority. You're put in the uncomfortable position of needing to teach your child an important life lesson. In your heart, you know that the best solution is to take away a privilege, something he or she truly loves. Your child, of course, voices his strong objection and tries to make you feel guilty. He yells and screams and gives you a dozen excuses. While he's pleading, he promises never to do it again. He then tells you what a rotten parent you are, and blames you for all of his unhappiness. You can feel yourself being drawn in. You are torn apart and hate being the bad guy.

If you're a parent, you know how easy it is to buckle under this type of objection, and how hard it is to know what to do. It's never easy to be unpopular, and this is especially true with regard to our own kids. If you don't remain calm, you can lose your bearings and even your temper. How many examples of this do we see each and every day? On the other hand, without resolve you can easily give in to the pressure, in which case you would be too lenient. Unfortunately, your child then learns that he can manipulate you, and doesn't learn his lesson. How often do you see a parent genuinely and lovingly stick to his or her stated consequence?

With calm resolve, however, it's easier to have faith that you are doing the right thing, and to stick to your guns. The calm part of the equation means that you are committed to keeping your cool. You know that you make the wisest choices when your mind is clear and you are not agitated and bothered. When you feel yourself getting off track, you use those feelings to remind yourself of the power of staying calm. You make gentle adjustments to guide yourself back toward a calmer feeling.

Resolve comes from reminding yourself over and over again that you are doing the right thing and that your heart is in the right place. The decision you have made came not from reacting impulsively, but from being in a quieter place of wisdom. You know that by pointing yourself in the right direction—and being committed to that direction—everything will work out fine.

Having calm resolve is helpful, almost irrespective of what you are going through. I met a woman who survived the huge Oakland Hills fire in Northern California, one of the worst in history. Her home as well as all of her financial and insurance records were destroyed. There was no denying the fact that it was a nightmare. However I'll never forget the calming influence she had on other victims as she reminded everyone, "Don't worry, we will get through this mess. It will work itself out." You could tell that even though she didn't have a clue as to how something this serious could be resolved, she really *did* know that it would be. More than a friendly overture, her words were a true source of comfort. She had calm resolve. She knew in her heart that if she stayed calm and took it one small step at a time, eventually all the pieces would come together.

You've probably had friends who have said to you a hundred times, "I'm going to quit smoking" (or drinking, gambling, cheating on their spouse, or something else). After a while, even though you love them, you start to tune them out. You know they don't really mean it. You're heard it all before.

But then one day, they say it to you again. Only this time, it's different. You don't know what it is—but you are certain that they really mean it. Their voice isn't louder. Their circumstances haven't necessarily changed. But something in the way they say it convinces you that they not only can do it, but they will do it. That "something" is calm resolve. Something inside of your friend—their confidence, wisdom, strength—had been touched, and perhaps for the first time, they feel it and they trust it.

It's the same quiet confidence that allows us to get through all "big" things. Whether it's an audit from the IRS, or planning a funeral for a loved one, we need faith that we can manage. When we have that faith, we make the best choices possible, given the circumstances. I think it's safe to say that if you can't get through something with calm resolve, then it probably can't be gotten through!

I'm not aware of a technique that can give you calm resolve. Rather it comes naturally when we trust that this is the best we can do as human beings. There is something within us—an inner intelligence and source of wisdom—that is activated when we trust that it exists. When this trust is genuine and our heart is in the right place, our wisdom opens and the sky's the limit. We gravitate toward the wisest and most appropriate decisions.

I was once on a backpacking trip with a good friend of mine. On the way out, we became lost. Luckily, he knew how to use a compass and how to identify landmarks. Even though he didn't know exactly where we were headed, he had absolute confidence that we were moving in the right direction. To him, that was all that mattered and all that was necessary. At his sole discretion, we simply put one foot in front of the other until—eventually—we knew exactly where we were. I've always admired him for that quiet, accurate confidence.

I often reflect on that backpacking trip when I think about calm resolve. It's a similar type of trusting in the unknown. It's not a matter of kidding yourself that you know something when you don't. That would be foolish. Rather, it's being willing to listen to that inner voice that knows what to do next. And when it doesn't know what to do—it knows that it doesn't know.

Being committed to calm resolve is one of the most comforting feelings imaginable. In an otherwise unpredictable and confusing world, it gives us hope that things will work out okay. It gives us a starting point, something to work with, when there are so many unknown variables. Give it a try—you'll be glad you did.

38. Forgiveness

I can't think of a more important ingredient for one's sanity and inner strength than the powerful practice of forgiveness. We forgive, not only for the benefit of others, but also perhaps primarily for our own peace of mind. Making forgiveness part of our daily life and spiritual practice is something we can do in order to let go of our anger, resentment, and fear. In its absence, our hearts and minds can, and probably will, become clouded with hatred, bitterness, and confusion.

In my estimation, there has never been a time in human history when forgiveness has been more important. After the barbaric acts of terrorism of September 11, 2001, many hearts have closed down. To many, the very thought of forgiveness is unthinkable. Unfortunately, the closing of the heart has gone way beyond our inability to forgive the terrorists, and has spilled over into aspects of daily living. Cynicism has taken over, which is truly a victory for the perpetrators of evil.

Whether we're talking about something as horrific as terrorism or something very painful, with far less magnitude, it's important to understand and acknowledge what forgiveness is *not*. Forgiveness is not the same thing as excusing, pardoning, or accepting unforgivable acts or behavior. It is not apathy, nor is it the same as saying, "Oh well, I'd better get over it." Forgiveness is not synonymous with weakness or lack of resolve. It does not mean you don't stand up and fight for what is right and punish that which is wrong. You can hate a particular act, work tirelessly to ensure it never happens again, yet hold the act in your heart in such a way that you can maintain your sanity and restore your sense of well-being. That way, you can get on with your life with renewed strength.

Years ago, I heard a story of forgiveness that changed the way I perceived many of the (far less serious) wrongs that have been done to me. A woman's child had been kidnapped and was never found. After a great deal of unimaginable agony, she opened her heart to forgiveness. She said that without it, her life would have been destroyed, along with everyone in her path. She said that without forgiveness, alcohol and drug abuse were as inevitable as the light of day. She described forgiveness as a caring hug from a loved one. It has the capacity to dismantle hatred, grief, and thoughts of revenge. It's a tremendous release of negative energy. Forgiveness allowed her to be open to the fact that life is "as it is." That doesn't mean we always like it—of course we don't. But forgiveness allows us to experience greater acceptance of "what is" and develop the ability to move on.

Another story brought tears to my eyes and perspective to my life. A grown woman shared with me how she was abandoned by her mother at birth—literally, she was left to die. As she grew up, she was filled with hostility, rage, and confusion. Her life was filled with unhappiness and trouble. Many people, including therapists, had given up on her potential for having an effective and happy life.

At some point she met a friend who, despite her strong and continuous resistance, somehow convinced her of the value of forgiveness. It took some time, but eventually she was able to find it in her heart—not superficially, but genuinely. She described her forgiveness in a manner similar to that of Christ himself. Specifically she said, "It's easy to forgive when *you* know that she knew not what she was doing." She realized that had her mother had the slightest warmth or compassion, she would have never done such an evil and selfish act. She knew that her mother was in intense pain. Was she condoning what her mother had done? Of course not. In fact, as many enlightened victims end up doing, she worked to help prevent others from having to go through the same ordeal. She didn't forgive her mother as an overture or as a gesture of kindness, but as a means of reigniting her passion for life. It was a means of survival.

Then there is the powerful story about a Buddhist monk. He and his friend, another monk, had been prisoners some years earlier. Both had been mistreated and tortured. At some point, the friend asked his fellow monk whether or not he would forgive his captors. "Never," replied the monk. The Buddhist's response speaks volumes to the heart of this strategy. "Then I guess you will always be a prisoner," he replied.

I once heard that the Dalai Lama referred to his "enemies" as "my friends the enemies." I've never questioned his resolve to make things right. Yet, I've always sensed that he knows that resentment and hatred will get him nowhere. Advocating violence and hatred is perhaps even more futile and counterproductive.

After a lecture, a man once came up to me privately and told me that while it might be easy for me to talk about forgiveness, I obviously didn't have the parents that he had! He was arguing that forgiveness sounds good in theory, but in some cases it's unrealistic. I shared with him the above-mentioned story about the woman and her kidnapped child, and I told him that I acknowledge that I've never been through anything remotely that painful. I have, however, heard many people share healing stories of forgiveness. In all these years, I've yet to hear one person say, "I was able to forgive—and I regret it." I never expect that I will. Like you, I can only hope to learn from those who have transformed their pain into forgiveness.

The truth is that forgiveness is about as practical a tool as we can possibly create. In fact, one of the strongest arguments in favor of forgiveness is that it's ultimately in our very best interest. Think about it. What other single practice has the potential to help us heal from such immense pain? What would it be—exercise, eating right, counting our blessings, expressing our anger, thinking positively, collecting achievements? I can't think of anything more ultimately powerful or effective than the conscious decision to forgive.

Whether we've experienced a divorce, a robbery, or a tragedy of some kind, forgiveness is essential to one's inner healing and ultimate happiness. I'd go so far as to say that the simple act of growing up, rebelling against our parents, and becoming adults requires at least some forgiveness. In my estimation, we either learn to forgive in a conscious way, or we suffer in agony. Our suffering may be silent or vocal—but it will be present.

Forgiveness is a central theme in my life. It's not that I've been treated badly or suffered greatly—far from it. It's just that in all of our lives, things happen, mistakes are made, we are disappointed, and resentment creeps into our hearts. It doesn't matter who you are—if you're human, it's there. If you're honest, you'll probably admit that there are times when you resent even those you love the most—your parents, spouse, children, even your best friends. No one is exempt. Even those of us who seem to have great-looking lives experience pain and confusion.

Admitting this makes the practice of forgiveness much less daunting. It enables you to see that part of the human predicament is disappointment and resentment. All of us experience pain. As hard as we try and as much as we wish it were different, there's no way to avoid it 100 percent of the time. The reality is that there are times when people will let us down—and we will do the same toward others. Acknowledging this reminds us that we're all human and we're all in this together. With this perspective, it's easier to forgive ourselves when we prove, once again, that we're only human. And when others prove the same to us, we can see that the same holds true.

I once experienced a weird coincidence having to do with the painful subject of infidelity. I was listening to a talk show when a married woman called in to share with the host her confusion about the fact that she had met another man to whom she was drawn. The host ranted and raged about how evil and wrong it was (even though nothing physical had happened). She hung up the phone sounding guilty and confused.

No more than two hours later, I was talking to a woman who told me essentially the same thing. My advice and reaction were very different. Although I'm no expert, I always feel that heartfelt honesty works best. To me, we're all humans, subject to similar, if not identical, issues. I suggested she talk to her husband about her feelings and about what happened. I thought a heart-to-heart was in order.

While I obviously never heard about what happened to the woman who called the radio talk show, I did hear back from the woman with whom I had spoken. She said that not only had her husband forgiven her, but the incident had also brought them ten times closer than ever before. She said that when he heard what had happened, tears had come to his eyes. He confessed that although, like her, he had never had an affair, he had experienced similar feelings in the past. In a strange way, under less than perfect circumstances, a near-affair had actually been a catalyst to a better marriage.

What if instead of having a forgiving heart, that woman's husband had become stubborn? What if he had forgotten that he too was human and wasn't able to see his wife's humanity? He and his wife never would have enjoyed their renewed closeness.

I'm not suggesting for a moment that it's okay to cheat on your partner or do anything that would be immoral or painful to someone else. I am suggesting, however, that knowing we are all human makes it much easier to forgive and move on. By admitting that "we" are "them," we are able to experience our shared humanity. Once in a while, we can even see the humor in the predicament of being human.

There are several levels of forgiveness. The first level is to consciously forgive yourself. Forgive yourself for the wrongs you have committed—the mistakes you have made and the decisions that turned out to be wrong. Forgive yourself for not being perfect, for being human.

Next, forgive others—everyone—for being human. Forgive your parents for not being perfect, your siblings for not always sticking up for you, and your friends for betraying you at times. Forgive your neighbors, associates, coworkers, and everyone else for acting in self-interest. Remind yourself that no one is perfect—no one. Remind yourself that being angry never, ever lives up to its promise of making you happier. In fact, the more you hang on to your anger and resentment, the more unhappy you will become.

Finally, forgive the world for not being perfect. Forgive the universe for making mistakes and for not putting you first. Forgive the chaos and everything that doesn't seem to make sense. Know that, despite the evidence to the contrary, God knows what he is doing. Somehow, it all makes sense. This is true, even though we can't always see it. There are various meditations that work on this type of multiple forgiveness. In a deep state of relaxation, you first start by asking forgiveness for all those you have harmed. Then you ask for the ability to forgive anyone who has harmed you. Finally, you ask for forgiveness for any harm you may have perpetrated on yourself. In some ways, this is the hardest part. We're so darned hard on ourselves!

The effective practice of forgiveness starts with our willingness to see that it's in our best interest. We have to know that love and forgiveness are the cornerstones of mental health and happiness. When we want to forgive, it's easy to use the words, "I forgive you." That, in fact, is the next step—the willingness to say, "I forgive you," or "I forgive myself" for being less than perfect. As simple as it seems, it's a huge relief to forgive.

The Bible says, "Forgive, and you shall be forgiven." This isn't a cop-out that means, "If I forgive others, then I can do what I want." Instead, it's merely a way of reminding us that none of us are perfect. We can easily justify, in a reactive manner, our own imperfections and say (or think), "What I did was not so bad, but let me tell you what was done to me."

Sometimes the hardest thing is to admit that, like everyone else, we are human beings—with human flaws. We mess up, make mistakes and bad choices. What if, instead of being resentful that others do exactly the same thing, we instead practiced the art of forgiveness? What do you suppose would happen to the hatred of the world if we were the first to forgive? It might be unpopular to believe that it's best to be the first to forgive, but so be it. I'd like to think that if forgiveness were to start at home—with each of us—then the world would be a better place. And we'd all be a lot happier.

39. Become Aware of the Mind-Body Connection

I've been interested in the connection between the mind and the body for more than twenty years. It's a thrill to finally have an opportunity to share some of those thoughts.

In college, I knew a woman who was a health advocate. She was as kind as she was vibrant and healthy! She could sense, just looking at me, that I needed some help. I remember her saying in a kind tone, "For your age and athletic ability, you're simply too tired and don't have enough energy." At the time, I wasn't sleeping very well, and my mood and patience were strung too tightly.

She knew a doctor who administered a series of food allergy tests. The results opened my eyes to the amazing connection between the body and the mind. The tests showed that I was either sensitive or allergic to a whole bunch of foods. It was suggested that I eliminate those foods for a while until it was safe to reintroduce them slowly, over time.

I can only tell you about my own personal experience, which was dramatic, to say the least. In addition to losing weight and sleeping better, almost immediately my mood shifted upward and I became far less tense. There was no question in my mind that eliminating those foods from my diet made an enormous difference in the quality of my life, both physically and emotionally.

About twenty years later, our ten-year-old daughter was having symptoms of her own. She has had a lot of trouble with her breathing, and had a tendency toward sudden frustration. We asked a physician what he thought about her symptoms, and we were asked if we were open to doing food allergy tests. Because of my earlier experience, we were absolutely willing to try.

Our doctor sent us to a lab where our daughter had the tests. The results showed a major allergy to certain food groups. Unfortunately, many of them were her favorite foods!

The story is ongoing but seems to be progressing well. According to her and her doctor, and all that we can observe, her symptoms have continued to improve. She even seems to feel happier as well.

Of course, foods are only a tiny part of the mind-body connection. What we've learned in the past twenty years, however, is that the mind and body are intricately linked. Therefore, what's good for one is often good for the other.

I love bodywork, for example—massage, chiropractic, and deep tissue work. I've had sessions with a top therapist when, all of a sudden and for no apparent reason, I started to cry. The sobbing wasn't a result of any physical discomfort, but was simply the result of "held" and stubborn emotions being released from inside my body. A cynic, of course, could make fun of this connection and deny any validity. I might have too, had I not experienced it myself and, as further evidence, seen and heard dozens of similar stories. Sometimes a good bodywork session is like peeling an onion. Layer after layer unwinds, and with each layer comes a sense of emotional release; sometimes subtle, other times more dramatic. When the session is over, I feel lighter, happier, and less stressed and burdened.

My favorite form of bodywork is Rolfing. It's a sophisticated form of deep bodywork named after Ida Rolf, its founder. Rolfers are trained at the Rolf Institute in Boulder, Colorado, as well as at other training locations. I'll never forget my first session with my now best friend, Benjamin Shield. Located in Los Angeles, he is one of the finest professionals in the field anywhere in the world.

I walked into the session tense and in a hurry, wondering how long it was going to take. I was cynical about being there—but due to some injuries, I was willing to give it a try. About an hour and a half later, when I walked out, I was a changed person. My body structure had gone through enough change, in a single session, to remove the layer of tension from my entire being. I can honestly say that I've never been as tense since that time. The results, for me, were permanent. As my body let go, so too did my mind. The biggest shock wasn't to me but to Kris, who was driving me back home after my session. She couldn't believe the shift that had taken place, and how much more relaxed I had become. That single experience was one of the most powerful of my young life. It opened my eyes to the magical world of the mind-body connection.

As I continued my sessions, I also continued to become more relaxed. My priorities began to change. I became less interested in competition and more interested in helping others. It's quite possible that had I not had that experience, way back in college, I would have taken a different life direction and wouldn't be writing this book today. The mind-body connection was that important for me, and it might be for you.

I'm certainly not qualified to offer any type of scientific explanation, but I can tell you that after a good bodywork session such as massage, Rolfing, or chiropractic, I can feel noticeably more relaxed for as many as two to three days. The same things that ordinarily "get to me" don't bother me at all. Once, Kris and I had side-by-side massages by two very good therapists. We became so relaxed that we noticed our defensiveness had disappeared. Our communication, which is already pretty good, soared to new heights. There was an invisible connection between our bodies being more relaxed than usual and our ability to have heart-to-heart, loving communication. To me, that's a practical example of the mind-body connection.

During a meditation course, I was introduced to a form of very deep breathing. I don't even remember what it was called, but I can tell you how effective it became in my life. The suggestion was made to spend two or three minutes taking deep, nurturing breaths before entering the house after a long day of work. The idea was that the breath has the capacity to create feelings of relaxation. So instead of charging into the house in a mad rush, with shallow breaths, therefore greeting my spouse and children impatiently, I would be able to enter the house in a relaxed state of mind. Wow! What an immediate difference it made. Not only me, but also my entire family became instantly calmer. And the only thing that had changed was my relationship to my body. I relaxed my body, and my mind followed suit. Again, the mind-body connection in action.

One of the most obvious applications of the mind-body connection is, very simply, exercise! It's long been known and accepted that physical activity releases endorphins, which can help increase a person's sense of well-being. I've met some pretty grouchy people who decided to start exercising at lunch instead of filling up on food, and what a difference it has made. The same people—but with different outlooks. I know that I feel much better when I prioritize exercise in my life. Even fifteen or twenty minutes a day makes an enormous difference. My advice is to check with your physician and discover the exercise that is best for you.

To me, perhaps the most dramatic examples of the mind-body connection are found through yoga and meditation, two practices that have changed my life forever. Both help us find and maintain inner peace, even in the midst of chaos. There is no question in my mind that these ancient practices can help anyone deal with and prepare for the inevitable big stuff of life.

I have two school-aged children. While I support all the hard work and everything they are learning, in some ways, I'd be in favor of a little less intellectual effort if it were replaced with a tiny bit of emotional education—namely, yoga, meditation, and prayer. As I look around at young people, I see students who don't necessarily know how to deal with conflict, disappointment, and frustration. Not all, but many simply react to their environment. Often those reactions are negative and aggressive. Meditation and yoga teach us to stay centered within ourselves. We learn to make decisions from a calm place of responsiveness, instead of from a heated place of reaction. Can you imagine what would happen to our world if our children could learn, not only the necessary scholastic cornerstones, but the ability to remain calm and happy as well? Just as reading, writing, and math are the cornerstones of a good education, yoga and meditation are, in my eyes, two of the cornerstones of kindness and cooperation.

Of course, it's not just kids who find themselves in the midst of unwanted drama and conflict. It's the rest of us too. Our minds are filled with conflicting desires, wants, and needs. Our impulse is usually to strive toward those desires at any cost—and to become frustrated or aggressive when we can't get what we want. What yoga and meditation teach us is the art of patience—knowing when to strive and when to back off. It gives us inner options. It teaches us to diffuse conflict by being able to maintain a calm state of mind.

Yoga and meditation demonstrate the mind-body connection in many ways. Two of the most notable developments that occur in people who study these ancient arts are patience and presence. It was Ondrea Levine who said, "You are either patient, or you're waiting." When I heard those words, I laughed because I realized she was absolutely right! In other words, you can't be patiently waiting! There's no such thing. "Waiting" means you're looking forward to changing conditions. You desire things to be different. There's a certain anxiety, an impatience because you're not where you want to be.

Patience, on the other hand, is the ability to accept things as they are. If you're in a long line and you're patient, you simply allow the line to move as it moves, without mentally urging it forward. There's a lack of anxiety and frustration. It simply is what it is.

That same quality brought to other, more important aspects of life can make the difference between a successful and peaceful inter-action and one that destroys us. Think of the value of patience when dealing with others—whether at the workplace, where you might have conflicts of interest to deal with, or at home, where you might be dealing with a stubborn teenager. The quality of patience allows you to peacefully, without losing your bearings, issue consequences instead of lectures, keep your cool instead of losing it, and make wise instead of reactive decisions. Ironically, there is no more powerful antidote to negative behavior than a calm state of mind.

Presence is another gift that often results from meditation and yoga. Presence is the ability to "be here now," to be where you are—and not wish you were somewhere else. How often are you talking to someone and, at the same time, glancing at your watch, wishing so badly that you could get on with your day? But by the time you reach your next destination, it starts all over again. Other than a few fleet-ing moments, you're usually not quite satisfied with where you are because you're always one step ahead of yourself—thinking about what's next. But when "next" arrives, you find yourself engaged in the same inner dynamic.

Learning to meditate or practice yoga won't mean you'll never be short of time, or in a hurry. It will, however, greatly reduce your tendency to feel rushed, even when it's not helpful or necessary. The anxiety will disappear. Have you ever been with someone who, while they are with you, is totally satisfied and happy to be there with you? You can tell there is no place they would rather be! It's one of the most comforting and satisfying aspects of being human. This is a quality that you can learn to bring to your life most of the time. You can get to the point where others will feel that you are the one who supplies that beautiful and supportive quality called presence.

Presence is a magical tool that brings you closer to everyone—your spouse, children, coworkers, friends, even strangers. But it's most valuable when the stakes are high. When you or someone else needs a loving hand, someone to be supportive, someone to listen or to lean on—that someone can be you. It all starts with the recognition of the mind-body connection. It results from finding ways to use the body to serve the mind—and vice versa.

A dear friend of mine is a prominent yoga teacher whose life is very much dedicated to his work and practice. Recently, he experienced the horrible pain of the loss of his father. I would never tell you that he, or anyone else, escaped the pain associated with the death of a loved one. I can tell you, however, that his inner beauty and compassionate heart enabled him to make the best of a difficult time. His practice of yoga had taught him to be centered and to keep his heart open, even during times of pain. His words, even in the midst of his pain, were comforting and meaningful to everyone around him. His dad would have been proud.

Both yoga and meditation have become very popular and accessible, which I think is great news for everyone. Currently, my favorite yoga magazine is called *Yoga Journal*. It's filled with great articles, ideas, and products to get you started. You can also find fine magazines and books on meditation at your local bookstore or library. I strongly encourage you to take this information to the next level and find the practice(s) that are right for you. You'll feel a significant difference almost immediately. Beyond that, however, you'll be preparing yourself for bigger things. When you read magazines like *Yoga*

Journal (and other good ones), you'll expose yourself to a wide assortment of great health- and healing-related ideas.

The mind-body connection is both mysterious and exciting. The possibilities are endless. To me, it's worth any effort it takes to become more familiar with it. The integration of body and mind gives us a needed edge in life—a peaceful weapon against the barrage of big stuff headed in our direction.

40. **Happiness**

When my daughter Jazzy was a little girl, one of her friends asked her what her dad did for a living. She said, "He teaches people to be happy." Her friend said, "That sounds like fun." Her little friend was right—it's not only fun, it's a privilege. In fact, the subject is so near and dear to my heart that I thought I'd end this book by sharing a few thoughts about it. In this final strategy, I'll use the words *happiness, contentment,* and *peace* somewhat interchangeably. To me, they are pretty much one and the same.

After many years of quiet reflection, I've learned a number of important things. Two, in particular, come to mind right off the bat. First, I believe that anyone can learn to be happier and more grateful—two qualities that go hand in hand. I'm confident, as one of my earlier book titles suggests, that *You Can Be Happy, No Matter What.* Many people have written to me to tell me that they have learned to be wiser and more peaceful, in spite of the fact that some horrible things have happened to them. Their increased levels of understanding and wisdom have exceeded life's ability to dish out damaging blows. Inner peace and wisdom not only enable a person to get through life's toughest challenges, but they also increase one's capacity for compassion, thereby making it possible for a person to be available and helpful to others.

Secondly, it's important to acknowledge that no one is happy all the time. I'm certainly not, nor have I ever met anyone else who is. In fact, one of the first things you'll notice when you're around believable people who describe themselves as "happy" is that they don't pretend to be happy when they're not. They don't make a big deal out of it. It's ironic to me that this may be one of the primary reasons they *are* happy. That is, when they're feeling down, they acknowledge and accept it—but they don't overanalyze or make too much of it either. One of the most peaceful people I've ever met once said to me, "When I'm down, I try not to treat it like an emergency." To him, it didn't seem much more important than a decision about which restaurant to attend. He said he never likes being "down," but he felt confident that "what goes up usually comes back down and, luckily, it usually goes back up again too."

As I thought about what he said, I realized he was right. I thought about the hundreds of times I've been in low moods, but I've always bounced back eventually. Like him, I don't minimize my lower states of mind—nor do I deny their existence. I simply try to remember that my "home base" is one of contentment. I'll always drift back toward that feeling if I allow myself to do so. I do get off course; sometimes more than I'd like to admit. Yet, I now have the confidence that I can make the necessary adjustments.

I once heard Rabbi Harold Kushner on the radio. He said something to the effect that "people are so busy chasing happiness—if they would slow down and turn around, they would give it a chance to catch up with them." Happiness is within the grasp of anyone. One of the keys, however, is to stop grasping.

Happiness is a state of mind, not a set of circumstances. If circumstances and getting what we want were the keys, then most of us would already be euphoric! It's interesting to think about how many times you've gotten exactly what you wanted. You felt a temporary sense of joy from an achievement, an accomplishment, or the fulfillment of a desire—only to return to a state of longing. What happened to the happiness it was supposed to bring? Why does it never last very long?

Don't get me wrong. I'm the first person to admit that I love getting what I want, and I love to achieve my dreams and goals. I absolutely encourage you to do the same. But what I've learned is that to equate the fulfillment of these desires with happiness is a mistake. What's more, it's not necessary. The turning point in my own journey toward becoming a more satisfied person was the moment I accepted this truth into my life. It was when I realized that life is a game that is played from the inside—out.

There's an old saying, "There is no way to happiness. Happiness *is* the way." Happiness is a feeling that exists in the present moment. That's really all it is. From my perspective, there are essentially two starting points, or ingredients, that enable us to experience this feeling more often in our lives. As long as we have either one or the other, at any given moment, happiness is never more than a thought away.

The first is to take our attention off of our concerns, worries, problems, regrets, and frustrations, and allow our minds to be clear. This clarity enables a natural state of contentment to begin to surface, which includes the ability to have perspective, compassion, and a sense of humor. Does this mean we don't have problems and major issues to deal with? Of course not. It's merely the awareness that allows peace to exist and to develop. When you consciously back off from your concerns, you're not doing so forcefully—or in order to pretend that the problems aren't there—but rather as a means of bringing more peace into the moment. Like the tide of the ocean bringing wave after wave to the shore, thoughts will continuously fill our heads. If we're wise, we learn to let most of them flow back to wherever they came from.

Obviously when it's necessary or helpful to focus on a problem, then that's what we need to do. There are many times when that's the only thing we can do. That's a totally different issue. What I'm talking about here is the conscious ability and willingness to back off of inner concerns instead of delving even deeper into them.

The second "ingredient" of happiness is a variation of the same awareness, but is perhaps even more important. It's the ability to recognize the troublesome thoughts that are in our minds—even if we can't or don't want to dismiss them. If we recognize our thinking as mere thinking—instead of something to fear—we can avoid becoming lost in our thinking and overwhelmed by it. We can step back from our thinking and relate to it differently—less personally. It's like the difference between being in a movie and watching the movie. When you're even slightly detached, it enables you to become the observer of your thoughts instead of being controlled by them. You start to relate *to* your thinking, and not from your thinking. That changes everything. It allows you to become far less reactive, and to make much wiser choices.

We either experience happiness right now—or not at all. If you find yourself saying or thinking things such as, "I'll be happy later on," watch out! What you're really saying is, "Someday—later on— I'll make the conscious decision to take my attention off of my current problems, concerns, and sources of stress, and I'll therefore be able to be happy." In effect, you're saying, "I can't or won't do it now—but I will later on." You're merely postponing what needs to be done.

The problem is that the same rationale preventing you from doing so today will exist later on, guaranteed. That is, there will always be issues in our lives and valid external justification for being serious, worried, resentful, or unhappy. There will always be concerns that seem to, or actually do, require our attention. We will always have the same personal history—the same parents, and so forth. If you had a horrible experience when you were young—and today you're forty—that same experience will have happened, even when you turn sixty. I don't say this sarcastically, but rather as an important reality to take into consideration. Unless something shifts inside of us, there is no way to become contented.

Logically, most of us acknowledge that we will always have problems. Ten years from now, our problems might be less or more severe than they are today. Either way, chances are they will be different. But one thing is certain—they will exist. Yet, despite this acknowledgment, many of us convince ourselves that if we are going to experience happiness, we will experience it later. There is good news and bad news. The bad news is: It won't work! Eventually, sooner or later, if you want to be happy, you're going to have to do so, in spite of it all. The good news is: It can be done—today. Right now.

Confucius said, "Happiness does not consist in having what you want, but in wanting what you have." Exactly! Many of us do experience moments of happiness. The moments are there, but they drift away with our thoughts, leaving us, once again, chasing that feeling. It has been helpful for me to remember that happiness is nothing more than a feeling that is experienced in the present moment. This moment.

One of the most important things I've learned is that feeling contented is one of the least selfish things we can do. When we have what we need on the inside, our natural response is to give to others or open our hearts to causes we believe in. Many would argue that compassion is what's most necessary for one's happiness. I absolutely agree. However, I don't think it's necessary to force oneself to be more compassionate because, when we are happy, we can't help but be filled with compassion. Aldous Huxley once said, "It's a bit embarrassing to have been concerned with the human problem all one's life, and find at the end that one has no more to offer by way of advice than 'Try to be a little kinder.' "

I often ask the question, "What would you say if I offered you a thousand dollars for everything you could think of to feel grateful for?" My guess is, you would run out of paper to write your answers on before you ran out of thoughts! That's because deep down, we all know that it's a miracle to be here. Life is a gift to be treasured. It was a gift when you were born, and it has been a gift ever since. Let's spread that message together, to create more kindness and happiness in our world. My hopes and prayers are that you will discover happiness in this life, starting right now. You're worth it.